Biracial Unions on Galveston's Waterfront, 1865–1925

Biracial Unions on Galveston's Waterfront, 1865–1925

CLIFFORD FARRINGTON

Texas State Historical Association
Austin

© Copyright 2007 by the Texas State Historical Association.

Printed in the United States of America.

Library of Congress Cataloging-in-Publication Data

Farrington, Clifford.
    Biracial unions on Galveston's waterfront, 1865–1925 / by Clifford Farrington.
      p. cm.
    Includes bibliographical references (p.) and index.
    ISBN 978-0-87611-217-5 (cloth : alk. paper)
      1. Stevedores—Labor unions—Texas—Galveston—History. 2. Cotton trade—Employees—Labor unions—Texas—Galveston—History. 3. African American steve-dores—Labor unions—Texas—Galveston—History. 4. African American labor union members—Texas—Galveston—History. 5. Galveston (Tex.)—Race relations—His-tory. I. Title.
    HD6515.L8F37 2007
    331.88'11387164—dc22   2007026467

5   4   3   2   1   07   08   09   10   11

Published by the Texas State Historical Association.

∞ The paper used in this book meets the minimum requirements of the American National Standard for Permanence of Paper for Printed Library Materials, z39.84—1984.

Frontispiece: "The Queen of the Gulf," Christmas Eve, 1870. *Courtesy of the Rosenberg Library, Galveston, Texas.*

Contents

Acknowledgments

I would like to express my gratitude to the staff at the following libraries for their help during my research: The Center for American History at the University of Texas at Austin; the Special Collections Division at the University of Texas at Arlington; the Galveston and Texas History Center at the Rosenberg Library, Galveston. Individual thanks go to Alan Scattergood, Prof. Peter Way, Prof. Mark C. Smith, and Jeanne Farrington. Lastly, my thanks to the Texas State Historical Association, particularly Holly Taylor and Janice Pinney.

Biracial Unions on Galveston's Waterfront, 1865–1925

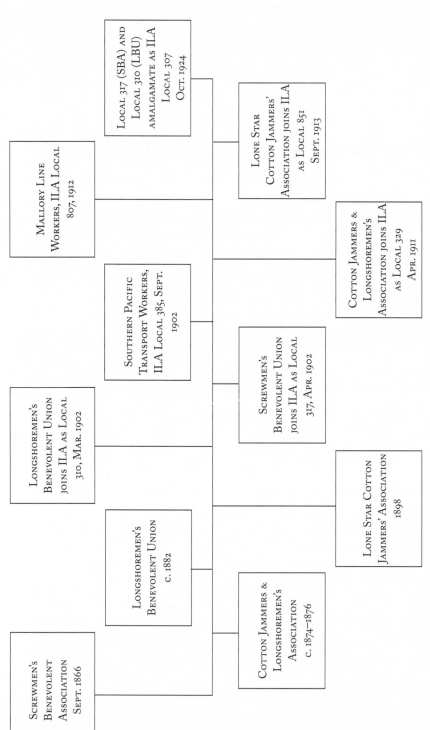

This timeline outlines the formation of Galveston's leading waterfront unions and their designation as ILA locals.

Introduction

"A significant strategy"

Here was a remnant of haunted beauty—gray, shrouded,
crumbling . . . of what did the city remind me? Miss
Haversham of course. That was it. Miss Haversham the
spectral bride in Great Expectations.

Edna Ferber, A Kind of Magic, 1963[1]

Although an air of ossified Dickensian glory haunts Galveston
to this day, Edna Ferber's image of Galveston belies the time
when the city was the most important commercial center in
Texas and one of the nation's leading seaports. At the end of the Civil
War, city boosters declared their expectation of turning Galveston into
a seaport serving the vast hinterland west of the Mississippi. Their
vision of a Galveston era flourished over the next several decades as railroads advanced the frontier of commercial agriculture, particularly cotton, across the Southwest. Cotton shipments rose steadily and The
Strand, Galveston's commercial center, became known as the "Wall
Street of the Southwest." The port, the docks and wharves at the core
of Galveston's rise, earned the city the title of the "Queen of the Gulf."
Ornate mansions and sturdy mercantile buildings arose as the symbols
of burgeoning prosperity. By 1900 a large percentage of the Texas cotton crop as well as wheat and other produce from as far away as California and Colorado left Galveston for destinations around the world.

For the next quarter of a century, Galveston reigned as the nation's leading cotton shipping port.

Many factors contributed to Galveston's commercial success—the port's location, the vision and commercial acumen of local businessmen, investment by northern capital and the federal government, expanding railroad networks, and the production of and demand for cotton all played their part. The literal driving force, however, was provided by the waterfront workers, the men who loaded the 3 million-plus bales of cotton exported a year and unloaded incoming agricultural and commercial goods.

Galveston's waterfront provided a lively scene in the decades around the turn of the twentieth century, particularly during the cotton season from September to March. Sailing vessels and steamships lined docks along the island's sheltered western shore where wharves were piled high with thousands of bales of cotton. Teams of freight handlers, cotton pressmen, yardmen, weighers, checkers, and draymen moved the cotton from freight cars to ship side where cotton screwmen took the bales on board to stow. The clamor of locomotives and railway cars switching from pier to pier, drays and hand trucks carrying cargo, steam winches dragging great bales of cotton aboard ship—all added to the cries and industry of the hundreds of dockside laborers.

These men, with their muscle, sinew, sweat, and, sometimes, blood, propelled the Galveston era, yet their labors have not received the attention they deserve. Histories of Galveston have tended to focus on the city's commercial success, its great mercantile families and their architectural legacy, the Great Storm of 1900, or the city's high tolerance for illegal gambling, liquor, and other vices.[2] Some recent works have included the social history of the island, but even these give scant attention to the waterfront or the men who toiled there. Yet the history of these men provides an important chapter in the underdeveloped field of Texas labor history in a place that was very different from other Texas cities, and even other ports such as Houston, Beaumont, and Texas City. Some of the state's earliest and strongest labor organizations began on

Galveston's waterfront as, uncoincidentally, did the state government's policy of staunch antiunionism. These waterfront organizations provide a study in how a particular laboring community in an industry with its own contours and intricacies dealt with such issues as the transition from benevolent societies to job-conscious unions; the role of the broader labor movement such as the Knights of Labor, the American Federation of Labor and International Longshoremen's Association; new technology and the struggle for workers' control; and the open shop movement. Historians have paid attention to certain aspects, a particular organization or individual strike in Galveston, but no one has written from a broad perspective and across a substantial time period. Moreover, no one has paid full attention to one of the central topics in Galveston's labor history, the interaction between black and white workers and the intersection of race and class.

Steam winches and locomotives aside, mechanization had little effect on the waterfront until containerized cargoes drastically reduced the labor force in the latter part of the twentieth century. Waterfront work relied upon large amounts of casual labor where the main requirement was manual strength, particularly when handling bulky raw materials such as cotton. Such tasks required a certain experience but not the lengthy apprenticeship associated with a craft industry. The work was irregular and depended upon such variables as seasonal and economic fluctuations as well as the tide and winds. The characteristic pattern of dock work was "hurry up and wait"—periods of idleness followed by long hours of hard and hazardous labor when a ship docked. Earnings were similarly erratic and, on average, low. The ready availability of unskilled, casual labor as well as ethnic and racial divisions only added to the economic insecurity of longshoremen. In many ports, the early morning ritual of the "shape-up" came to characterize the intense competition for jobs. Men seeking work formed a rough semicircle or "shape" at the pier gates each morning for the foreman to select the number of workers required for that day, a system as much open to favoritism and bribery as it was to skill or seniority.[3]

Waterfront labor was generally regarded as unskilled, but the work itself could be highly specialized and the workforce highly stratified. Longshoreman is a broad term that covers a wide variety of tasks and skills as workers usually handled only one class of goods, often at a particular stage of the loading process, and were employed by a small number of firms. Every major port developed its own particular division of labor, its own working practices and language, and its own hierarchy of specialized tasks and wage differentials according to the types of cargo handled. In addition to specialization by cargo, the workforce was divided into deep-sea longshoremen working only on vessels serving foreign ports, and coastwise longshoremen working on vessels serving American ports. Longshoremen usually worked in gangs with three gangs per hatch: pier men prepared the cargo on the dockside to be hauled aboard ship by the deck gang, who transferred the cargo to the hold gang for stowage. The work required coordination and judgment, particularly when moving heavy, bulky staples, to avoid damaging the cargo or injuring oneself or one's fellow workers. The hold gang, in particular, required a high level of experience to securely stow the maximum amount of cargo into an often irregularly-shaped hold. In 1915 sociologist Charles Barnes, in one of the first studies of American longshoremen, recognized that such work could require judgment, responsibility, and years of training. Historian Eric Hobsbawm compared the qualities of nineteenth-century British dockworkers to those of the skilled iron puddler, requiring physical strength as well as craft skills, experience, initiative, and teamwork. Moreover, even if longshoremen were not skilled by conventional standards, they nevertheless held considerable bargaining strength.[4]

As John Lovell explained in his account of early dock unionism in Britain, technology had little affect on dockwork, thus requiring management to rely heavily on the skill of the workforce. With little technological or managerial structuring of work, dockworkers could organize themselves according to craft principles and establish their own control over wages and, especially, working conditions. While the ready availability of casual labor made the replacement of longshoremen an easy matter in theory, even the limited skills of a general cargo long-shoreman could take many weeks for a new hand to learn. A ship's turn-around time in port was a major factor in profitability and employers could ill afford the time necessary to train green hands. Using untrained hands risked at best, loss of time, damaged cargo, and inefficient stowage, which ultimately cost money. At worst, a badly stowed cargo could shift in transit and possibly even cause a ship to sink. According to Barnes, steamship companies dreaded hiring untrained men, whose inefficiency incurred heavy losses. Occupying a strategic link in the transportation chain, longshoremen could use collective action to pressure employers into making concessions. While a determined employer with a large reserve of casual labor held the long-term advantage over most longshoremen, the skills of some groups made them almost irre-placeable. The specialization of tasks and the associated skills enabled some waterfront workers to form some of the earliest and strongest labor organizations.[5]

In Southern cotton ports such as Galveston, cotton screwmen formed the most powerful unions. Before the introduction of high density cotton compresses, screwmen used large jackscrews to force the maximum number of cotton bales into a ship's hold, thus playing a vital role in maximizing the cargo's profitability. Cotton screwing required a particular strength and experience that attracted high wages and earned screwmen the respect of employers and fellow longshoremen alike. Organized screwmen were able to exercise a similar degree of control over their working practices and wages as a more traditional craft union. Like many craft unions, screwmen's organizations sought to protect their position by controlling the labor supply through strict member-ship requirements and the closed shop. Although immigrants, sailors, and migrant labor provided competition in Southern ports, the screw-men's main challenge came from black labor. While Southern racial mores supported the exclusion of black labor from skilled or highly paid labor, white labor sometimes recognized that exclusion was not the only policy open to them.

C. Vann Woodward outlined the pattern of Southern labor and race relations in his seminal study, *Origins of the New South*. Two challenges confronted white labor as the Southern economy slowly recovered in the decades following the Civil War. From above, a new commercial and industrial class allied with Northern capital sought to establish a new social, political, and economic order across the South. From below, a newly freed black labor force directly competed for work with white labor. The renewal of large-scale immigration further heightened the competition for jobs. Woodward argued that white labor had two options to meeting the challenge from black labor: "eliminate the Negro as a competitor by excluding him from the skilled trades either as an apprentice or a worker, or take him in as an organized worker committed to the defense of a common standard of wages." David Roediger also recognized that the notion of black-white labor unity was a post–Civil War innovation. The racism of white labor, however, severely limited the potential of such collaboration, particularly as immigrant groups adopted anti-black racism as a means of asserting their own "whiteness." Moreover, employers willingly exploited racial, ethnic, and national divisions, placing rival work gangs in competition "not only to undermine labor unity and depress wages in the long run but also to spur competition and boost productivity every day." Woodward acknowledged that race consciousness would divide far more than class consciousness could unite but, still, Southern labor wavered between these two contradictory policies. The South's racial ideology sanctioned the exclusion of black workers from many occupations, but in certain industries their presence was too strong to be ignored.[6]

Between 1865 and 1913 a tradition of biracial unionism developed in the South, particularly among lumberjacks, miners, and longshoremen. White and black workers were organized into separate locals, but these locals crossed the racial divide by working together in a common economic cause. Biracial unionism thus both upheld and pushed the boundaries of white Southern racial practices. Moreover, biracial unionism was symptomatic of the broader popular discontent aroused against the new order. This discontent found its widest expression through the Knights of Labor and Southern Farmer's Alliance in the 1880s and the American Federation of Labor and Populist Party in the 1890s. At times, these movements pushed the races toward cooperation. These fragile experiments in white-black working-class unity ran counter to the racial assumptions of the South, yet all-told they involved many thousands of Southerners. Perhaps no group of workers pushed these assumptions further than the longshoremen in Gulf Coast ports such as Galveston and New Orleans.

Historian Eric Arnesen has revealed much about the development of biracial unionism in Gulf Coast ports, particularly New Orleans. Arnesen, like Woodward, concluded that "southern longshoremen adopted racial practices that differed sharply from those of other trade unionists and that violated some of the central tenets of the age of segregation." Biracial unionism developed relatively early in New Orleans with the formation of a Cotton Men's Executive Council in 1880. This initiative was led by the all-white Screwmen's Benevolent Association, which was forced to confront the issue of race when employers tried to break their control by using black screwmen. The Cotton Council, which included most of the port's white and black labor organizations, provided an institutional framework for regulating wages, working conditions, and work-sharing agreements. The council successfully mediated racial tensions until the mid-1890s when, under the pressure of a severe economic downturn, cooperation foundered amid a series of strikes and racial violence. The Cotton Council reemerged in 1901 with the International Longshoremen's Association to provide a broader institutional base for such local organizations. The ILA, perhaps more than any other labor organization of the time, pursued a policy of overcoming occupational and racial divisions through interracial collaboration. With the ILA acting as mediator, efforts toward biracial unionism

sprang up in ports all along the Gulf Coast, including Galveston. Biracial unionism was an imperfect, but nevertheless significant, strategy
that broke racial barriers and revealed much about how both black and
white workers balanced their class and racial identities.[7]

Labor historians have been slow to investigate this intersection of
race and class in the past although, as Arnesen points out, the topic is
now central to the field of labor history. Herbert Gutman and his followers were among the first historians to examine race and class, and
Gutman himself pointed to the urgent need for a more detailed knowledge of the interaction between black and white workers and particularly of the "local world" of the black worker. However, early studies in
the "new" labor history tended to emphasize the role of skilled white
artisans to the exclusion of unskilled and black workers. Critics such as
Herbert Hill and David Roediger, among others, have argued that the
emphasis Marxist scholars placed on class ignored white racism altogether or replaced it with a mythologized past of working-class solidarity. As Barbara Fields and Arnesen have pointed out, however, such
critics have themselves been guilty of turning class and race into wholly
separate and deterministic categories. Stressing white racism alone
ignores the ideological perspective of those black workers who participated in the labor movement, whether in wholly independent unions or
through biracial unionism.[8]

Although a majority of both black and white workers remained outside the ranks of organized labor, or even chose to act as strikebreakers,
black activism within the labor movement provided an important alternative for some. For this significant section of black workers, labor
unions represented a means to further their own goals and although
white labor variously reacted with hostility, neutrality, and only occasional support, biracial unionism was a part of that strategy. Evidence of
this "local world" of black labor is often difficult to uncover, and labor
historian Robin Kelley has suggested that we approach the topic through
"hidden transcripts." However, unionism was a part of this world of
black working-class culture and a part for which union records, newspa-

pers, and photographs provide at least some hard evidence. Moreover, as Arnesen emphasizes, the details of this activism, rather than broad, deterministic categories offer an opportunity to pose important questions on the nature of working-class relations and black labor activism. Neither class nor race are, by themselves, sufficient categories for analysis—nor are they the only categories since we all occupy multiple and intersecting identities. Rather, it is through the connections between economic and racial issues that we can reach a fuller understanding of race and the labor movement and workers' consciousness.[9]

The development of biracial unionism in the South was as varied and complex as the industry itself. While economic self interest was always at the forefront of white workers' motivation, Arnesen also charts the range of other factors that shaped the particular course followed in each port. The character of employment relations, the power of employers, the prior history of racial division or segmentation of labor, the strength of black unions themselves, and the culture of longshoremen both black and white all played a part. Besides these local factors, the longshoring industry by its nature is part of a geographically broader movement. Local unions became bound to the ILA yet retained a measure of local autonomy through the South Atlantic and Gulf Coast District Association. Thus, as Arnesen argued, a whole range of experience, not abstract categories, influenced both black and white workers. And while race and class experience directed the thoughts and actions of both sets of workers, to understand why any particular component of these identities operated at any one time the dynamics of class and race must be studied over a period of time, and across a range of social, political, and economic developments.[10]

The early history of Galveston's waterfront has never been covered from the broad perspective Arnesen described although the subject has not been entirely ignored by scholars. In the 1930s economic historian Ruth Allen gathered information on Galveston's longshoremen for inclusion in her groundbreaking *Chapters in the History of Organized Labor in Texas*. Allen recognized that "Racial recriminations and perse-

cutions do not build the subtle shadows of the Southern scene. Not bit-
terness but harmony limn the picture." Interaction between white and
black unions depended upon local conditions and black unions used
organizations such as the State Federation of Labor to push for equal
rights within the union movement. Philip Foner, in his extensive study
of the black worker, acknowledged the strong commitment among
many black workers to the ideals of unionism. Foner uses an 1898 strike
by coastwise longshoremen in Galveston to demonstrate "a clear case in
which black workers placed union loyalty above racial identity." Broad
studies by F. Ray Marshall and Lawrence Rice devoted paragraphs to
the subject based largely on Allen's work, but Allen Taylor provided the
first in-depth study of Galveston's waterfront workers in his "A History
of the Screwmen's Benevolent Association." Taylor's dissertation gives
the most complete picture of the task of cotton screwing, particularly its
economic importance, as well as covering aspects of the association's
development as a job-conscious union. The writings of labor historians
James Reese and James Maroney provided further background on
organized labor in Texas and Galveston as well as the early development
of the SBA, the role of the ILA on the Gulf Coast, and a 1920 strike by
Galveston's coastwise workers. Works by Ruth Kelly and Thomas
Barker covered the commercial development of Galveston as a port.
Most recently, Arnesen himself has included sections on Galveston in
several articles that begin to draw comparisons between Galveston and
its chief commercial rival, New Orleans.[11]

Robert Shelton's dissertation contains a great deal of statistical evidence on Galveston's population before 1860 and focuses on four of the
strikes that occurred in Galveston between 1865 and 1920. However,
Shelton does little to explain the particular conditions that existed on
Galveston's waterfront and how these conditions affected white and
black longshoremen. More importantly, he relies heavily on a few secondary sources rather than the extensive union records. Consequently,
Shelton's work does not sufficiently explain the motivation of these
workers, particularly the black unions, and why biracial unionism in

Galveston took the form it did after 1900. Ernest Obadele-Starks's work similarly fails to make full use of sources or to take account of the intricacies of waterfront labor, particularly the distinction between coastwise and deep-sea longshoremen. Obadele-Starks does recognize that black workers saw unions as a way to combat the racism of white labor. Instead of unionism, however, he sees strikebreaking and working below recognized wage scales as the chief tactics of black labor, thus missing the extent to which many of Galveston's black unionists pushed for economic equality through biracial cooperation. None of these works gives a complete picture of Galveston's waterfront workers over an extended period of time paying particular attention to the intersection of race and class. Some were written from the perspective of economic, rather than labor, history or focused on a particular group of workers or incident. Consequently, we have a fairly detailed knowledge of the port's labor aristocracy, the white screwmen, and the strikes of 1898 and 1920. Strikes, however, were not typical of Galveston, and little has been written about white longshoremen in the deep-sea and coastwise trades or, more importantly, the struggle of black screwmen and longshoremen to gain a place on a waterfront dominated by white labor.[12]

The story does, however, revolve around the white screwmen. The Screwmen's Benevolent Association, formed immediately after the Civil War, was Galveston's first and most powerful waterfront labor organization, which exercised a craft-like degree of control over wages and working conditions for many years. Since cotton was by far Galveston's most important export, the SBA was at the center of most major developments on the waterfront, drawing the other waterfront unions, white and black, into its orbit. The SBA first set the pattern as an independent labor organization but later led the way in the organization of local, district, and international associations under the auspices of the ILA. Similarly, the SBA was the first union to turn away from the policy of exclusion and recognize the necessity of including black workers into the fold of organized labor. The SBA's manuscript archive held at the University of Texas at Austin is also the most extensive of all Galveston's waterfront unions, with records of union meetings dating back to the very first meeting in 1866. These minutes are often frustratingly terse when it comes to the details of decision-making, but, supplemented with local newspapers and other sources, they reveal an organization in an almost constant ideological tug-of-war. While economic self-interest prompted union officials to recognize the necessity of coming to terms with organized black labor, race consciousness motivated rank-and-file members to be more reluctant to make concessions to black workers.

Each chapter of this work corresponds to a period in the development of the SBA and is framed by the commercial development of Galveston as a port. Piloted by the city's leading commercial families, the period from 1865 to 1924 was one of almost uninterrupted growth for the port, even though underlying trends presaged its eventual decline. As the port's economy began to prosper from the westward spread of cotton farming from 1865 to 1880, so the SBA grew from a benevolent society into a fully job-conscious union. The SBA adopted a policy of excluding black labor in these early years, but this did not hinder the appearance of the first black labor organizations by the mid-1870s or strikes by longshoremen and black laborers during the Great Upheaval of 1877. By the 1880s, the SBA had fully established its control over the loading of cotton but with cotton exports continuing to rise, the SBA could not maintain its monopoly. Norris Wright Cuney, a leading black Republican, won a contract for black cotton workers in 1883 despite a strike by the SBA. Two years later, Cuney, this time aided by the anti-union Mallory shipping line, successfully broke the monopoly of white coastwise longshoremen. Black workers had secured regular employment, but in Galveston, as elsewhere, their world was not simply bound by "white racism, economic institutions and Negro middle-class organizations."[13] Black workers made choices for themselves based upon their own experience and situation and, again as elsewhere, one of those choices was unionism. Although employed by Cuney, the leader of Galveston's black middle class, black waterfront workers took their own initiative in forming unions and seeking recognition from the SBA and other longshoremen's unions as well as inclusion in Galveston's Trade and Labor Assembly.

In the 1890s changes in technology and the structure of the shipping industry added to the commercial pressures facing the SBA. Like craft workers elsewhere, Galveston's white screwmen had successfully exploited employers' dependence on their skills to uphold their own definition of fair wages and work practices. Also like craft unions, they now faced their own twin challenges from technology and management rationalization.[14] With cotton exports continuing to rise, employers began to mount their first serious challenges to the workers' control of the screwmen and one firm of shipping agents began to exclusively employ the leading black association, the Cotton Jammers and Long-shoremen's Association. Employers also began using ordinary long-shoremen to load cotton, thus bringing the SBA into conflict with the other leading white union, the Longshoremen's Benevolent Union. Similar pressures during the previous decade had prompted waterfront unions in New Orleans to form a biracial Cotton Men's Executive Council to successfully mediate work and racial divisions. The SBA now cautiously followed a similar path by seeking a working agreement with the Cotton Jammers, a move the black association welcomed. Ironically, biracial unionism in New Orleans disintegrated amid mounting employer opposition and a deepening economic depression, further convincing the SBA of the need for some kind of biracial coop-eration in Galveston. In 1898 black longshoremen on the Mallory docks organized and joined the American Federation of Labor in their unsuc-cessful bid to win better wages. However, not all of Galveston's black longshoremen held the same faith in a white-dominated labor move-ment and this ideological divide among black workers was demon-strated in 1898 when a breakaway group from the Cotton Jammers formed the Lone Star Cotton Jammers Association. The Lone Stars chose to secure work by working below the recognized wage scale, thus competing with both the SBA and Cotton Jammers. This move created an often bitter divide between the two black associations and would hinder attempts to build a working coalition such as had existed in New Orleans on Galveston's waterfront.

By 1900 Galveston had achieved its long-standing goal of becoming a deepwater port serving the trans-Mississippi West. As commercial and technological pressures continued to erode the screwman's craft, the SBA began to sacrifice its long-held independence by seeking a bulwark in broader organizations such as the State Federation of Labor and the ILA. The SBA also continued to seek agreements on wages and working sharing with the Cotton Jammers and Lone Star Association. In New Orleans, waterfront associations had healed the divisions of the previous decade; in 1902 they reached an unprecedented agreement that black and white gangs would work side by side, or "abreast" one another. Similar efforts in Galveston failed, however, largely due to the intransigence of the Lone Stars. In 1908 the SBA made a determined effort to reach a joint agreement, and the two black associations used the opportunity to push for the adoption of the New Orleans plan of amalgamation. Although SBA officials persuaded their members that amalgamation was the only solution, black officials were less successful and the lengthy negotiations faltered without agreement. The SBA was more successful in forming a local Dock and Marine Council comprising ILA locals and, in 1911, a Gulf Coast District Association. The formation of these local and district ILA councils led to renewed efforts to recruit black workers, particularly the Cotton Jammers and Lone Stars. The Cotton Jammers joined the ILA in 1911 and almost immediately used the District Association to raise the issue of amalgamation. Following a directive from the District Branch, the SBA and Cotton Jammers reached an agreement, and, despite opposition from employers, white and black screwmen in Galveston began the 1912 season working abreast one another. However, the agreement could not last while the independent Lone Stars continued as a thorn in the flesh of both sides, and the SBA reneged on the work-sharing agreement after just one season. This decision resulted in SBA's suspension from ILA amid much denunciation and recriminations on all sides. The situation was only resolved when the Lone Stars finally agreed to join the ILA.

The war years were lean ones for the longshore industry as foreign shipping declined, but Galveston quickly recovered its trade after 1918. The postwar years brought a renewed effort by employers across the country to break union power. In Galveston, the Southern Pacific and Mallory companies provoked white and black longshoremen into a joint strike in 1920 by refusing to implement a wage rise set by the wartime National Adjustment Board. Faced by a united front of white and black labor, business interests leading an open shop campaign called on the power of the state government to impose martial law in Galveston over the protests of city government and citizens. The strike was defeated and union power in the coastwise trade broken. Such coercion was not required to subdue the SBA. Since the late 1890s, cotton screwing had been a dying craft made obsolete by high-density cotton compresses and larger capacity steamships that rendered the screwman's time-consuming skills unnecessary. Following several years of pressure from employers, the SBA finally agreed to merge with the deep-sea longshoremen's union to form a new ILA Local 307 in 1924. As part of this agreement, the new local signed a fifty-year agreement to share work with the Lone Star Association on a fifty-fifty basis. Henceforth, white and black gangs would work aboard the same ship, but they would work separately, taking turns to work the fore and aft holds. Ironically, it was not the unions who insisted on this work-sharing agreement, but the employers, who had for so long tried to exploit racial divisions to their advantage. The employers, in fact, had been too successful with their practice of giving the larger percentage of work to black labor, and they now wished to restore a more "equitable" distribution of their large payroll. Even more ironically, the Cotton Jammers, who had once led the push for recognition as part of the union movement, chose to remain outside this agreement and contract independently.

Galveston's waterfront workers shared the same concerns as other longshoremen along the Gulf Coast: they held similar class and racial attitudes, faced the same pressures from employers, and developed their own unique pattern of biracial unionism. Galveston thus provides a study of how a particular laboring community organized to deal with issues such as class, race, changing technology, and employer hostility. Galveston also provides a significant point of comparison within the broader movement of biracial unionism along the Gulf Coast, particularly when compared to New Orleans, a much larger port with a greater volume of trade and more diverse cargoes. Competitive pressures were much greater, particularly in the deep-sea sector, where black labor presented a large and well-organized threat to the control of white unions. With employers more than willing to exploit racial divisions by playing one race against the other, job competition threatened workers' control over wages and working conditions and led to strikes and racial violence. These very conditions, however, also led to an early realization by white and black unions that working together was essential if they were to combat exploitation by employers. With Galveston's trade dominated by cotton exports, job competition was less intense as white and black labor each settled into their own corners of the labor market. Employers were less able to exploit racial divisions; strikes were rare and serious racial conflict almost unknown on Galveston's waterfront. Although leaders of white and black screwmen came to recognize the need for interracial cooperation, rank-and-file members on both sides were often reluctant to follow. Steps toward biracialism were halting and the ultimate goal of amalgamation only briefly realized. Galveston's longshoremen never reached the same depths of confrontation and racial violence as in New Orleans; neither did they reach the same heights of cooperation.[15]

CHAPTER ONE

"No persons of Color"

The Screwmen's Benevolent Association and the
White Labor Monopoly

Galveston is a barrier island, created over the years by the deposition of sand and silt carried in by the currents of the Gulf. Twenty-seven miles long and between half a mile and three miles wide, situated two miles offshore parallel to the Texas coast, the island protects Galveston Bay from the Gulf. In the early nineteenth century, the island lacked water and was isolated from the mainland; yellow fever and hurricanes were other perennial problems. Yet Galveston Island protected the best natural harbor on the Gulf Coast and was close to Mexico, the West Indies, and the Gulf Stream flowing north. Antebellum visitors were impressed by Galveston's potential as a port, despite the obvious danger high tides posed to a low-lying island. Thomas North, a New York journalist viewing the island from a Morgan Line vessel in 1860, saw a "mirage" suspended in the air:

> On nearer approach the illusion disappears, and there
> stands before you, on a small piece of nature's ground work,
> and as though painted by a fairy hand, in spirit and shad-
> ows, on the low extended horizon beyond, Galveston,
> exciting the strange beholder into the romantic feeling that
> it is a city of fairies.[1]

Even allowing for North's hyperbole, Galveston's origins were steeped in romance. The pirate Jean Laffite was among the first to recognize Galveston Bay's advantages; legends of buried treasure are a part of his legacy. In the 1830s Galveston quickly graduated from pirate base to legitimate seaport, particularly as the young Republic of Texas sought a vital trade link to the north. The Morgan Line sent the first steamboat from New Orleans in 1837, thus linking Galveston to New York. Although called a city, Galveston consisted of little more than two or three houses and the frames of several others, yet even Houston, Galveston's great rival and eventual nemesis, recognized the importance of a natural harbor. According to the *Houston Telegraph*, the port was destined to soon become:

> the center of a commerce rivaling in extent that of many of
> the first commercial cities in the world. The products of
> many millions of acres of the most fertile lands in the
> globe, and of many rich mines of gold, silver, and iron, will
> necessarily be wafted to this port rendering Galveston City
> the commercial emporium of Texas.

The first cotton bound for Liverpool was shipped in 1839, thus establishing the basis of this future prosperity, as 228 vessels entered the port that same year, bringing freight and 4,376 passengers. Although the port had outgrown its pirate roots, it took more time to shake off its frontier image and not all antebellum visitors shared Thomas North's ethereal vision of the island. Charles Hooton, visiting the island in 1841, agreed that from a distance Galveston appeared as a fine city:

> but its glory vanishes gradually in proportion to the near-
> ness of the approach of spectator, until on his arrival at the
> end of one of the long, rude wooden projections, called
> wharfs, which shoot out some quarter of a mile into the
> shallows of the bay, he finds nothing but a poor straggling

Many publications extolled Galveston's commercial success, particularly around the turn of the twentieth century. Rarely, however, was much prominence given to the waterfront workers behind that success. *Courtesy of the Rosenberg Library, Galveston, Texas.*

collection of weather-boarded frame-houses, beautifully embellished with whitewash.[2]

• • •

By the time of the Civil War, however, Galveston had developed into a busy port of several thousand inhabitants as agricultural products from the interior flowed out to Northern and European ports in exchange for farm supplies and general merchandise. The city took on a more refined air as it grew into one of Texas's principal commercial centers and became a home to merchants, bankers, shippers, and foreign consuls. Immigration added a cosmopolitan flair to the commercial and official functions as the town developed its own distinct visual and social character. As Donald Meinig's history of early statehood described it: "In the whole structure and fashion of its community life, Galveston was not so much a culmination of Texas culture as a combination of Texas wealth and the elements of many cultures, a product impressive and unusual to Texans and foreigners alike."[3]

From the first, Galveston attracted entrepreneurs keen to realize the extravagant vision of Galveston's destiny. In 1853 four dry goods merchants, George Ball, John H. Hutchings, and brothers John and George Sealy, helped to finance the construction of Galveston's first railroad, the Galveston, Houston and Henderson line, which began operating in 1860. Determined to expand Galveston's commerce, the four men also founded the banking firm of Ball, Hutchings and Company in 1854 and the company that was to become known as the Galveston Wharf Company. The object of the company was to consolidate all of Galveston's wharves under common quasi-public ownership and control. The wharf company paid the city an annual dividend of around 6 percent in exchange for control over almost all of Galveston's wharves. Hutchings acted as president of the company and a director of the railroad; John Sealy was vice president of the railroad and a director of the company. The wharf company's monopoly, and the prices it charged for its facilities, eventually drew criticism from merchants and shippers and became a target of Granger discontent. The Grange movement began in 1867 as an agrarian fraternal organization but quickly became a vehicle for farmers' grievances, particularly against the financial power held over them by large corporations. The Texas Grange singled out the Galveston Wharf Company for using its monopoly to charge farmers high rates for handling cotton. However justified such attacks, it was the wharf company that began to finance the integration of the port's rail and water facilities and attract Northern capital. In time, Ball, Hutchings, and the Sealys were joined by other leading commercial families, notably Henry Rosenberg, William Moody, and the Kempner family. These names came to dominate the city's leading commercial and political organizations; the Cotton Exchange, Deep Water Committee, Relief Committee, and the progressive Commission Government of the early 1900s. This internecine pattern was perhaps unsurprising in such a relatively small community as Galveston, yet it was the willingness of these men to invest time and money in the port and its facilities that played a large part in the port's success. However, their unwillingness to invest in and develop a broader industrial base was one element in the city's eventual decline.[4]

Galveston's rise as a port was aided by a relatively quick recovery after the Civil War and its own ambition. The port was briefly occupied and blockaded by Union ships throughout the war, but Galveston's isolation from the main conflict left the city itself largely untouched. In contrast, Union troops occupied New Orleans, Galveston's great rival on the Gulf Coast, early in 1862. Although many citizens left Galveston for the duration, they quickly returned at war's end. Galveston's leading newspaper, the *Daily News*, was soon reporting that "All is bustle and activity, the wharves are crowded with shipping, the stores are filled with goods, buyers from the country are in force and our merchants jubilant." Barely a year later, the newspaper outlined the city's great destiny: "It may look extravagant to hold up Galveston as destined . . . to be the sea-port of half a continent, and yet all the premises and existing facts lead to that conclusion." The only barrier preventing Galveston from fulfilling her destiny was physical: ironically, the same sand barrier that sheltered the harbor from the ocean restricted the shipping lane to a shallow channel. Larger vessels thus prevented from entering the port were forced to anchor in the Bolivar Roads beyond the sand bars where lighters ferried cargoes to them, a costly and time-consuming process. Given the national importance of the project, the *News* thought it reasonable to assume that the government would undertake the deepening of the channel through Galveston Bay. There was, after all, scarcely a Northern harbor of any importance on which the government had not expended far more money than would be required to make the port of Galveston the best on the whole Gulf: "as it is the most convenient of access for the whole extensive, varied and productive region west of the Mississippi." The cost, estimated at $2 to 3 million and equal to the amount spent per day in the late war, was trifling when compared to the benefits. Despite its faith in the justice of Galveston's claim on the national purse the *News* could not help but goad the federal conscience by playing the injured party: "But the policy of the party in power is to bring utter ruin to the South, even though the North must suffer almost as much, rather than give prosperity to the whole country by a just and liberal course towards the Southern people."[5]

It would be several decades before Galveston received the necessary federal aid; until then the city's leading businessmen relied on their own efforts in attracting Northern capital to invest in the port. Galveston's prosperity would be based upon cotton: the demand for cotton was growing, the crop was easy to raise, and railroads were opening up large new areas of production, particularly along the Texas-Arkansas frontier. Moreover, it was also the one crop an impoverished South could grow on credit. Cotton production in Texas approached its prewar level by 1870 and then approximately doubled every decade, reaching a high of 3.5 million bales in the 1900–1901 season. However, rivers in Texas were largely unnavigable, and hauling by freight was slow and expensive, as was shipping on the few railroads built prior to the Civil War. Before Galveston could begin to tap the developing market, new railroads and cheaper transportation were required to open up the hinterland. The Galveston, Houston and Henderson Railroad was just a first step toward the railroad boom of the 1880s that pushed the line of commercial agriculture further west. In the meantime, the port's own transportation and commercial facilities had to be developed in order to attract and handle trade. To this end, the Ball, Hutchings, and Sealy partnership sought to attract Northern capital. While railroads would be a key factor in the development of the New South, in the immediate postwar period water transport held the advantage.[6]

Shipping firms like Charles Morgan and C. H. Mallory and Company benefitted from the construction of steamships during the war and the slow speed at which Southern railroads were rebuilt and integrated in the postwar period. Mallory based its trade upon providing regular coastal services. This liner service had the advantage of regularity, but it was more expensive to run than a tramp fleet that relied upon special charters or chance to pick up a cargo. As James Baughman, historian of both Morgan and Mallory lines, explained: "Since success depended on maintaining a regular volume of mixed trade, [Morgan and Mallory] worked constantly to attract and hold permanent customers and to concentrate traffic at ports most convenient to themselves and to a majority of shippers." Although most of Galveston's cotton would be shipped to Europe and elsewhere by tramp vessels and, by the 1890s, liner service, a regular coastwise service provided an important link to markets in the North. Moreover, since Galveston would never attract a large volume of foreign imports, this service remained especially vital for bringing finished goods to merchants in the city and interior.[7]

Prior to the Civil War, the Galveston Wharf Company offered preferential treatment to the Morgan Line, which had run regular service between Galveston and New Orleans since 1837. Charles Morgan dominated the coastal trade of the Gulf and the quick resumption of his Texas services after the war required the enlargement of his port facilities in that state. In 1867 Morgan received exclusive four-year rights to Galveston's best wharves, Central and Brick wharves, and to one warehouse. In the longer term, however, Galveston's businessmen planned to end their traditional dependence upon New Orleans as a supplier, consumer, and re-exporter of goods by linking a direct service to New York. As the wharf company later revealed: "It became an object of the first importance to our company to get the [New York] steamships to land at our own wharves, and at the same time to get more and more and better vessels in the business." Morgan remained the wharf company's main customer until 1870 while other New York-to-Galveston lines docked at Bean's Wharf. During the first months of 1870 the wharf company negotiated with the Galveston, Houston and Henderson railroad to extend its tracks directly to the waterfront and appointed a committee to report on the best ways "to secure the NY trade." With improvements to its facilities in hand, the Galveston Wharf Company entered into an agreement with the Mallory Line to use those facilities.[8]

The Mallory company had focused business on both New Orleans and Galveston after the war but Galveston offered less competition and more potential. Through determination and superior vessels, Mallory quickly overcame most of its competition and secured a large share of the port's trade. The next step was to improve Galveston's dock facilities and develop railroad connections to the hinterland. Together, Mallory, the Galveston, Houston and Henderson Railroad, and the Wharf Company constructed a rail and water terminal in 1873 and negotiated expeditious through-freight handling at favorable rates with connecting railroads. Improving the port's shipping capacity was also essential. The Wharf Company offered the Mallory Line favorable wharf rates, and the Ball, Hutchings Company bought a $20,000 interest in three Mallory vessels. Moreover, the Wharf Company and its financial friends took a quarter interest in financing the construction of four new Mallory steamships. On August 12, 1871, the *City of Houston*, an iron steamship specially constructed to navigate Galveston's shallow shipping channel, made its first voyage to the port. As Baughman points out, Mallory emerged as the winner among half a dozen rival steamship lines partly as a result of expertise in ship operations but mostly from the pooling of their interests with those of the Galveston Wharf Company and the Galveston, Houston and Henderson Railroad.[9]

One unintended consequence of Galveston's alliance with Mallory was to push the Morgan company toward rival Houston. Although Galveston was Texas's most important connection to the outside world, the city relied on nearby Houston, whose better location made it a hub for railroads, for its connection to trade with the interior. Commercial rivalry between the two cities began as early as the 1840s, when inland planters and Galveston merchants tried to save time and handling costs by shipping cotton directly to Galveston, using steamship lighters to avoid Houston altogether. From that point on, each city sought to bypass the other—Galveston by using railroads and Houston by building a ship canal. The Houston Direct Navigation Company began taking cotton by ship and barge to be loaded directly onto ocean vessels in Galveston Bay, thus avoiding Galveston altogether. Beginning in 1870, vessels arriving in Galveston from the ports of Brashear and New Orleans were subject to a twenty-five-day yellow fever quarantine. The quarantine, timed to hit at the start of the commercial season, was clearly intended to favor Mallory's direct service from New York at the expense of Morgan's New Orleans route. Morgan won a court decision against the quarantine but then found that rebates granted by the Galveston Wharf Company were withdrawn in 1874, thus again placing the line at a disadvantage to Mallory. Frustrated with his treatment in Galveston, Morgan turned his attention to Houston.[10]

When the Missouri, Kansas and Texas Railway reached Denison, Texas, in 1873, railroads could now offer a through route to New York. The Galveston, Houston and Henderson, meanwhile, refused to alter to standard gauge tracks until 1876. In 1874 Morgan invested in the new routes and in the Buffalo Bayou Ship Channel Company, an operation run by many of the same men involved in the Houston Direct Navigation Company. Morgan provided a dredging fleet to deepen the ship channel from Houston to Bolivar Channel east of Pelican island in Galveston Bay, thus bypassing Galveston's quarantine, wharf company, and railroad. The Ball, Hutchings Company responded to this challenge with its own four-point plan. The strategy involved further improvements to the physical facilities of Galveston's dockside and the Galveston, Houston and Henderson line, and closer financial and traffic ties to Houston railroads in competition with Morgan. Further financial support was given to the Mallory Line to help offset losses from price competition with Morgan at sea. Lastly, a new Mallory liner service began to challenge Morgan's monopoly in the other Gulf Coast ports. A rate war, however, served neither shipping line's purpose in the high-cost liner trade and competition turned to cooperation when Charles Morgan died in 1878. In a secret traffic agreement designed to exclude other competitors, Morgan's son-in-law agreed to concentrate on the company's rail link from Houston to New Orleans, leaving Mallory in control of the coastal trade from Galveston. Morgan's decision to cooperate with Mallory was decisive in the subsequent course of development in the Gulf Southwest.[11]

Visitors to Galveston in the 1870s were impressed by signs of the port's burgeoning economy. A correspondent for *Scribner's* magazine told his readers that 'Latterly [Galveston] has assumed a commercial importance which promises to make it a large and flourishing city. . . . Few cities with a population of twenty-five or thirty thousand are more spirited; though manufacturing, as a solid basis, is nevertheless a supreme need." This caveat, which exposed one of the long-term weaknesses of the city's economy, was well founded. Moreover, the railways still threatened to siphon away business and Houston's ship canal remained another long-term problem. Norwood Stansbury, a former Louisiana planter, noted both these threats when on a visit in 1876: the railroads were taking enough business to affect both the Mallory and Morgan lines, and, because of the exorbitantly high wharf rates, Morgan was vigorously pushing his scheme to make Houston a port of entry. However, as one of the many seeking a fresh economic opportunity in Texas, Stansbury was more impressed by the port's wonderful growth since 1861 and the continuing air of commerce and prosperity:

> The business portion of the city cannot be surpassed for the elegance and solidity of its structures. The private residences are neat and often showy, with tasteful yards and shrubbery. Long lines of steamers and vessels give evidence of the large commercial and business transactions of the place. Galveston is truly the Queen of the Gulf.[12]

Thus enthroned, Galveston typified the dynamism, economic

opportunity and social mobility of the New South while retaining a social and cultural air that had more in common with older southern ports such as New Orleans, Savannah, and Charleston. Like the city's commercial ambition, this genteel air was cultivated during the antebellum period. Galveston's ethnic background was rooted in the Old World of northern and western Europe with around 40 percent of residents claiming German, English, Irish, or French ancestry. Early on, Galveston became a city where old money did not mix with new, although both funded the city's economic aspirations; a city ruled by a social elite who readily adopted European customs and taste. Although Roman Catholics outnumbered Protestants by three to one, elite status was reserved for Episcopalian, Presbyterian, or Jewish families. Germans were the most influential immigrant group, and it was they who constructed the park and pavilion of the Garten Verein, which became a social center for the city's elite. The opera house, the first built in Texas, also catered to refined tastes with performances by artists as varied as Buffalo Bill, Lillie Langtry, Sarah Bernhardt, and Oscar Wilde. Each ethnic group formed its own social club or benefit society to accompany an array of Masonic and fraternal orders, brass and string brands, and other clubs and societies. Less rarified entertainment could be found at the many flourishing beer gardens such as Weirylouis, Dalian's, and Schmidt's, or among the growing scene of organized sporting events.[13]

The opera house and other social, economic, and technical innovations distinguished the ascent to the throne of Texas's most important commercial and cultural center. Galveston would boast, among other things, of the first private and national banks in the state of Texas, as well as the first cotton exchange, telephone, electric lighting, hospital, historical society, and country club, as well as the opera house. This progress was also marked by the formation of some of the state's earliest and strongest labor organizations as Galveston became not only the state's leading commercial center but also its most strongly unionized city.

Labor organizations in Texas, like the state's economy in general, lagged behind the rest of the nation. The ports of Houston and Galveston were the only Texas cities to develop any kind of diversified economy prior to the Civil War. Even after the railroad building of the 1870s and 1880s, Texas remained a primarily agricultural economy, with little large-scale industry or concentrations of workers. Isolation was a further barrier to organization, and newspapers carried few reports of labor associations and activity in other states. Ethnicity, rather than occupation, provided the basis for early benevolent and social societies in Texas from the 1850s on; German groups in particular formed Workingmen's or Mechanics Associations to provide a range of social, educational, and welfare benefits. Houston formed a Workingmen's Association in 1857, but a similar effort in Galveston proved short-lived. Printers and carpenters were the only purely craft groups to form in either city prior to the Civil War. However, postwar economic growth was matched by a growth in organized labor, and by 1872 Galveston had a dozen or more labor associations. The New York trade and cotton exports fueled Galveston's growth, and it was on the waterfront where the greatest concentrations of labor were to be found. And it was on the waterfront where one of the first, and certainly the strongest of Galveston's early labor organizations, the Screwmen's Benevolent Association, formed in September 1866.[14]

· · ·

The primary aim of the twenty-three white screwmen who met on the evening of September 11, 1866, was to form a benefit society. The association agreed to hold regular meetings on the second and fourth Friday of each month and adopted a constitution and bylaws based upon those of the New Orleans SBA. Membership cost ten dollars and was restricted to men over the age of twenty-one and under forty-five who had worked for at least six months as a screwman in Galveston. Strict entrance requirements limited new membership; nominees had to pass an investigation committee and receive fewer than four black balls from the general assembly before being initiated. Fines were imposed for recommending "unworthy" candidates. Any member found guilty of "habitual drunkenness or other disorderly or dishonorable conduct," or "wicked or notorious practices" was liable for suspension, loss of benefit, and even expulsion. Meetings were governed by strict rules of decorum so that "the most prominent objects of our Association 'Harmony, Benevolence and Union' be not defeated." To ensure harmony, "No subject of a sectarian religious or political character shall be introduced before this Association." Fines were imposed for any infraction of the rules, including nonattendance at meetings and members' funerals. In early 1869 a permanent Relief Committee began to oversee the payment of benefits. Monthly dues were fifty cents, with a one dollar levy on the death of a member and fifty cents for a member's wife. After twelve months, a member could receive up to six dollars a week in sickness benefit, forty dollars in funeral expenses, and twenty-five dollars for a wife's funeral. Forty dollars went to the widow and orphans of a member who drowned without the body being recovered.[15]

Harmony and union were not always characteristics of the SBA's early years. According to Allen Taylor's history of the association, many of the first members were established foremen and stevedores, men in relatively secure positions who primarily saw the SBA as a benefit and social society. Membership quickly rose to fifty-three as ordinary gang members joined the organization, but they brought a different set of priorities with them. Screwmen were the highest paid waterfront workers, but the cotton season only ran from September to March. High wages were offset by the need to find alternative work, usually as longshoremen, during the offseason. Screwmen were not immune from economic insecurity and "Dropped from the Rolls for nonpayment of dues" frequently appeared in the association's minute books throughout the next thirty years. Consequently, many ordinary screwmen turned to the SBA for job protection. In January 1867 SBA members expressed concern at the amount of work going to nonassociation gangs. The following March they resolved: "That no member of this Association shall on any pretext, work sailors in a Gang either in, or outside the Bar, and further that no member shall work in a ship or for a Stevedore who employs sailors to work in a gang for the purpose [of] stowing cotton."[16]

Given the uncertain nature of dockwork, maintaining relatively high wages and restricting the labor supply were of particular importance to waterfront workers. For stevedores and foremen, however, sailors provided a convenient labor supply, particularly in Galveston, where many vessels were unable to reach the wharf until harbor improvements were made toward the end of the century. The tension between foremen and ordinary gang members caused the SBA to disband for the second half of 1867, but the association reformed the next January and withdrew the injunction against working sailors. The rule was reintroduced at the beginning of the 1869 season as ordinary screwmen again controlled the SBA. Benefit and social functions remained important, but from that time onward members became increasingly concerned with issues of job protection, wages, and working conditions. Two factors helped the SBA transform itself from a quasi-fraternal social society into a job conscious union: a sense of group solidarity and the economic importance of screwing cotton.[17]

Cotton screwmen stood at the top of Galveston's dock hierarchy. Their task was to move cotton bales from the wharf onto a ship and then stow the cotton into the hold. Screwmen worked in five-man gangs, with each gang led by an experienced foreman who picked the men to work under him. The screwmen were employed by stevedores, middlemen who either contracted with, or were employed by, local shipping agents and brokers to arrange the loading and unloading of their vessels. Stevedores chose their foremen, supplied costly tools and equipment, supervised loading, and paid the screwmen's wages. Nine gangs worked the early sailing vessels, while up to twenty-five were used on the much larger steamships. Three gangs would work at each hatchway, with one gang loading the cotton from the wharf to the deck, another taking it to the hold, and a third gang stowing the cotton in the hold, wedging each bale into place using a system of jackscrews and posts. In larger holds, several gangs worked at stowing. In an industry characterized by manual labor, the screwmen required particular strength and stamina. As Allen Taylor explained in his study of the SBA, "In addition to moving cotton bales and 205 pound jackscrews about a ship, the screwmen had to be able to exert great force against the tool to properly stow cotton." In this way, screwmen could "jam" the maximum amount of cotton into even the most irregular-shaped holds. Their strength and experience, and the wages they commanded, placed the cotton screwmen at the head of the labor hierarchy in Southern ports.[18]

Cotton screwmen must have felt a particular sense of unity: they worked together in regular teams, often in confined spaces, and at laborious and dangerous tasks. Moreover, conditions in Galveston added to the difficulties and dangers. For many years, cotton bales were stored on the dockside, covered only by tarpaulins, and rain made bales heavier, especially when a norther blew the tarpaulins away. Loading ships from lighters to vessels in the Bolivar Roads was anything but a simple matter with squalls and choppy seas making the task even more difficult. Not only were ships' holds irregularly shaped, but there was no standard size of cotton bale until after 1880, when the Galveston Cotton Exchange succeeded in standardizing the product of newer steam-driven cotton compresses. Gangs relied on the industry and competence of each member to perform the work efficiently and safely, yet injuries were commonplace. Foremen usually picked the same men for each new job, and stevedores similarly employed a regular group of foremen.[19]

Beyond the physical difficulties of cotton screwing was the skill and experience required. Although Taylor gives a detailed description of the tools and techniques of screwing taken from personal interviews with ex-screwmen, it is not clear to a layman quite how the screws were removed as the final bale in a row was jammed into place. Gilbert Mers, a Texas longshoreman in the 1930s, gave a description based upon first-hand accounts:

A row of bales (a "tier") was laid from either side ("wing") of the vessel, to meet at midship. At a certain point before that meeting the jackscrews were set. The cotton was screwed back to make a larger gap. How they filled that gap, "keyed" the bales that were to fill it, released the pressure on the screws and retrieved them without that pressure in turn kicking those midship bales out of place, how they forced those bales down into the tier, is the secret that made the screwmen true aristocrats of labor.

It was these mysteries that made the screwmen's craft so important to employers.[20]

The shipping industry represented a major capital investment and profitability depended upon a number of fixed and variable costs. Two of the most important variables were time spent in port and load capacity. Any unnecessary time spent at dock was money lost, yet the more cargo taken on, the more profit to be made. Screwing cotton cost more than hand-loading and took two to three days longer, so less voyages were possible in any given period. However, until the widespread use of high-pressure cotton presses after 1900, cotton bales were soft and bulky, and screwmen could increase ships' loads by between 10 and 20 percent. Profits per voyage increased by a similar amount. On coastal vessels tied to a regular sailing schedule, cotton was generally hand-loaded because time spent in port outweighed extra cargo, but on the longer transatlantic routes cotton screwing yielded a 4 percent increase in yearly profits. Thus screwmen occupied a specialized and important link in the chain of transportation.[21]

Sociologist Raymond Miller contends that dockworkers formed an "occupational community" with a strong sense of group solidarity. These communities are found in highly skilled trades, such as printing, or among isolated workers such as miners, sailors, and longshoremen. Miller contends that the widely prevalent conditions of dockwork even created a universal dockworker subculture. Beginning with the casual nature of dockwork, he identifies a number of factors commonly found on the waterfront. The work was exceptionally arduous and often dangerous, and although work was varied, there was only a limited occupational hierarchy through which a worker could progress. There was no regular contact with one employer, yet longshoremen were continuously in contact with foreign goods, seamen, and ideas. Finally, longshoremen tended to live near the docks and shared the belief that outsiders saw them as a low-status group. The clearer the boundaries of job territory, the stronger the ties of solidarity. Miller argues that "As casual laborers in constant fear of underemployment dockers learnt that solidarity was even more vital to them than it was to the ordinary worker; and as a tight community . . . they learnt the importance of loyalty and the fear of ostracism."[22]

Some historians have taken this idea a stage further, arguing that because these industrial communities were insulated against the conservative values of the surrounding society, they provided fertile ground for radical politics. However, in his study of West Coast longshoremen, Howard Kimeldorf contends that while this is sometimes true, at other times workers were insulated from left-wing political groups as well, "in which case isolation can become an obstacle to radicalism. In short, the mere fact that a group of workers is isolated tells us next to nothing about the content of their politics." New York's dockworkers, for instance, lived in an insular community yet belonged to one of the most conservative unions in the country. In contrast, San Francisco's dockworkers mingled freely with the larger community, yet they were among the most radical unionists.[23]

Certainly respectable society kept longshoremen as a group at a distance, regarding them as being among the lower elements of society. This undesirable reputation was partly due to the casual nature of dock work with its periods of enforced leisure and to the "shenangoes," the lowest and most casual section of waterfront labor. According to Charles Barnes's study of New York, "Though shenangoes wear longshoremen's hooks, hang about the waterfront, and handle the cargoes of barges and lighters, they must be distinguished sharply from the skilled and semi-skilled workmen whose good name they have helped to tarnish." In contrast to this flotsam and jetsam of the pier, a regular longshoreman was a hard-working family man—one who swore and fought hard but drank no more than any other worker. With few facilities on the piers, saloons were one of the few places where men could gather while waiting for work or to get a meal. This view was echoed in another study of New York by muckraking journalist and author Ernest Poole. Longshoremen worked long, hard hours, sometimes thirty or more at a stretch, in dangerous conditions. The strenuous work caused men to wear out at an early age, and those who were not capable of performing this work had no place on the docks:

> In gangs at every hatchway the four hundred men were
> trundling, heaving, straining, a rough crowd, cursing and
> shouting at the rough shouts of foremen . . . far from being
> the drunkards and bums that some people think them,
> [longshoremen] are like men of the lumber camps come to
> town—huge of limb and tough of muscle, hard-swearing,
> quick-fisted, big of heart.[24]

Cultural anthropologist and former longshoreman William Pilcher described the dockworker subculture in Portland, Oregon, in terms of masculine self-image. There are several facets to this self-image including a sense of independence. Because dockworkers are not tied to one employer or stevedore they tend to identify themselves by the class of longshore work they perform rather than as workers for a particular employer. Moreover, they can choose whether to work or not. The most important element, however, is an air of self-confidence. Working in highly coordinated teams in hazardous conditions, a longshoreman must not only have confidence in his own physical abilities but be able to convey that confidence to his fellow workers. This ability to take care of oneself and others is essential to avoiding accidents while a "devil-may-care" attitude helps to relieve on-the-job anxiety. Longshoremen thus place a high value on physical strength and courage and consequently on the ability to fight. Group norms are reinforced by hostility to outsiders and through work socialization such as in-group joking behavior and language. The saloon and the ability to gamble and drink large quantities of alcohol serve similar purposes away from work. While this rough culture reinforces group solidarity, it does not necessarily promote radicalism or even class consciousness.[25]

Labor historian Peter Way has argued that a culture based upon "excessive drinking and interpersonal violence" serves to subdue, rather than promote class consciousness. Way's study of Irish immigrant canal laborers corrects the discipline's focus on skilled workers whose culture served as a source of strength in their struggle to improve wages and working conditions. This focus ignores the much more numerous ranks of the largely powerless common laborer. As unskilled workers, their world was determined by material conditions of industrial capitalism and the struggle to maintain employment. The culture of Way's nineteenth-century Irish canal workers is much the same as that of Pilcher's twentieth-century longshoremen. Arduous and often dangerous manual labor bred a culture of rugged individualism that valued the ability to work and play hard. The emphasis on physical strength, drinking, gambling, and fighting provided an important, if typically male, means of self-definition, which was at the same time a means of self-exploitation. This rough side of workers' culture is "the negative side of class struggle" in which a culture determined by material forces directs anger and frustration inward rather than at the inherent exploitation of the capitalist wage labor system.[26]

Seaports were notorious for catering to the rougher elements of working-class culture, and Galveston had a reputation for providing more in the way of rough entertainment than many other ports. According to one recollection of the city's early years, "The saloon was the first institution in Galveston." The number of saloons in the city began to increase with the influx of German and Irish immigrants after 1850, especially along Water Street by the docks. By 1880 Galveston had

489 saloons, more than any city of comparable size and more than New
Orleans or any other Gulf Coast port. Certain sections of the city were
known for accommodating this less respectable side of the port's economy. Fat and Tin Can Alleys in the Fifth Ward held a particular noto-
riety along with the saloons, boardinghouses, gambling halls, and
brothels concentrated in "the district" north of Avenue E. A section of
Post Office Street held a reputation as a red-light district. One contemporary account cited the New London Theater, a large two-story frame
building on the southwest corner of Bath Avenue and Market Street as
the principal place for the large number of sailors usually in port and
"others of that horizon":

> It was strictly taboo in society to even mention this place,
> much less speak of what went on in the Theater. Then the
> large number of saloons and gambling halls, for gambling
> was legal, and other places of like character took care of the
> entertainment of those who wanted it very nicely.

Police and community leaders were generally willing to tolerate these
less savory entertainments as long as they remained confined. Attempts
during the early 1900s to enforce Sunday laws and other restrictions
resulted in a fall in arrests for public intoxication, but the city could not
easily shake off its past reputation.[27]

There is little direct evidence as to how far Galveston's waterfront
workers participated in the masculine self-image or the rougher elements of working-class culture, although official figures suggest that at
least some were eager participants. Out of 2,564 white and black males
arrested by Galveston's police force in 1905, 700 gave their occupation as
either screwman or longshoreman. More significantly, some of these
values were transmitted through the working practices and rules of both
screwmen's and longshoremen's unions. Most of Galveston's waterfront
unions either owned or rented their own hall but official notices were
still placed in dockside saloons. Union meetings were themselves an

occasion for social drinking, both during and after the meeting. It was also customary for the men to drink while at work. In the early 1900s, employers made several attempts to limit or end the practice of fetching beer at quartering time in the morning and afternoon, but this was one concession the men refused to make until Prohibition. A similar attempt to ban drinking during union meetings was amended to allow beer. The unions established fines for fighting at work, although a man was expected to defend his reputation. If a fight was caused by a member being "grossly insulted" by another, then only the party giving the insult would be liable to fine.[28]

Although Galveston's waterfront unions perpetuated certain less-reputable male values, they were also concerned with providing respectable alternatives. The saloon might have provided longshoremen with a refuge, a "poor man's club," providing a separate and autonomous male realm of leisure activities and social functions that reinforced working-class values; a drunkard, however, was a liability at work and tarnished the public reputation of an organization. Union members were fined for overindulging at union meetings, work, or the annual Labor Day parade. Unions also provided more family-oriented entertainment by organizing events such as annual picnics and balls. The Labor Day parade was followed by a picnic at Wollams Lake with foot races and other competitions and a regular tug of war event pitting a team of screwmen against the longshoremen. Women's auxiliaries provided a social setting for wives who were otherwise excluded from the male realm of the waterfront.[29]

A corollary to this respectable image was a sense of the workingman's rightful place within the community. Whatever the role of culture and working conditions in promoting group solidarity, the lack of space on the island made it difficult to maintain a wholly isolated community, and Galveston's waterfront unions did consider themselves as separate. Union constitutions sermonized on the monopolistic nature of capital and recited a litany of in "union is strength" and the duty to:

rescue labor from the condition into which it has fallen and to raise ourselves to that position in society to which we, as workmen are justly entitled, to place ourselves on a foundation sufficiently strong to insure us from further encroachments.

The objection to monopoly capitalism was a common refrain among American workers in this period, but unions like the SBA had no program to achieve their broader aims, focusing instead on the narrow self-interest of job protection and working conditions. Although several longshoremen served as city aldermen during the 1890s, unions themselves demonstrated an almost pathological avoidance of political matters. More significantly, at heart the SBA and Galveston's other waterfront unions shared a belief in the fundamental harmony of interests between labor and capital. One indication of this conservative attitude came at the annual Labor Day celebration. While attendance at the parade was compulsory for many years, the afternoon's speeches were delivered by politicians and businessmen who, while allowing the right of labor to organize and receive a fair wage, spoke at length on this commonality of interests. Unions did claim the right to a voice in the community, either singly or through local and state federations, and even on rare occasions to call a strike. However, even during labor disputes, Galveston's waterfront unions were usually willing to accept arbitration by a citizen's committee constituted of local businessmen. When they eventually looked beyond themselves by seeking ties with the broader labor movement through the ILA, and even agreements with black unions, Galveston's white unions were still motivated by self-interest rather than class solidarity.[30]

Despite its essentially conservative nature, the SBA was willing to use its strength to improve wages and working conditions. In August 1870 the SBA became the first labor organization in Texas to receive a state charter. A charter gave the SBA the right to conduct business transactions, to sue and be sued, and to receive donations, legacies, and bequests. During the 1870s the SBA's membership grew to include most of Galveston's white screwmen, and, as numbers increased, the association extended its control over working conditions, wages, and the labor supply. Less strict entrance requirements enabled membership to increase from around one hundred men in 1872 to between one hundred and fifty to two hundred by the mid-1870s. In 1875 the black ball rule was raised from four to fifteen, increasing membership still further. In March 1871 new work rules included setting a nine-hour day, with seven hours for night work, and "time shall count from leaving to returning to the Wharf." By the mid-1870s the SBA adopted the outward trappings of unionism, with caps and badges and an annual parade wearing "suitable uniform and regalia." In the late 1870s employers agreed to a wage increase from five to six dollars a day, with seven dollars for foremen. In September 1880 the SBA imposed a seventy-five-bale limit for a day's work. Any foreman or gang asked to do more was to leave the job forthwith. A few months later, a special meeting considered the complaint of "Bro. Charles Newell and gang" who were replaced after quitting a ship for having no cook. Newell's gang returned to work, and stevedores were made responsible for supplying a cook to gangs working in the outer harbor. These work rules were rigidly enforced, and members were heavily fined for infractions.[31]

Although entrance requirements were eased, rules such as the six-month apprenticeship still ensured that only competent local men became SBA members. Moreover, screwmen remained in short supply in southern ports. Requirements could be raised or lowered to meet the demand for labor but, overall, they kept only a limited number of skilled men available to employers. Other rules, such as the injunction against working sailors, were more directly aimed at enforcing a closed shop. In late 1870 the SBA notified stevedores that all stages of loading were to be considered as cotton screwing and tried to prevent the hiring of nonunion men during the slack season. After 1875 the SBA widened its boycott of nonunion labor.[32]

As early as 1869 the SBA had amended its rules to bar members from working "with or for, any person or persons, who shall employ to work on Shipboard, persons of Color." Despite barring "persons of color" the association worked in a cosmopolitan seaport. Galveston had a reputation for tolerance both in its indulgence of less reputable forms of entertainment and in race relations. Galveston's black population prior to the Civil War was not as significant as in other Southern cities. Slaves were illegally imported through Galveston, but the city took measures to curtail its free black population. According to the somewhat unreliable census figures of 1850, Galveston had 678 slaves and 30 free blacks, or 16 percent of the city's total population. In 1860 Galveston's 308 slave and 2 free blacks comprised only 4 percent of the total. In contrast, the South's largest free black community in New Orleans was well developed and stratified. In the decade after 1860, the Louisiana city's black population doubled to 50,456, increasing from 14.6 percent of the total population in 1860 to 26 percent by 1870. Galveston's slaves chiefly worked as domestic servants or dock laborers, and indulgent owners apparently used their domestics for ostentatious displays of their own status. A visiting British army officer noted: "innumerable Negroes and Negresses parading about the streets in the most outrageously grand costumes—silks, satins, crinolines, hats with feathers, lace mantles etc., forming an absurd contrast to the simple dress of their mistresses. Many were driving about in their masters' carriages."[33]

Like many southern cities, Galveston's black population rose after the Civil War as freedmen, many of them young men, moved to urban areas to seek work. By 1870 the city's black population stood at 3,007, or 21 percent of the total. The number of black citizens continued to grow for the rest of the century, although the percentage remained constant at around 20 percent. Despite their relatively small numbers in the antebellum years, Galveston's black community had already begun to form their own institutions. The first black church was organized for slaves by white Baptists in 1840, but the congregation built its own First Missionary Baptist Church in 1850. The Reedy Chapel on Broadway became the first black Methodist Church in Texas in 1848. After the war, the Freedman's Bureau established itself in Galveston, opening the first black school in 1865. As reconstruction ended and segregation began to take its place, Galveston's churches, schools, and most public buildings became racially segregated by the mid-1880s. While separate churches and schools were often a matter of choice, the Civil Rights Act of 1875 encouraged black citizens to protest against discrimination on railroads and in other public places. In 1875 two black women sued the manager of the Galveston Opera House after being ejected from the ladies circle. Although the manager was convicted and fined the case was eventually dismissed by a district judge.[34]

Housing was less segregated than in other Texas cities, particularly among the laboring classes, partly because of the lack of space on the island. According to one architectural historian, most houses east of Twelfth Street and south of Avenue J were inhabited by white and black laborers, with the poorest families living closest to the water. Laborers also occupied landfill areas on the western and southern edges of town. Many families lived along the city's back alleys, where converted stables and slave quarters stood at the rear of the large houses fronting the main street. Although blacks tended to live in pockets around black schools in the eighth, ninth, and twelfth wards, there were no predominantly black wards. The black population of the wards lay between 9 and 29 percent, with an upper limit of 47 percent by 1890.[35]

There were eight black churches and three schools in Galveston in 1882. The following year the *City Directory* listed twenty-one different black societies. Some of these societies, such as the Knights of Pythias, Rising Sons and Daughters of Progress, or the Garrisson Club, formed by young black men to cultivate taste for music and literature and all subjects that would tend to advance its members, catered to the small black middle class. Other clubs, such as the Hawley Guards, Excelsior Band, or the Colored Cadet band, which was often employed at big white funerals and in street parades, perhaps had a less limited membership. These societies served to foster cultural identity and racial uplift among the city's black population, but they also were a means of isolation.[36]

Racial lines were perhaps less clearly drawn in the city's lower forms of amusement, which were not solely reserved for the white population. According to one of Galveston's black middle class leaders, the Rev. Ralph Albert Scull, by the 1870s saloons and gaming were lucrative businesses and "The majority of the laborers drank and played cards or bet on monte." Scull listed several of the livelier black hangouts including Ike Rector's "flourishing place" at Post Office and Twenty-fifth Street, "Soup and Bully" at Market and Twenty-seventh Streets, and Bailey Sparks's "lively corner" at Avenue L and Twenty-eighth street. According to Scull, these and dozens of other smaller places in all parts of town providing "Drinks, women and games anything on the sport line." The most notable participant in this sport was Jack Johnson, the first black heavyweight boxing champion of the world, who worked on Galveston's waterfront for several years while developing his pugilistic skills. Jack "Lil' Arthur" Johnson described his fellow longshoremen as being:

> some of the toughest and hardest-boiled men imaginable. To them, fighting was one of the important functions of existence. They fought upon every occasion and on any pretext. They shot craps and indulged in other forms of gambling with almost as much ardor as they fought.[37]

Black laborers had worked on Galveston's wharves since the antebellum period. Before piers were constructed, black draymen would unload cargo and passengers in shallow water. Given the casual, unskilled nature of dockwork and the relative cheapness of black labor, freedmen probably found work on the waterfront in the years immediately after the war. While the *Daily News* editorialized on the need to compel freedmen to work, nothing suggests that the SBA, or any other class of white labor, was threatened by black labor until the organization of the first black unions after 1870. As in New Orleans, white labor dominated the waterfront. Cotton screwing was a white preserve, and the SBA was determined to keep it that way. The SBA's decision to exclude black workers appears to have stemmed from racial motives rather than a genuine economic threat.[38]

Before the 1890s very few of Galveston's screwmen were native southerners. The screwmen were an ethnically diverse group and overwhelmingly foreign-born, coming from England and Ireland as well as Germany and Scandinavia. Socioeconomist Herbert Bloch suggested that "These workers, primarily German and Irish, came equipped with a disposition towards competition and the ideology of a free-labor system and an unfortunate belief in black inferiority." This conditioning in job competition and work scarcity derived from European conditions where a labor surplus and shortage of agricultural land made the perception a reality. New Orleans also experienced considerable immigration even before the war, and Irish and Germans dominated certain sectors of dock work such as screwing and cotton yard work. Arnesen argued that many of these immigrants were opposed to slavery, either because they came from a radical democratic background or because slavery competed with free labor. They also opposed the power of the old planter class. None of this, however, implied sympathy or understanding for free blacks. Immigrants following the tradition of artisan republicanism identified labor as the source of wealth and civic virtue. Blacks without independence or property did not possess civic virtue— an assumption reinforced by racial attitudes in the South. While white laborers sought to protect their jobs and raise the dignity of labor with the eight-hour day, blacks simply wanted the right to work and protection from violence. While exhibiting few, if any, radical tendencies, the racial sympathies of Galveston's white waterfront workers were readily apparent.[39]

The Colored National Labor Union formed in late 1869 as a response to the exclusion of black workers by white unions. The CNLU's aim was to improve the working conditions of black labor, but it did not discriminate against race, sex, or skill, and even accepted Chinese labor. The union included industrial, agricultural, and common laborers as well as skilled artisans and mechanics, and, although black workers were the primary focus, it knew that it could not reject sympathetic whites. The union made an effort to organize state associations among southern black workers although its principles, "the chance to work and rise in American society through industry, temperance, frugality, and education," reflected the ideas of individual effort propounded by the black elite rather than of workers themselves. However, black dockworkers in Southern ports were taking collective action and organizing independently of the CNLU. In Charleston, black longshoremen mounted successful strikes in 1867 and 1868 and formed a Longshoremen's Protective Union Association in 1869. In New Orleans, black screwmen and longshoremen had struck in 1865 and 1867. A Screwmen's Benevolent Association No. 2 formed in 1870 and a Longshoremen's Protective Union in 1872. Black workers organized regardless of whether the cultural and ideological gap between white and black labor was too wide to be bridged by unionism. They did, however, see unions as a collective means to fight against exclusion by white labor and even to gain a measure of acceptance as organized workers with a common interest in wages and job security. Political polarization also drove a wedge between white and black labor, with freedmen supporting the Republicans and Reconstruction and whites the Democratic party. Arnesen points out that both black and white labor clung to party loyalty, regardless of their needs as laboring men. This point is illustrated in Galveston and Houston, where organizing black workers also served to bolster the position of black Republican leaders.[40]

Both Galveston and Houston had formed local CNLU associations by 1871. The Galveston branch was formed under the guidance of George Ruby, a black carpetbagger who had moved from New York to Louisiana before arriving in Texas. Ruby was a state senator, an influential Republican figure, and the leader of Galveston's black community. According to Carl Moneyhon's study of early Republicanism in Texas, Ruby organized the black labor force on the docks, with the Negro Longshoremen's Benevolent Association as an important part of his political machine. In a study of Texas's black leadership, Merline Pitre argues that while Ruby accepted the aims of the national CNLU, he also saw local organizations as a means of enlarging his own urban power base. According to Pitre, black workers began to move onto Galveston's waterfront after 1870 despite the hostility of white long-shoremen. Although these black longshoremen welcomed organizational efforts, Ruby's leadership tied these local associations to the Republican leadership. At the annual labor convention held in Houston in 1870, Ruby focused on party politics, urging black workers to vote for a party nominee rather than discussing the political, economic, and social needs of blacks. The Galveston Union proved short-lived, as did a branch of a white socialist International Workingmen's Association formed in 1872. The IWA disintegrated when some members argued for the inclusion of black workers. As one opponent of the proposal explained, "if the colored man is to be taken into full fellowship in this society, socially and politically, I must decline to become a member." Any effort to organize a more permanent laborers association would have to come from within Galveston's black community.[41]

Although Ruby's Negro Longshoremen's Benevolent Association had organized as early as 1870, the first evidence of collective action by black labor came during the Great Strike of 1877 and had no apparent connection to a black organization of the elite.

The labor turmoil that swept the country in 1877 was a source of some anxiety to Galveston's business community. The *Galveston Daily News* tracked the contagion and sought to quiet local fears when the strike reached railroad workers in Marshall, Texas, on July 25. "Everybody seems to be busy," reported the *News,* "and consequently happy, with not even the whispered mutterings of a strike to be heard along the entire sweep of the wharf." Despite this optimism, rumors of a strike were already circulating and three days later the newspaper's headline announced, "It Is Here." The first outbreak began on the Morgan Line wharf as a crowd of white and back laborers, thickly interspersed with police officers, moved along the wharf hoping to persuade other workers to join them. Police offered protection to non-strikers but the strikers appeared in a buoyant rather than threatening mood. After a brief counsel with the strikers, Morgan agent Captain Fowler acceded to their demands and they returned to work "laughing and looking right jolly to the discharge of their duties." The *News* made no mention of any black organization but it did report a rumor that Morgan's black laborers had been induced to strike for higher wages by white men on the Mallory Line wharf. Longshoremen's union officials denied any direct involvement but expressed sympathy with the strikers: "thirty cents an hour was not reasonable compensation for the sort of work required of the negroes, and that as they were getting forty cents an hour they thought it but just that the colored laborers should receive the same price." This minor dispute is the first example of the two contradictory impulses within white organized labor. On the one hand, the white longshoremen's support for the Morgan workers may have been genuine since lower wages for one group could depress wages all round. Alternatively, however, the white organization could have been playing to employers' racial sympathies, reasoning that at equal wage rates employers would choose white labor over black.[42]

Rumors of further action circulated over the weekend and on Monday, July 30, about fifty black laborers downed tools at the Giradin building. Marching in a body down the Strand, the men toured other sites to enlist support for their claim to a two-dollar daily wage. Accompanied by a police detachment, the well-ordered strikers patiently listened to a speech by the mayor, which failed to deter them. Later that day, police and citizens armed with pistols and batons quickly suppressed scuffles between strikers and draymen at a cotton press yard. At a mass meeting that afternoon, the strike's white leaders urged the men to remain peaceful and appointed a committee to meet with contractors. That evening, black washerwomen joined the protest by attacking a white steam laundry and forcing the town's Chinese laundries to close. The mood of the strikers hardened the next day after a wharf-front altercation between a white man and a black striker. Police arrested the white man, but when a group of strikers threatened to seize the man and lynch him, the police fired their pistols into the air, wounding one man. The incident prompted the enlistment of one hundred special police officers and the town's "citizen soldiery" to patrol the town. At a turbulent meeting that evening, 250 strikers heard that some contractors were paying or had agreed to pay the two dollars while others refused. White and black speakers condemned the police shootings but urged the continuance of the strike. One black speaker, however, rose to condemn both the threats and the strike.[43]

Norris Wright Cuney was a rising figure in the local community and state Republican party. Cuney's mother had been a slave and his father a white planter who made sure that Cuney received a good education. Cuney proved to be an able politician and, under George Ruby's guidance, quickly established himself in the Texas Republican party after the Civil War. Cuney's biographer, Virginia Hinze, suggests that for long periods in the 1860s and 1870s Cuney had no visible means of support, although he might have been connected to the Belle Poole Establishment, the "worst set of Gamblers and whiskey men in the country." Cuney did operate a tobacco and liquor establishment in 1875 and was twice arrested by the United States Marshal in Galveston for violations of revenue laws. He held several minor customs posts granted by the governor but this patronage ended with the election of a Democratic governor in 1874. When Ruby left Galveston for Florida in the early 1870s, Cuney remained as heir apparent. Cuney made his first bid for local respectability in 1875 when he ran for mayor of Galveston. Cuney lost the race, but his demeanor and political skill won the respect of his white opponents. According to Hinze's assessment, Cuney was an energetic climber and hustler whose hearty manner and heavy smoking and drinking were qualities well suited to the horse-trading of the political arena.[44]

Addressing the meeting, Cuney told the strikers that three hundred men could accomplish nothing "except riots and bloodshed" when there were more than fifteen hundred laboring men in the city willing to work. Moreover, there were seven hundred armed men in Galveston, with one thousand more in Houston, ready to "annihilate them all in an hour": According to the *Daily News* reporter:

> He deprecated in the severest terms the follies into which
> the colored men had fallen, and said they were not sup-
> ported by the white men, nor by the full strength of their
> own color . . . and in an elegant and forcible manner
> appealed to his countrymen to heed his warning and go
> peacefully to their homes and stay there.

Although "treated with contempt by the rabid faction in the crowd," the strike was over and Cuney received credit from a grateful white business community. Hailing Cuney as "one of the most intelligent of his race in the state," the *Daily News* editorialized: "Mr. Cuney knows but too well that the poor, deluded colored men who are now on strike in this city are but the tools of some few designing white men who have aspirations—political and otherwise." According to the *News,* Galveston's "bona fide workingmen" were hardworking and law-abiding until led astray by the ideas of outside political agitators, Communist Interna-tionals and Molly Maguires. Inflammatory rhetoric aside, Cuney's speeches did demonstrate his concern for the consequences of black workers inciting trouble, particularly given the rabid anti-labor senti-ment of the time. He may also have had the more personal motive of building his own stock among the white business elite. Cuney, however, was no puppet, seeking instead to advance both his own personal inter-ests and those of his race. He took a personal stand against segregation and always insisted that blacks be given equal educational and work opportunities. Within a few years Cuney would lead the challenge by Galveston's black longshoremen against the dominance of white labor on the waterfront.[45]

Cuney was aided by the men of the Cotton Jammers and Long-shoremen's Association and the first sign of a new assertiveness on their part came in early October 1879. The SBA called a special meeting to discuss taking action against and application by the Cotton Jammers for a state charter. By granting legal rights, a state charter would recognize the black association as a well-established institution. The SBA appointed a special committee with full power to take "such action as they deem proper." An appropriation of one hundred dollars, and more if necessary, underscored how seriously the SBA took the threat from the Cotton Jammers. The organization's charter was read at the next meeting, but there is no record of any further action being taken. There was perhaps little action the SBA could take because its own success was now beginning to work against it. As cotton production and exports rose so the demand for screwmen increased, yet the SBA stuck to its strict controls, particularly the seventy-five-bale loading limit. That January local businessmen had complained about the SBA's restrictive practices, and, with the demand for skilled labor rising, stevedores were increasingly tempted to look beyond the SBA.[46]

• • •

The port of Galveston made great strides between the end of the Civil War and 1880, developing from a regional port into one of national importance. Local businessmen pushed for Galveston's success, confident that they and the city were destined for great things. They built on the island port's natural advantages by investing in the commercial infrastructure of banks, railroads, and shipping facilities, which attracted Northern capital in the form of the Mallory company. Mallory's regular coastwise service established an important direct link with New York, but real economic success depended upon foreign exports of cotton. With the Texas cotton crop growing exponentially and commercial agriculture spreading further westward, the port's future seemed all but secured. The task over the next decade would be to attract federal money for harbor improvements to ensure that Galveston would fulfill her destiny.

The port's commercial growth brought increased opportunities on the waterfront, particularly for the cotton screwmen. In southern ports, screwmen were the aristocracy of the segmented and hierarchical world of waterfront labor and their skill in "jamming" the maximum number of bales into a hold played a vital role in a ship's profitability. Cotton screwing was the province of white labor, and Galveston's white screwmen organized themselves into the first and most powerful union on the waterfront. The SBA quickly developed from a benevolent society into a job conscious union that exercised a high degree of control over wages and working conditions. Like other craft unions, the SBA also sought to control the labor supply and barred sailors, nonunion men, and other "outsiders" from working as screwmen. The union also enforced Southern racial mores by prohibiting members from working for any employer who hired black labor.

Union rules alone, however, were not enough to exclude black labor in the South, particularly in such a segmented and expanding labor market as Galveston's waterfront. By at least the mid-1870s, black workers not only found work on the waterfront, they were forming their own waterfront associations. Moreover, during the Great Strike of 1877, black longshoremen and other laborers demonstrated their willingness to strike for higher wages. However, the most important developments for black labor during this time were the emergence of Norris Wright Cuney and the Cotton Jammers and Longshoremen's Association. Cuney, a black Republican who successfully established himself among Galveston's white business elite, would play the central role in securing work for black screwmen and longshoremen during the next decade. The Cotton Jammers may not have been the first black association on the waterfront, but it was to become the most well established and longest lasting. Within the next few years, the Cotton Jammers emerged as a permanent competitor to the white screwmen: a competitor that the SBA could either work with or against but would not be able to ignore.

CHAPTER TWO

"The colored men along the shore"

The Cotton Jammers and the Longshoremen's Association and the Challenge from Black Labor

G alveston's trade grew during the 1880s as the city's business community continued its efforts to expand the port and its trade. This growth in trade was reflected by a growth in organized labor on the waterfront and the emergence of a permanent black labor force. Aided by Norris Wright Cuney's influence in white business circles, black workers successfully challenged the monopoly of the white screwmen in 1883 and then the coastwise workers on the Mallory docks in 1885. In 1883 the continued rise of cotton exports strengthened Cuney's hand by undermining the SBA's ability to enforce a closed shop. In 1885 the willingness of the staunchly antiunion Mallory company to exploit racial divisions to secure cheaper labor gave Cuney and his men another opening. In New Orleans, waterfront workers had learned the consequences of a divided workforce by 1880, when the port's first biracial waterfront organization began to mediate racial divisions. Nationally, the Knights of Labor were organizing all workers, regardless of race, skill, or gender, yet this enlightened policy was circumscribed by the structural and ideological weaknesses of the order. The Knights had a strong presence in Galveston, yet white screwmen and longshoremen continued to fight to exclude black labor from the waterfront and even won support from the Knights during the 1885 strike. A citywide boycott called by the Knights failed to prevent Mallory from hiring black longshoremen but succeeded in breaking apart Galveston's only biracial labor assembly. By 1886 Cuney had achieved his goal of securing an income for himself and work for black laborers. These men were not content to find regular employment—almost immediately black workers under the banner of the Cotton Jammers and Longshoremen's Association began to seek recognition from white unions as a legitimate part of the union movement.

Galveston's continued economic growth faced a major challenge at the beginning of the 1880s as the development of a national railroad network provided a mixed blessing. With more than 6,000 miles of track laid in Texas during the decade, 1,527 miles put down in 1881 alone, the port benefited from the railroad boom. Galveston was the only Texas port with significant connections to this network via Houston while smaller ports such as Beaumont and Corpus Christi remained relatively isolated until the turn of the century. Cotton production in Texas also continued to increase, tripling to more than 1.2 million bales between 1870 and 1880 and reaching 1.6 million before the end of the decade. The expansion of a national railroad network also provided Galveston with increasing competition. The city's rivalry with New Orleans increased as each port's hinterland expanded, particularly once a Houston to New Orleans rail link was established. More importantly, an all-rail route to New York via St. Louis offered a cheaper alternative to water transport. New cotton markets and presses opened in Denison, Dallas, and St. Louis during the mid-1870s, reflecting a shift away from a reliance on seaports as the only conduit for trade. Moreover, since the smaller railroad lines serving Galveston could not compete with the rates offered by the large networks of Jay Gould and Collis P. Huntington serving St. Louis, it cost less to ship through St. Louis to New York than through Galveston. As the *Daily News* complained in late 1879, "We don't wonder at Galveston getting no cotton from northern Texas, where rates of

Cotton screwmen pause for the camera while unloading cotton bales from a sling. A jackscrew sits in the right foreground. *Courtesy of the Rosenberg Library, Galveston, Texas.*

freight are proportionately four times the through rates from points in northern Texas to New York."[1]

Galveston's business community responded to this new threat by renewing its efforts to win federal support for harbor improvements. The disadvantages of the sandbar that restricted the approach to Galveston Bay became more pronounced as larger iron and steel-hulled steam vessels began to replace wooden sailing ships. After several failed attempts to provide a deepwater channel, businessmen at the Cotton Exchange organized a "Committee on Deep Water" to commission an engineering study and to lobby for federal money. The committee's members were cotton brokers, bankers, lawyers, and land developers, and, since congressional support for the New South largely came from Republicans representing Northern capital, the election of the Republican R. B. Hawley as representative for Galveston may partly be attributed to a need to further the cause. A deepwater harbor could turn Galveston into a focal point for railroads carrying western minerals and grain to meet ships to transport these products to growing overseas markets. As local boosters argued, a deepwater harbor was vital if Galveston was to overtake its greatest rival, New Orleans:

> Either Galveston or New Orleans must become the great
> city of the Gulf, the metropolis of the empire west of the
> Mississippi and Missouri. . . . The city that shall stand sec-
> ond at the first, will stand so far behind it as to be wholly
> out of comparison with it, a mere satellite, so to speak, of a
> great planet, entirely by it and in its power.[2]

The Deep Water Committee sought support from a coalition of Western and Southwestern states whose grain and mineral sources, unlike the seasonal cotton crop, could provide year-round work for the port. California, for example, had become one of the nation's leading wheat-producing areas by the 1880s, and Galveston had taken steps to promote the grain trade from the mid-1870s with the formation of a Produce Exchange, the Galveston Elevator Company, and the Texas Star Flour Mills. Politicians and businessmen across the west were eager to find another outlet to the East Coast and Europe for their produce, and Galveston offered the shortest connection to shipping. John Evans, territorial governor of Colorado, became a leading promoter of Galveston, and his portentous rhetoric matched that of Galveston's business leaders in the quest for a direct route from "summit to sea":

> we will, in a short time, work a wonderful change in the
> relation of the mountain and of the Gulf, so clearly indi-
> cated by the wise Creator when he put the treasures of the

mountains, and brought the great arm of the Atlantic
Ocean so far West toward them, for their distribution.

With the flow of Manifest Destiny thus reversed, and Galveston's deep-water harbor as the nearest port of entry and Denver as a central interior point of delivery, the two would become among "the greatest cities on the Continent."[3]

A less grandiloquent and more business-minded support came from the railroads as both Gould and Huntington were attracted by Galveston's strategic position. Gould planned to run a steamship line from Galveston to Vera Cruz, thus improving his connections to Mexico. He hoped to persuade the Wharf Company and the local business community into providing terminal facilities for his proposed line. More significant was the interest of Collis P. Huntington's Southern Pacific railroad. Although interested in New Orleans, Huntington also knew that Galveston presented a shorter haul by railroad from California. Like Gould, Huntington made public his interest in Galveston as a terminal facility for the Southern Pacific. Huntington, however, made a deepwater harbor a precondition of his choosing Galveston over New Orleans.[4]

The expanding railroad network also presented a threat to Galveston's regular coastwise carriers, Morgan and the now-dominant Mallory Line. The two lines met this threat by plotting a step-by-step course from competition to cooperation as rail and water carriers in the Southwest engaged in a complex web of agreements to equalize freight rates and eliminate competition during the 1880s. Beginning in the late 1870s, both lines sought to improve their own rail connections. Morgan promoted its Houston to New Orleans connection while Mallory invested in the Gulf, Colorado and Santa Fe. They had also reached a secret agreement equalizing their respective sea rates between New York and the Gulf. Rate cutting would henceforth only be used against third-party competitors while Morgan and Mallory restricted their competition to services and railroad connections. By the mid-1880s Mallory was linked to the Gould system and Huntington's Southern Pacific had acquired Morgan's railroad interests. The Southern Pacific also swallowed up Morgan's shipping line, although it retained the Morgan name. All that remained was to equalize railroad freight rates, which was achieved by a series of agreements in the late 1880s. Freight costs were fixed around rail rates from St. Louis and Mallory's shipping rates, with a change in either rate leading to a compensatory change in the other. Consequently, all traffic originating west of a line running from Buffalo down to the lower border of North Carolina, traveled east via the Texas rail-sea link. The formation of the Southern Railway and Steamship Association similarly equalized competition between Southern carriers.[5]

• • •

The SBA was a well-established union by 1880, with assets of $10,000 and a membership of around 225 men, rising to 300 by mid-decade. The association now included most of the port's white screwmen and operated as a craft union controlling wages, working conditions, and the labor supply. A new work rule introduced at the beginning of the 1879–1880 season emphasized the SBA's strength. Seventy-five bales per gang would now be considered a day's work and gangs would only load more if paid overtime. Stevedores were warned that if they discharged any foremen or gangs for working to this limit, they would have all their gangs withdrawn. By restricting the amount of work per day, the new rule ensured that all SBA members could receive a fair share of available work. New Orleans had introduced a similar limit two seasons previously, and through such measures longshoremen in Galveston and New Orleans avoided the indignities and corruption of the daily shape-up. For stevedores and shipping agents, however, a seventy-bale limit increased labor costs and loading time. Perhaps most galling to employers was the sight of screwmen, having stowed their seventy-five bales by midday, strolling off the wharf boasting of working only "banker's hours." Moreover, the shortage of skilled labor meant even the SBA's own foremen found difficulties reaching the limit. In March 1881, a Brother Wilson complained that he found it impossible to find enough

SBA men to do the work and wanted permission to employ nonunion men. Two weeks later, another foreman asked if there was a limit under seventy-five bales for shorthanded gangs.[6]

Local cotton merchants and shipping agents complained of the SBA's restrictive practices and the high price of cotton screwing, but to little effect. In January 1879 a committee of the Cotton Exchange met to discuss the high cost of shipping cotton, particularly when compared to New Orleans. Committee members proffered several causes but were most "evidently impressed" by shipping agent J. Moller's attack on the SBA. According to Moller, the loading of cotton was "one of the most exorbitant charges" because the screwmen were paid their six dollars from the moment they set foot on a lighter rather than from when they began stowing. They were also paid during bad weather when no cotton could be loaded, yet the vessel even had to feed the idle men. Moreover, the SBA was trying to expand its control by taking steps to prevent ordinary laborers from loading cotton. Moller argued that the work could be done for half the cost by men from other ports, but it would take a joint effort from all the agents to successfully challenge the SBA.[7]

Although Moller declared his willingness to lead an attack, there seemed little to challenge the SBA's power as long as the port's trade continued to grow and the demand for skilled labor remained high. The employment structure of the waterfront also helped screwmen, and to a lesser extent longshoremen, maintain their position. Waterfront workers were hired by stevedores, who in turn contracted with a shipping line operating a regular service or agents who commissioned tramp vessels. Only Mallory dealt directly with its workers at this time, giving that company a greater say in wages and working conditions. Some stevedores still used sailors and other nonunion labor but, despite their constant appeals to the SBA to ease working restrictions, stevedores made no concerted effort to break the SBA's control. One reason for this reluctance was the close personal relationship between employers and employed. Many of the port's stevedores had risen from the screwmen's ranks and were still active SBA members and usually employed the same foremen and gangs from job to job. John Lovell points to several other factors that helped unions gain the ascendancy during the age of sail. Stevedoring firms were usually small and in competition with one another and so lacked both the resources and will to mount either an individual or united challenge to union power. Many stevedores, in fact, preferred to work with unions because by regulating wages and working conditions they eliminated competition. The balance between employer and employed would shift in the next several decades as large, foreign-owned steamship companies and more intense commercial pressure came to dominate over the irregular tramp service. These companies were more prepared to exert their influence over the stevedores when negotiating wages and working conditions and, most importantly, were more than willing to hire black labor. For the time being, however, Galveston's stevedores appeared more or less willing to maintain the status quo.[8]

While stevedores were reluctant to challenge the SBA, the Cotton Jammers' application for a state charter in 1879 was just one sign of the growing presence of black labor on Galveston's waterfront. Although probably formed by Norris Wright Cuney in the mid-1870s to bolster his political and economic ambitions, the application indicated the association's growing assertiveness. Another sign came in September 1881 when black longshoremen working for the Morgan shipping line asked for a wage raise to fifty cents an hour for day work and seventy-five for nights, which was granted without any confrontation. Draymen and streetcar drivers also sought wage raises but met with mixed success. A strike by 280 white cotton handlers the following year failed to prevent the hiring of black workers.[9]

Despite these gains, it would be far more difficult to break the SBA's monopoly, as stevedore Gus Lewis discovered when he set a black gang to work loading cotton in 1882. The black gang quit work when confronted by a white screwmen's delegation, but this did not prevent a general walkout by SBA men. No reason was given for the walkout, although Lewis claimed the action was aimed at him for hiring black labor even though there were no available SBA men. According to Lewis, a return to work was conditional on him quitting as a stevedore, which he would do if the SBA was willing to buy out his $2,500 investment in tools. Lewis's claim of a labor shortage was probably justified, but when questioned about the cause of the stoppage the SBA simply replied that they were "just taking a holiday."[10]

While the SBA's response to the use of black labor was entirely predictable, Galveston's business leaders attacked the union's control of the labor supply as well as the cost of screwing cotton. More importantly, they were now themselves willing to take a hand in breaking the SBA's monopoly. Reporting a labor shortage in January 1883, the *Daily News* announced that at the request of the stevedores the SBA had voted to allow five additional gangs. Despite this concession, the *News* hinted at a "new phase" in stevedoring labor. While acknowledging the strategic importance of skilled cotton labor to the port, there was enough work over the next several months to employ fifty extra men. Why then, queried *The News*, should the port be subservient to the rule of one organization:

> The SBA . . . has no right to assume to dictate what class
> of labor shall do service in response to the calls of com-
> merce. The report is . . . that an opposition to the associa-
> tion is to be organized, with both capital and influence to
> support it. Should the report prove to be true . . . it is likely
> that there will be a lively stir in some quarters.[11]

The man providing this capital and influence was Norris Wright Cuney whose star had continued to rise after 1877. His political skills within the state Republican party earned Cuney federal recognition with an appointment as customs inspector in Galveston. By 1881 he was a chief inspector, and his appointment the following year to the new post of special inspector reflected both Cuney's political acumen and Galveston's commercial growth. Cuney was forced to relinquish this well-paying federal position in 1883 when elected as alderman to the City Council for the predominantly white Twelfth Ward. Cuney served for four years, during which time he assumed the leadership of a state Republican party dominated by blacks. In 1889 Cuney became Galveston's collector of customs, a highly paid and important post, particularly for a black man in the South.[12]

Needing to supplement his alderman's salary, Cuney entered the stevedoring business in 1883. Before contracting for work, he used his influence with the white business community to lobby for support for his new enterprise. In a letter to William Moody, head of the Cotton Exchange and one of Galveston's leading business figures, Cuney emphasized the commercial disadvantages caused by the shortage of skilled screwmen. With this shortage jeopardizing next season's success, Cuney concluded:

> I have thought it proper to call your attention to the fact
> that there are a large number of laborers admirably adapted
> by the character of their pursuits to supply this necessity. I
> allude to the colored men who have a scanty livelihood by
> hard labor along the shore.

Cuney's "new association" was, in fact, the Cotton Jammers Association. Moody and the other members of the Exchange "heartily welcomed" Cuney's offer, adding that in their opinion there was enough work to go round. Thus reinforced, Cuney gathered about three hundred black workers from Galveston and New Orleans, purchased tools worth $2,500 and secured a contract on the Morgan wharf by underbidding the white stevedores. The *News*'s earlier prediction that such a move by black labor would create a "lively stir" among white labor quickly proved accurate.[13]

Cuney's men, including members of the Cotton Jammers, began loading cotton aboard the *Albion* on April 2. The SBA responded by walking out. Cuney quickly returned to Moody for support, explaining that he only sought a fair proportion of work for himself and his men.

The Cotton Exchange backed the introduction of lower-paid black workers, describing the SBA's actions as "unreasonable and detrimental to the best interests of this port." At the next SBA meeting, a motion "to notify all Stevedores and Ship Brokers that we are ready and willing to proceed to work, providing that there are no negroes employed" was withdrawn, but the decision not to work stood. Some members proposed that the SBA buy their own jacks, hoists, and posts, "so that we may be prepared at all times to solicit for and obtain vessels to load them should necessity arise for so doing." The tools would allow the SBA to bypass the stevedores and contract directly with the shipping lines. Three thousand dollars was set aside to purchase stevedoring equipment, but it was not put to immediate use. In addition, a request went out to all white cotton screwmen to join the SBA.[14]

Tension dissipated as the season ended and SBA members sought other work, but not before the SBA received an ironic lesson. In late May a special meeting was called by the Picnic Arrangement Committee. The committee was unable to find a white band for a forthcoming picnic and so requested a change in rules to allow them to employ a black band. The committee's request was granted. With the advent of the cotton season, however, a resumption of work was not so easily settled. On August 26, a special meeting called to discuss a return to work grew so heated that it was forced to adjourn. The next day, the SBA resolved to return to work, but not to "work in any vessel, consigned to or chartered by any Broker, Shipper, Buyer, or Agent, who may from this date employ any labor, white or black, who are not members of this Association." All "white stevedores" were to be notified of the decision, which only passed by a vote of seventy-nine to seventy-two. Although clearly divided by the issue, the SBA accepted the presence of Cuney and the black screwmen. At a special meeting in October, called because "the colored Stevedore had a Steamer to load and had sent colored gangs on board to do the work," the white screwmen again resolved to continue working, but only for stevedores who employed SBA men.[15]

Cuney had established a regular place on the waterfront without provoking a major confrontation with white labor. In truth, black labor still could not threaten the SBA's dominance. In Allen Taylor's estimation, the majority of Cuney's men were ordinary longshoremen rather than experienced cotton screwmen. Longshoremen hand-loaded cotton onto coastal vessels and for many years the SBA classed this work as screwing in an effort to maintain wages and a share of the work for its members. The coastal trade provided regular work but paid less than the larger oceangoing vessels loaded by skilled screwmen. Cuney was the only stevedore hiring black labor while Galveston's other stevedore firms continued to only hire SBA men. Thus, his organization offered little direct or immediate threat to white labor but did establish a potential base of strikebreakers and supply of alternative labor whenever more might be needed. This pattern of firms hiring either only white or black labor would continue as trade expanded in the 1890s.[16]

Racial antagonism undoubtedly played a major part in the SBA's opposition to Cuney's men, but it was also symptomatic of the reluctance of a craft union to participate in a broader labor movement. The SBA regularly exchanged invitations to picnics, balls, and other social events with local labor organizations but generally rejected any more formal ties. Perhaps the closest links were with the New Orleans SBA, which had been the model for the Galveston association. In 1878 Galveston sent five hundred dollars to its "Sister Brotherhood" when yellow fever struck New Orleans. During the course of the 1883 strike, the SBA received messages of support from the Mobile Baymen's Benevolent Association and the Galveston Knights of Labor Lodge 2376, a mixed-trade assembly that included longshoremen. The New Orleans SBA also sent a telegram to their brother screwmen offering assistance against the "usurpers and unskilled workingmen" attacking their joint interests. The SBA, however, refused to translate these joint interests into a formal alliance. The Mobile Association proposed uniting screwmen in all the Gulf Coast ports in 1878 with no result. In June 1881 the SBA received a letter from the Cottonmen's Executive Council of New Orleans suggesting that Galveston form a similar body.[17]

In New Orleans, waterfront workers had begun cooperating across racial and occupational lines the previous year. The structural core of this cooperation was the Cotton Men's Executive Council, formed in December 1880 upon a tide of unionization and successful strikes, including one biracial and multi-trade strike of the cotton presses. The Cotton Council acted as a coordinating body for individual unions that initially included white and black unions of screwmen, longshoremen and yardmen, white weighers and classers, and black teamsters representing approximately thirteen thousand men. The council, according to Eric Arnesen, "ended the fragmentary nature of waterfront unionism, making solidarity, or at least collaboration, between the different dock trades possible for the first time." Exactly why this organization occurred at this time is uncertain since no union records or any other first or secondhand accounts survive. Arnesen argues that collaboration made sense given the weakness of a largely unskilled labor force split along occupational and racial lines. This segmentation and the ready supply of alternative labor gave individual unions little chance of winning concessions from employers. The cotton screwmen, by contrast, were able to exercise control over the labor supply and working conditions and so they set a significant example. Shortly after the formation of the council, the screwmen allied with black and white longshoremen and black teamsters to impose a uniform wage scale for the loading of cotton by both black and white workers. Arnesen concludes that, although the Cotton Council did not eliminate job security, nor erase racial and occupational divisions on the waterfront, it did bring a degree of stability and improvement by codifying and enforcing work rules and wage rates, regulating the size of the work force, and overseeing interunion relations.[18]

Galveston's screwmen, however, felt that they had nothing to gain from such a coordinating body. The committee appointed to consider the New Orleans proposal concluded that as the only chartered organization handling cotton in Galveston "it would be useless for us to amalgamate with uncorporate bodies." In 1883 Mobile and New Orleans renewed the proposal of forming a joint association, but the offer was again rejected despite the Galveston SBA being in the middle of the dispute with Cuney. These decisions reflected the SBA's strength and insularity and the weakness of the port's other waterfront organizations, whose combined total membership barely equaled the SBA's membership of around three hundred. Moreover, with a surplus of work while Cuney was the only black man in Galveston with the money and influence to take up stevedoring, black labor did not present the same challenge as it did in New Orleans. Although the black population in the two cities was similar in percentage, New Orleans had a longer history as a port and a greater volume and diversity of trade. These factors enabled earlier and more significant participation by black labor on the waterfront. A strong black presence and employers willing to exploit racial divisions made biracial cooperation in New Orleans imperative.[19]

The SBA proved almost equally reluctant to associate with Galveston's non-waterfront locals. In the summer of 1881 the city's oldest labor association, the Galveston Typographical Union, called on other local unions to form a joint body. The resolution was couched in the familiar language of the craft worker whose main goal was to earn an independent livelihood:

> the only way to consummate this end is by putting into
> practical effect the old axiom that in "Union there is
> strength" therefore be it resolved that a committee of five
> be appointed to confer with the different trades-unions of
> this city for the purpose of soliciting their co-operation in
> uniting the interests of the working classes, of whatever
> calling, and organizing what is known as an "Amalgamated
> Union."

• • •

After some initial apparent support for the idea from other unions, the GTU committee reported that "apathy took the place of enthusiasm." The idea resurfaced in November 1883, when nine local organizations, including representatives from both the SBA and LBU, met to discuss the formation of a labor assembly. This meeting led to the formal organization of a Trade and Labor Assembly, which included the SBA, in January 1884. In March the SBA, after considerable debate and various motions, instructed its delegates to the TLA to vote in favor of admitting black organizations and the black screwmen, and possibly a longshoremen's association that joined soon after. This decision was the first indication that some SBA members were prepared to grant recognition to black organizations, but clearly many were still not ready to take this step. A little over a year later, in May 1885, the SBA withdrew from the TLA. The cost of membership, the TLA's involvement in political matters, and improper use of the strike defense fund were among the reasons given for the withdrawal. Given the SBA's insularity and rigid avoidance of politics, these stated grievances were perhaps genuine grounds for withdrawal. However, the Cotton Jammers' presence in the assembly was again heavily debated, indicating that race too was a factor in the decision.[20]

The formation of the Labor Assembly coincided with a growing presence of the Knights of Labor in the city, although the Knights' influence among the waterfront associations is difficult to gauge. Galveston had at least two locals by 1882, the Telegraph Operators Local 2042 and a mixed Local 2376, which included longshoremen. During the peak of the Knights' national popularity from 1884 to 1886, the city had around a dozen locals. These locals included the all-black mixed-trade Local 3440 organized in 1884, a screwmen's Local 4583 organized in 1885, and longshoremen's Local 5057 organized in 1886. District Assembly 78, based in Galveston, claimed nearly nine thousand members in 190 locals in 1886, the largest numbers outside of the northeast. According to Arnesen, in New Orleans it was the Cotton Council and the Trades and Labor Assembly that controlled organized labor in the 1880s because their formation preceded the KOL's peak years. In Galveston, events appear more convergent with KOL membership figures rising from 35 in 1882 to 220 in 1884 and 336 by 1885. Galveston's locals had a high membership turnover. In 1885, for instance, the total membership of Local 2376 was forty-nine, but while eighty-one members joined that year, ninety-seven left. Similarly, membership in black Local 3440 totaled twenty-three, with twelve new members and six resignations. What is clear is that the screwmen's and longshoremen's locals had little influence in changing the racial attitudes of their main bodies. Local 5057, in fact, was formed after the strike of 1885 when longshoremen on the Mallory wharf turned to the KOL for support in their struggle against black labor.[21]

The Knights of Labor, which began organizing in the South in 1878, aimed to unite all laborers irrespective of skill, race, or gender. Their intention to recruit black workers was unequivocal:

> We should be false to every principle of our Order should we exclude from membership any man who gains his living by honest toil, on account of his color or creed. . . . Why should workingmen allow a foolish prejudice against color to keep out of our organization any one who might be used as a tool to aid the employer in grinding down wages? . . . will your employer stop to inquire the color or nationality of any man who will take your place at the reduction offered?

While a few, more advanced labor leaders recognized that to degrade one section of labor would degrade all, their appeal was to the self-interest of white workers. The reaction of white workers, however, was dominated by racism, particularly in the South. The Knights' leadership made no determined effort to overcome racism, preferring to avoid the stigma of promoting social equality by accepting separate white and black locals. Nevertheless, black labor in the South generally responded favorably. Many skilled and unskilled blacks entered the ranks of a predominantly white labor movement even though many were forced to organize into separate assemblies. At their peak in 1886, the Knights had as many as 60,000 black members in a total membership between

700,000 to 1 million. For black workers, the Knights offered the chance to improve working conditions; more importantly, it was perhaps seen as a means to achieve civil, if not social, equality.[22]

According to Knights historian Melton McLaurin, the organization in the South walked a fine line between recruiting black members and accommodating white racism and consequently pursued a contradictory dual strategy. On the one hand, racial divisions were subsumed by emphasizing the purely economic nature of grievances. At the same time, the Knights' Northern antebellum reform heritage forced them to confront race but in ways that would not antagonize Southern white laborers. As a result of this dual strategy, integrated locals were rare but many district assemblies were integrated. In 1886, for instance, at a meeting of District Assembly 78 in San Antonio, two thousand black and white members marched, gave speeches, and ate together. According to a San Antonio newspaper, "it was perhaps the most unique gathering ever seen in the city, white ladies and gentlemen sitting at the same table and eating with their colored and mexican brethren." However, this optimistic picture of racial harmony was not borne out by the District Assembly's intervention in the Mallory strike. In Galveston, as in other instances across the South, the combination of a weak national organization and inexperienced local leadership compounded the Knights' ambivalence over race and led to ill-advised and disastrous strike action.[23]

The 1885 strike began when white longshoremen working on the Mallory Line's New York wharf walked out in a wage dispute. In May of that year, the longshoremen had accepted a temporary cut in wages from forty cents an hour for day work, and sixty cents for Sundays and night work, to a flat rate of forty cents. On Saturday, October 11, the men demanded the promised restoration of the old rate. In the absence of Capt. J. N. Sawyer, the Mallory Line's long-serving agent, the contracting stevedore offered a fifty-cent flat rate. When he returned the following Sunday, Sawyer denied any knowledge of an agreement to restore wages and refused to pay the fifty-cent rate. The 150 white longshoremen refused to continue working at the forty-cent rate. At first, black longshoremen on the Morgan wharf suggested they had no wish to take over the work of the white longshoremen, but by October 21 Cuney was providing the Mallory Line with 120 black laborers to unload the *State of Texas*. Cuney insisted that his men would not merely be "the catspaws to pull the chestnuts from the fire." His men should receive the same rates as on the Morgan wharf and were to be given an equal showing with white longshoremen in the future. Cuney's men went to work protected by a squad of police.[24]

The Mallory company had a history of strikebreaking and anti-unionism. In New York, Mallory combined with other steamship operators in using scab labor to break union strikes and impose new rates in the mid-1870s. In 1879 and 1880 a series of wildcat strikes for a ten-cent rate increase and union recognition hit Mallory in New York. Mallory's attitude to labor relations with longshoremen was "violent and unenlightened," a situation made worse by the rise of the Knights of Labor. Charles Mallory himself commented that "I know of no good reason why I should not have the privilege of employing whomever I wish, and hardly think it right that I should be compelled to discharge men at their dictation." In Galveston, Mallory had to face its workers alone, but the company was in a strong position with its virtual monopoly on the coastal trade. The Mallory Line claimed to be paying forty cents for day work and sixty cents for night work in Galveston, rates equal to if not ten to twenty cents higher than those paid by other steamship lines in the coastal market, although Mallory had successfully driven down these rates in New York. Convinced that the strike was unprovoked by management, Mallory openly condoned violence during the strike. The striking longshoremen, perhaps encouraged by an easy victory against Jay Gould's Wabash Railroad earlier that year, turned to the KOL to help present their case.[25]

On October 18 a three-man strike committee from the Mallory longshoremen's New York Wharf Association accompanied by a KOL delegation met with Sawyer. Since the Galveston men were not KOL

members prior to the dispute, the KOL representatives were only acting as advisors, although they were in sympathy with the Galveston
men. Admitting that they had made a mistake, the strikers asked to be
reinstated to their former positions. The following day, the committee
made a further offer of sharing the work with black labor on an equal
basis, either by working alternate weeks or ships. In a conciliatory letter
to Sawyer, the union rehearsed the KOL's rhetoric of equality, declaring
that employment should be impartially distributed based upon natural
right and justice not artificial and inequitable lines of race or color. Ability to do the work, not race or color was the sole qualification:

> Believing this we certainly could not insist upon the exclu-
> sive employment of any class of labor to the exclusion of
> others. . . . We think that you will agree with us that these
> views are most equitable where labor is dealing with labor.
> It is true that these views have not always obtained, but it
> has not been our fault that they should not have obtained.[26]

• • •

Cuney was prepared to accept this unprecedented offer of work sharing,
despite its denial of responsibility for the exclusion of black labor. Cuney's
men agreed to accept the principle of equality but, having been promised
exclusive employment while their work remained satisfactory, they were
unwilling to relinquish the advantage. They determined to abide by
Sawyer's decision, arguing it was not the province of labor to dictate
terms. Sawyer referred the dispute to his superiors in New York and
within the week the decision was made to continue with "colored laborers for the time being, to make a thorough test of their capabilities."[27]

Cuney's men remained at work under police protection. The strikers
offered no violence, but Cuney became a particular target of their
insults. When rumors circulated that a mob would attack his house,
Cuney's friends gathered to protect him. While business friends waited
inside, longshoremen patrolled the street in front of the house and hid
among the salt-cedars opposite, determined to meet any lynch mob

coming to attack their friend and leader. According to Cuney's daughter's recollection, the men carried guitars and other stringed instruments ready to form an unlikely "serenade" if challenged by police for loitering.[28]

When the strike committee next met Sawyer on Sunday, November 1, their attitude had changed significantly. The committee called for the reinstatement of those Knights dismissed from the Mallory wharf and an end to discrimination against KOL members. P. H. Golden, chairman of the Knights' local Executive Board, accused Mallory of "discriminating against this order by discharging and refusing to allow them to work upon the Mallory or New York wharf." Sawyer, mixing truth and sophistry in equal measure, pointed out that no one had been dismissed. Not only had the white longshoremen walked off the job, they were not even members of the Knights at the time:

> We have never discharged a man because he was a Knight of Labor or belonged to any other society. . . . The assumption that the Mallory Steamship Line is antagonistic to organized labor is gratuitous, unjust and unfounded. The strikers have applied to us for positions . . . but our answer has been that there were no vacancies.

As a final embellishment, Sawyer claimed a "moral obligation" to continue employing the black longshoremen.[29]

The Knights responded by calling a city-wide strike for the following Tuesday. According to the *Daily News*, between twelve hundred to fifteen hundred cotton pressmen, railroad men, screwmen, longshoremen, and even barbers joined the strike. There were sufficient KOL members among the screwmen and longshoremen to force an almost total suspension of work on the waterfront. That evening, a meeting attended by five to six hundred Knights called for a general strike throughout the state. The Knights portrayed the strike as a struggle by organized labor against unorganized labor, thus ignoring the black waterfront unions and the refusal of the white associations to accept black members. The Knights appealed to Galveston's business community for support. Wholesale merchants affected a lack of concern, preferring to wait out the strike, although railroad chiefs were less sanguine. From the commencement of the strike, no freight trains on the Gulf, Colorado and Santa Fe, or the Missouri Pacific companies were permitted to leave Galveston. However, feeling did not run unequivocally against the strikers. The *Daily News* commented that "the absence of agitation or disturbance is quite remarkable" and further suggested that although the strike was unfair and excessive, it was up to the Mallory Line to compromise. The newspaper, however, was in no doubt as to the root cause of the strike: "There is no question of labor involved in the present movement, and the race question seems to be the one that prevails as the basis of grievance."[30]

Just how far the Knights had shifted the focus of the strike from the original wage dispute was revealed on November 6 when the *Daily News* reprinted an interview from its sister newspaper, the *Dallas News,* with Henry Schuhl, Judge Advocate of the Texas Knights. When questioned whether the employment of black labor was the cause of the strike, Schuhl emphatically denied the dispute concerned black labor in any way. Instead, he characterized the dispute solely as a scheme by employers to break the Knights that predated the present trouble. Accusing the Mallory Line of referring to the Knights in "language unbecoming gentlemen," Schuhl continued: "The words Knights of Labor are repugnant to the minds of many employers, who associate with the order the ideas of communism and revolution." Schuhl's accusations were not unfounded, but the Knights' leadership preferred to overlook the racial dimension of the strike in favor of recruiting the Galveston men into their broader struggle against the railroads. Ironically, because Mallory shipped mainly local freight and general merchandise, which was being supplemented by barges from Houston, it was the only line still operating during the boycott.[31]

Despite the public statements to the contrary, the strike call circulated to Galveston locals by District Assembly 78 emphasized race while again ignoring the efforts of black laborers to organize:

> Whereas the Knights of Labor and other white labor are being discriminated against on the wharves and in the cotton presses by the importation of Colored Rat and Scab Labor from other counties. . . . lend us your aid in putting down and breaking up unorganized labor in this city.

· · ·

Despite the widespread support for the strike, the Galveston Typographical Union, at least, recognized that the KOL and Labor Assembly had no authority to call a strike when the strikers were not affiliated prior to the strike. When ordered to cease work, the GTU withdrew from the Labor Assembly, although this decision met with strong dissent from some rank and file members. At least one member declared he was ashamed of the actions of the GTU, which would be the subject of intense debate over the next few months.[32]

The strike was lifted on November 10, pending the outcome of arbitration between a Citizen's Committee and the State Executive Committee of the Knights. Such citizen committees became a regular feature of labor disputes in Galveston. Committee members—merchants, businessmen, and Wharf Company officials—all stood to lose financially by a strike, thus demonstrating the importance of trade to Galveston's economy and the spending power of longshoremen to local merchants. Workers' acceptance of these committees also indicated the essentially conservative nature of Galveston's unions. The Mallory Line, too, was willing to abide by the joint committee's decision. The black longshoremen were represented by Cuney, who took the opportunity to push the claims of all black labor. The division of work was only just, argued Cuney, and should be applied to other areas such as the almost exclusively white cotton presses as well. His men, however, may have been less willing than ever to accept work sharing. The Knights had demanded that Mayor Fulton dismiss four policemen, three of them black, for endeavoring to "incite violence among the colored people." The mayor dismissed the request but the incident aroused hostility among longshoremen on both sides.[33]

On November 12 the Arbitration Committee announced its decision: there should be "no discrimination against any one on account of race, color, or organization." The committee would further "recommend and request" that Sawyer, in addition to men already on the rolls, employ the men working before the strike when needed. The decision was ambiguous, allowing Sawyer to continue hiring only black longshoremen while claiming adherence to the Committee's decision. The Knights interpreted the ruling to mean the reinstatement of the striking men. Mallory only saw an obligation to rehire those men if and when vacancies occurred, meaning there was no need to discharge black labor. The strike was lost but, in a display of persistence if not realism, the Knights continued to press their cause. A token force of Knights continued to present themselves at the Mallory wharf thus maintaining a cause for grievance. On January 27, 1886, the Knights called for another boycott of the Mallory Line. Wholesale merchants dismissed the call as an absurdity, and even workers seemed reluctant to heed the order. As the Typographical Union's minutes revealed, the Labor Assembly was now solely composed of two longshoremen's societies. The Typographical Union had been refused reentry and all other societies had withdrawn, thus leaving the longshoremen isolated.[34]

Eighteen-eighty-six proved to be a pivotal year for the Knights of Labor, partly because of the reluctance among the state and national leadership to act against locals that maintained the color line. The issue came to a head at the Richmond convention in October. Frank J. Ferrell, a black delegate from New York, appeared at a local theater seated among the white audience. Ferrell also introduced the Knights' president, Grand Master Workman Terence Powderly, onto the convention platform. While the black press praised the Knights, Southern papers attacked the incidents as an effort to force social equality on the South. A typical reaction came from a "now and henceforth" ex-Knight of Labor who wrote to Powderly: "Since you have changed from a Knight of Labor advocate to a nigger social equality man I hereby denounce you as a low, vulgar buffoon than whom there is none more contemptible. A decent nigger would shun you." Powderly publicly praised the actions of white delegates from New York who had supported Ferrell, but he also wrote to the *Richmond Dispatch* disclaiming any intention of interfering with social relations in the South. The Knights suffered two other major setbacks that year. One was the Haymarket bombing in Chicago, which employers exploited to level charges of anarchy against organized labor. The other setback was the Great Southwest Strike, in which the Texas Knights lost their ongoing battle against Jay Gould. White membership declined nationwide after these events, leaving a concentration of segregated locals. For the next few years, southern black labor continued to join the fading organization in some numbers, but this support fell away as segregation and racial violence increased. Galveston's Trade and Labor Assembly was another, albeit temporary, casualty, as individual KOL locals, including the screwmen's, survived into the 1890s. The strike had, for the time being, only succeeded in destroying any hope of cooperation between trades and races.[35]

Historian Ernest Obadele-Starks argued that black longshoremen in Gulf Coast ports would continue to follow an adversarial strategy, using their numerical superiority to win economic concessions from employers and white unions. According to Odadele-Starks, Cuney's recruitment of workers from New Orleans "significantly increased the numbers of black workers available to employers and placed white workers at a serious disadvantage during labor strife." Black longshoremen, furthermore, used strikebreaking "as a basis for expanded protest and further resistance against biased white unions. Strikebreaking became an effective way for black dockworkers to resist unfair treatment by white unionists." This is an accurate assessment of the events of 1883 and 1885, and white unions clearly recognized the potential threat posed by the introduction of black labor. However, in Galveston at least, this threat was far from realized.[36]

There is no evidence to suggest that black longshoremen held a clear numerical advantage over white until the early years of the twentieth century. The New Orleans men were probably recruited to train the Galveston men in the art of cotton screwing, just as both white and black workers from Galveston later trained workers in other ports such as Houston. Moreover, unlike New Orleans, labor strife was rare on Galveston's waterfront. Black longshoremen, whatever their numbers, had little further opportunity to exploit strikes by white unions. More importantly, even when opportunities did arise in 1895 and 1907, Galveston's black longshoremen explicitly refused to act as strikebreakers, in both cases placing their union principles ahead of racial or economic advancement. Although 1885 is the only instance of black strikebreaking, undercutting union wage rates and the growing reserve of mainly nonunion black labor continued to be problems over the next several decades. These problems, however, were not simply a black versus white issue. Undercutting and nonunion labor, whatever the race, threatened both black and white unionists—a point that became increasingly apparent to both the SBA and the Cotton Jammers.

The introduction of black labor certainly did little to ease the pressure on the SBA, and, despite a steady flow of applications from new and former members, the association still struggled to provide enough gangs. In October 1885 stevedores were given permission to select foremen to make up new gangs and even use LBU members. The following September, foremen who released men to form a new gang were allowed to hire a nonunion outsider but were told to use "such men as are already broken in thereby avoiding the breaking in of any green man that can be avoided." Restrictions on Sunday working were also eased. These concessions were prompted by concern over work going to black labor. Prior to these new rules the names of the SBA No. 2 had been read out and a committee appointed to revise the working rules so "as would best serve this Assn with regard to the question of the SBA No.

2." This concern however, was misplaced: rather than competing with white labor, the black association sought to gain acceptance within the world of organized labor.[37]

On August 26, 1887, the SBA received a communication from "an organization styling and calling themselves the colored screwmen and longshoremen asking and petitioning us to admit them and organize a trade and labor assembly." The petition, at any rate, seems to have taken the SBA by surprise since it was considered "not being very plain and the object intended being more obscure." However, the application was received and referred to a committee, which met with the black screwmen, the first recorded meeting at this level. The committee's report understandably caused a great deal of discussion, although the minutes gave no details. There was a further meeting at which the black screwmen raised several questions. Again, no details were given but the committee's answers were "gladly received" by the black screwmen. Moreover, the committee was empowered to furnish the black screwmen with a copy of the SBA constitution and by-laws.[38]

Several authors have assumed that Cuney formed the No. 2 Association in 1883 and that he acted as its president. However, when Cuney referred to a "new association" in his letter to the Cotton Exchange that year, he meant new relative to the SBA. It is clear from contemporary accounts that No. 2 was not a new association but, following the practice of New Orleans and elsewhere, simply another designation for the leading black organization, the Cotton Jammers and Longshoremen's Association. The Cotton Jammers perhaps owed their existence to Cuney, who personally supervised his screwmen until 1894; several Cotton Jammers' officials acted as pallbearers at his funeral. However, whatever Cuney's role in the formation of a black organization and the procurement of work, there is no mention of his involvement in the approach to the SBA or in any subsequent negotiations between the Cotton Jammers and white labor. The initiative to approach the white association came from the ranks of the black workers themselves.[39]

According to Obadele-Starks, Cuney's role in 1883 and 1885 demonstrated the need for middle-class blacks to assist black laborers in their workplace struggles: "Black elites used their education, community influence, and resources, and often resorted to controversial protest strategies to achieve their goal of a well organized and racially unified black laboring class." Cuney not only built himself a lucrative stevedore business, by one estimate he also provided work that added from $75,000 to $100,000 to the income of Galveston's black population. However, even before Booker T. Washington's rise to prominence in the 1890s, black leaders were stressing an ideology based around anti-unionism, individual effort, economic self-improvement, and a reliance on the good offices of the better class of whites. Journalist T. Thomas Fortune, a political associate of Cuney's, was one of the few prominent blacks to speak in favor of labor unions. Black Republicans in Texas did put forward the most comprehensive and foresighted labor program in the state, including the need for legislation to protect the dignity and rights of labor and the right of labor to share in the profits that it helped to create. Cuney himself, however, viewed unions as a means to an end of exploiting white racial attitudes to black advantage. According to his most recent biographer, Cuney "did not foresee blacks becoming an important part of a Southern labor movement that whites dominated." This account brings Cuney into line with most other members of the black middle-class, many of whom saw little value in unions, particularly given the exclusionary policies of white unions. It was these middle-class leaders, as much as black workers, who advocated strikebreaking as a means of breaking through the white labor monopoly. In contrast, as Arnesen points out, it was working-class black activists who "contributed distinct ideas about the relationship between labor and capital that contrasted sharply with the ideology espoused by middle-class black politicians and journalists of the era."[40]

The Cotton Jammers' approach to the SBA was followed by a similar overture to the white longshoremen when committees from the Longshoremen's Benevolent Union and Cotton Jammers met in September 1887. The LBU had represented Galveston's white deep-sea longshoremen since 1882 and, next to the SBA it was the largest white union with around two hundred members. The black committee stated that they did not aspire to the Morgan or Mallory docks, although they may have been expecting the black coastwise workers to join their association. However, the Cotton Jammers were perhaps more interested in making inroads into the more lucrative and prestigious deep-sea work since they were willing to work for forty and sixty cents per hour, the LBU's rates. More ominously from the LBU's point of view, the Cotton Jammers were prepared to take work where they could find it. Rather than confrontation, however, the Cotton Jammers wanted to find the "ways and means that the laboring men could be a little closer committed," beginning with their applying to join the Trade and Labor Assembly. At the next meeting, the LBU informed the black committee that they had nothing against their joining the assembly. However, they had nothing else to offer them or any other organized body and "were opposed to letting any colored men in the union."[41]

Clinging to a policy of exclusion, however, did nothing to lessen the threat of black competition. The issue resurfaced in 1889, when the LBU was forced to confront the possibility of work going to the Cotton Jammers. The union's only solution was a resolution that "any member of this union who shall at any time work along . . . with these men that is known as No. 2 be expelled from this union." The less skilled deep-sea longshoremen of the LBU had more to fear than the screwmen from outsiders or undercutting of wages by another organized group. However, their rejection of working with the Cotton Jammers came amidst regular complaints about the use of nonunion labor, including the loading of coal barges by nonunion blacks. A more secure SBA seemed more willing to at least accept the presence of an organized black association, but if this seeming acceptance marked a shift in official policy, there was certainly no change in racial attitudes. In early 1888 Brother Charles Newman was charged with injuring the reputation of the association by living with a black woman. Newman was found guilty and called to the

center of the Hall "and in a few but well chosen words severely repri-
manded on the bad example and immorality of leading such a life."[42]

· · ·

The decade thus ended as it had begun with Galveston's white unions
pursuing narrow self-interest and exclusion, despite mounting evidence
that these policies were no longer tenable. In 1883 Cuney promoted
black labor as an alternative to the shortage of skilled screwmen caused
by the restrictive practices of the SBA. Cuney, with backing from the
white business community, secured a contract and set his men to work
loading cotton. The SBA responded with a brief, almost halfhearted,
strike before accepting that Cuney's presence offered no direct, immediate threat to its dominance. In 1885 the Mallory company used
Cuney's men when white longshoremen stopped work over a wage cut.
The longshoremen's union appealed to the KOL for support but lost the
strike despite a citywide boycott. Mallory had successfully exploited
black labor to break union power and lower wages; policies that would
continue in the next decade, thus ironically forcing a now all-black
workforce into their twenty-five-year struggle for union recognition
and better wages.

While the failures of 1883 and 1885 demonstrated that neither white
privilege nor union power were sufficient to prevent the hiring of black
labor, New Orleans and, to lesser extent, the KOL, provided alternatives
to exclusion. The Knights, however, chose to make race the central issue
of the Mallory strike, thus demonstrating the organization's structural
and ideological weaknesses in the South rather than its promise of
accepting all workers. The success of the New Orleans Cotton Council
in regulating wages, working conditions, and racial tension provided a
more compelling example of biracial unionism. The Cotton Council
was born out of intense competition between black and white labor, but
in Galveston an expanding labor market readily absorbed the limited
introduction of black screwmen. As an employer, Cuney was satisfied
with securing regular work but the men working under him, the Cot-

ton Jammers, wanted white unions to recognize them as a legitimate labor organization. In New Orleans, job competition and employer pressure had created the conditions that fostered biracial cooperation, but until those pressures approached the same levels in Galveston, the SBA could continue to be guided more by race consciousness rather than economic self-interest. Over the next decade, changes in technology and the shipping industry, as well as excess numbers of workers, would increase these pressures as Galveston fulfilled its destiny of becoming the nation's leading cotton shipping port. Within a very few years, the SBA would be forced to recognize that in order to maintain its position it would have to develop some kind of working relationship with the Cotton Jammers.

CHAPTER THREE

"For our mutual benefit and protection"

The Emergence of a Biracial Class Consciousness

A ll of Galveston's citizens had good reason to be optimistic at the start of the new decade as the Deep Water Committee's lobbying finally won federal approval. Galveston's water-front workers particularly stood to gain from the expected increase in the port's trade, although greater opportunities for black longshoremen meant a greater potential for racial conflict. In addition, changes in technology and the structure of the shipping industry were beginning to erode the power of the skilled screwmen and shift the balance of power towards the employers. In New Orleans, these changes coupled with a deteriorating national economy aggravated local conditions, causing racial violence on the waterfront and the disintegration of the biracial Cotton Men's Executive Council. Employers aggressively exploited the situation, playing one race against the other as workers' power to control wages and working conditions vanished with the Cotton Council. The depression had less effect on Galveston, although the port's white screwmen faced the same challenge from changes within the industry and the surplus of labor created by the economic slump. Rather than forcing the races further apart, however, conditions in

Galveston pressed the SBA into taking its first steps toward biracial cooperation with the Cotton Jammers Association. Conversely, as employers began using ordinary longshoremen to load cotton, the SBA was forced into a demarcation dispute with the white deep-sea long-shoremen. The power of employers in the coastwise industry was once again demonstrated on the Mallory docks, where workers lost a pro-longed and bitter strike against the company in 1898. The Mallory workers had affiliated with the American Federation of Labor during the dispute, thus demonstrating a commitment to class principles not shared by all black workers. While the Cotton Jammers welcomed negotiations with the SBA on wages and work-sharing, black long-shoremen who disagreed with this policy formed a breakaway group, the Lone Star Cotton Jammers Association. The Lone Stars chose to take advantage of the black worker's racial position as cheap labor to secure work by undercutting the wage rates of both the SBA and Cotton Jammers. This split exposed divisions in black society as a whole and created a long-lasting and often acrimonious breach in the ranks of the port's black waterfront labor.

• • •

Galveston's twenty-five-year-long campaign for a deepwater harbor ended in September 1890, when President Harrison signed the Galve-ston Harbor Bill appropriating $6 million for improvements. Galve-ston's citizens greeted the news with two days of street celebrations with fireworks, bonfires, whistles, bells, and shouts of "Hurrah for Galveston and Deep Water" filling the air. It would be another six years before the port reaped the full benefits from the jetty-building and dredging oper-ations that ensured a deepwater channel. In the short term, the severe economic depression that gripped the nation from 1893 to 1897 threat-ened the stability of both the port and organized labor. Galveston, how-ever, usually weathered such downturns more successfully than compet-ing port cities because it relied so heavily on cotton exports. Ports such as New Orleans were more vulnerable to economic cycles because they handled a greater percentage of general freight and imported goods.

After the completion of the deepwater harbor, Galveston exported more than 3 million bales of cotton per year. *Courtesy of the Rosenberg Library, Galveston, Texas.*

While some areas of Galveston's trade did suffer from the economic downturn, cotton exports continued to grow as cotton production in Texas far outstripped the previous decade, rising from 1,471,242 bales in 1890 to 3,364,055 bales by 1898. Exports from Galveston also rose as work on the harbor progressed and the increasing depth of the channel allowed larger and larger vessels to enter the port. Each year, 300 to 400 coastal vessels visited the port, as well as 375 foreign steamships and 130 sailing vessels. Annual trade figures released in 1894 reported a record year both in the number of vessels entering port and the amount of cotton shipped. The following year set another record for cotton shipment.[1]

Between 1893 and 1896, the Wharf Company spent close to $2 million on wharf improvements, deepening slips, extending railway tracks along docks and piers, and building storage sheds for 1 million bales of cotton. At the same time, two stone jetties were built on opposite sides of the channel extending eastward toward the Bolivar Roads, a project that finally cost $8,700,000. In 1896 the world's largest cargo vessel, the British steamer *Algoa,* navigated the completed deepwater channel and tied up alongside in what was now one of the best equipped harbors in the country. The effect of the deepwater harbor on Galveston's trade was immediate. A booklet publicizing the port's success and facilities proclaimed that, "Over 71,000 miles of railroad connect with the Texas Systems, all of which terminate at Galveston." The network of railroads included the Southern Pacific, which now agreed to construct terminal and wharf facilities covering five blocks from Forty-first to Forty-fifth Streets. Products from the entire West Coast, especially California's wheat, would now come through Galveston at Southern Pacific's piers A and B. Over twenty steamship lines served ports in northern Europe (particularly Liverpool), the east coast of America, southern Europe, Japan, and South America. "Due to deep water," the booklet added, "the increased volumes of business required the construction of grain elevators, additional docks, increased wharf trackage, and the building of miles of expensive sheds to protect goods."[2]

Exports from Galveston in 1898–1899 were valued at $78,470,375, more than double the 1895–1896 figure of $36,397,09. Foreign imports increased by an even greater percentage from $602,770 to $2,921,016. The total cotton shipment went from 1,664,129 bales in 1894–1895, to 2,318,995 bales in 1898–1899. That same season, Galveston surpassed New Orleans as the nation's top cotton port, handling about two-thirds of the Texas crop and one-third of the total national shipment. This was the climax of Galveston's thirty-five-year campaign to become the seaport of the

Great West. Surveying the port's progress, S. O. Young, secretary of the Galveston Cotton Exchange, rather disingenuously remarked that, "the city and port have been rather dragged into prominence by the course of events, and no people could be more amazed by the wonderful growth of the port's commerce than the people of Galveston."[3]

Secretary Young was being overly modest; Galveston's success owed much to the ambition and drive of its business leaders. The growth in trade, however, masked underlying weaknesses in the port's economy. Exports remained thirty times greater than imports, despite increases in both figures. This imbalance indicated Galveston's heavy reliance on the export of bulk commodities and its failure to develop a broader industrial base. Small manufactories were established before and after the Civil War but not on a scale to provide an alternative source of investment or employment. Printing was the largest industry in 1880, employing 107 people. The lack of a water supply hindered growth, but even the completion of the water system in the 1890s failed to stimulate significant investment. According to Galveston historian David McComb, even local financiers preferred to invest their money elsewhere. When they did invest locally, their money went to commercial facilities such as the Cotton Exchange, or to improvements in water transport. While these efforts ensured Galveston's success as a cotton port, the failure to develop better rail connections gave inland cities a long-term economic advantage. Shifts in population growth suggested this advantage. Galveston was the state's leading city in the immediate postwar period, but by 1890 population growth began to stagnate. Galveston's population was outstripped by both Dallas and San Antonio and, by 1900, Houston, whose location made it a more natural hub for railroads.[4]

Whatever the future prospects, Galveston's white screwmen shared in the air of prosperity that hung over Galveston at the beginning of the decade. Andrew Morrison, a local booster, wrote of the balmy winter season, "when the cotton 'is moving' and the streets are alive with 'samplers' and 'screwmen,' spending prodigally a weekly stipend that would be considered a handsome recompense in many of the learned professions. Nothing apparent here that the retail trade of the city is circumscribed at all by its insular position." Insularity, however, still characterized the screwmen's attitude towards the Cotton Jammers. In the fall of 1890 the reorganized Trade and Labor Assembly invited the SBA to rejoin the association. According to the SBA minutes, other labor organizations "very much desired" the SBA's cooperation but the SBA refused to affiliate unless any TLA delegates belonging to the "so-called No. 2 Screwmen" were expelled. SBA delegates attended TLA meetings soon afterward, although there is no evidence whether the Cotton Jammers were members of the assembly and, if so, whether the SBA's demands were met. In the early years of the decade, however, the screwmen faced other pressing problems besides competition from the Cotton Jammers that threatened their control over wages and working conditions.[5]

The SBA had always tried to restrict the supply of skilled labor by limiting membership to men of good character who fulfilled residency and apprentice requirements. Cuney and the Cotton Jammers had successfully exploited the shortage of skilled labor in the early 1880s and the SBA, itself, had been compelled to officially sanction the use of outsiders at the beginning of the 1886 season. Foremen who were required to release a regular hand to help form another gang could replace him with a nonunion man, giving preference to local men over migrant laborers. Working rules also stipulated that foremen should hire men "such as are already broken in thereby avoiding the breaking in of any green man that can be avoided." As cotton exports continued to rise, however, the shortage of skilled labor became more acute, and the SBA's restrictive practices became more counterproductive.[6]

By the early 1890s stevedores, and even SBA foremen, were increasingly forced to hire "outsiders," men with no affiliation to the association or even the city of Galveston. Longshore work had always provided a useful source of employment for off-season agricultural workers and other casual laborers, but, starting in 1893, the deepening economic depression created growing pools of surplus labor and tramps in cities. Cotton prices fell as production rose, creating the conditions that gave rise to the Southern Farmer's Alliance and Populism and forcing many mostly landless black farmers to move to towns. For employers, the ready availability of cheap, casual labor now offered a means to circumvent the restrictive practices of screwmen and longshoremen. To screwmen, outsiders threatened a loss of income and workers' control and the SBA introduced several temporary measures to counter "the competition of cheap labor that is becoming well-established." Four thousand dollars were set aside for purchasing tools and procuring vessels, thus bypassing the stevedores. Two walking delegates were appointed with the power to make decisions regarding the distribution and composition of gangs, which now only needed to include two full SBA members. By settling disputes on the spot, the walking delegates avoided the delay of work stoppages while grievances were referred to a full SBA meeting. Finally, nonunion gang members were levied 2.5 percent of their wages for the privilege of working cotton.[7]

Cheap labor was not the only threat facing screwmen; changes in technology and the shipping industry also threatened to undermine their control over the workplace. Mechanization had little effect on the handling of cargo itself, or the way in which vessels were loaded and unloaded. Steam winches were now used to haul cotton bales up the wooden stages and lower them into the hold, but the final stowing still relied heavily on the strength and skill of the men involved. By the mid-1890s, however, cotton compresses were turning out experimental bales of cotton tightly rolled in layers around a core. These round bales achieved a density of between 35 and 45 pounds per cubic foot as compared to the 22.5 pounds of the standard bale. The more compact round bale cost less to transport and was less at risk from fire or water damage, which lowered insurance rates. More significantly, the round bale required little or no screwing. The round bale was not widely accepted by the cotton industry, but it was an indication of the longer-term threat to the skills of the screwmen.[8]

The appearance of the round bale coincided with changes in the shipping industry. Deep water allowed larger iron-hulled steamships to enter the harbor, and the increased stowage capacity of these vessels significantly reduced the advantages of screwing cotton. While early sailing vessels held eight hundred to one thousand bales, later steamships held as many as twelve thousand bales. Wooden vessels remained a common sight in Galveston throughout the 1890s, with sailing vessels still in the majority as late as 1897. By 1900, however, sail and steam vessels were almost equal, and steam dominated thereafter. In his study of British ports, John Lovell explains that, besides the increased capacity, the emergence of steamships had two important effects on the employment structure. First, larger vessels usually went hand in hand with larger companies. While sailing vessels and smaller tramp steamers with no set sailing schedule benefited from the extra time it took to screw cotton, the larger steamships of foreign-owned companies were more interested in a regular schedule and a quick turnaround time in port. Second, some of these companies assumed more direct control of the loading and unloading of their vessels and were more hostile toward unions than local stevedoring companies. This direct control broke the personal tie between stevedores and screwmen that was an important element in workers' control. By mid-decade, employers were using ordinary longshoremen to stow cotton by hand for longshoremen's wages and with no bale limit.[9]

These companies were also prepared to circumvent the power of the white screwmen in ports such as New Orleans and Galveston by hiring black labor. In August 1893 a new firm of cotton brokers, Freeman and Parr, announced that they would employ Cuney and his men rather than white screwmen. The SBA immediately appointed a five-man committee to meet with the brokers and to try to persuade the Cotton Jammers to work for the same hours and wages as the SBA. The use of ad hoc committees, however, was growing increasingly inadequate as outside pressures mounted and the need to negotiate with other parties grew more compelling. That same month, the SBA selected an Executive Committee of twenty-one elected members to handle all matters pertaining to wages and working rules and to conduct all negotiations with employers and other unions. Led by SBA President J. H. Fricke, the committee met regularly and reported back at each full meeting, where any recommendations could be amended before approval or rejection by a vote of the whole.

The committee's first task was to continue negotiations with an executive committee from the black screwmen. The SBA's main concern at the first meeting on September 15 was still to persuade the Cotton Jammers to bring their wages into line with the SBA's rates. Equalizing wages served two purposes: it maintained existing rates by preventing undercutting; and for the same rates, stevedores would prefer to hire white labor. The Cotton Jammers seized the initiative by suggesting the appointment of two committees to reach an agreement on joint action. The Cotton Jammers, however, appeared more concerned with the threat from outsiders than equalizing wages, and several more joint meetings failed to produce any significant accord. Both sides, with some reservations, appeared willing to agree not to take work from each other, but the Cotton Jammers were not prepared to raise their scale of wages, arguing that they were already bound by a contract for that season. The Cotton Jammers were also more concerned with protecting their own position rather than having to compete on equal terms with the white screwmen. Consequently, the only resolution fully agreed to was "that both organizations employ Galveston labor exclusively in preference to outside labor, and that both organizations act in conjunction with each other in doing the same."[10]

Despite the initial lack of success, the appointment of executive committees formalized the relationship between the two associations and allowed the Cotton Jammers into the fold of organized labor. However, even this limited contact appeared to be too much for some white screwmen. During the course of the joint negotiations, a Brother Boyd complained that "some of the members seemed to be familiar with and conversing with the No. 2 Screwmen rather frequently of late." This discontent among rank-and-file members continued to be reflected by official policy, particularly when competing for work. In October 1894 stevedore John Young appealed to the Executive Committee to raise the day's work from seventy-five to eighty bales. Young argued that with this concession he could secure the work of the McFadden Brothers now being done by Cuney. The committee agreed to raise the limit provided that Young got the work, yet the SBA was still struggling to meet the current demand for labor. Just two weeks later, Young was requesting six more gangs, warning that he had already been forced to turn one ship over to the black screwmen and would lose another without the extra men. The SBA was prepared to use all means to prevent any ship being given to black labor and again resorted to temporary concessions to meet the emergency.[11]

Rumors circulating in the summer of 1894 presented a more serious threat to the fragile accord between the SBA and Cotton Jammers. According to one rumor, some black screwmen were going into the stevedoring business for an unnamed Galveston broker by undercutting the present wage rates. The second rumor was that a Thomas Gallagher was contemplating setting up as a stevedore and that his work would come from William Parr and Company. Parr had always employed black screwmen but, if successful, Gallagher wanted to have the work done by white labor. Events in New Orleans intervened, however, before the substance of either rumor could be established. New Orleans had reached a high-water mark in biracial unionism two years previously when forty-nine AFL unions and twenty-five thousand workers held a four-day general strike in support of three unions carrying a high percentage of black members. Moved by this display of biracial solidarity, AFL president Samuel Gompers declared it a unique moment in world history as white workers risked their livelihoods defending their black fellow wage workers:

> With one fell swoop the economic barrier of color was broken down. Under the circumstances I regard the movement as a very healthy sign of the times and one which speaks well for the future of organized labor in the "New South."

Circumstances, however, had changed by 1894 as biracial cooperation on New Orleans' docks collapsed amid the worst economic crisis of the century and rising levels of employer aggression and racial antagonism.[12]

As in Galveston, New Orleans's screwmen faced increasing pressure from employers to alter working practices, particularly lifting their seventy-five-bale limit. In addition, black screwmen were becoming increasingly dissatisfied with the division of work. Rather than an equal division of work, such as existed between longshoremen and yardmen, black screwmen were limited to a twenty-gang, or one hundred men, limit by the white association. In 1892 the black union split into two factions: a Screwmen's Benevolent Association No. 1 of around one hundred men willing to accept the status quo while a much larger No. 2 association rejected the gang limit. The No. 2 association was prepared to work for fifteen cents a bale below union scale and to abolish the seventy-five-bale limit; they quickly found an agent willing to hire them on these terms. The white screwmen responded with increasingly harsh denunciations of all black screwmen, making no distinction between either black association.[13]

By October, harsh words had turned to a policy of exclusion as the New Orleans SBA notified stevedores it would no longer work for employers who hired black labor. The Cotton Men's Executive Council, now dominated by white screwmen and longshoremen, disbanded soon after the ultimatum. From that point the situation rapidly deteriorated into open conflict as black workers sought to regain their jobs and white screwmen retaliated with strikes and violence. The situation grew even worse as white longshoremen followed the screwmen in attempting to exclude black workers. While some employers wanted a return to stability, others were eager to exploit racial divisions to lower wages and break the control of the white screwmen. The No. 2 association continued to be willing to accept lower wages and less job control in exchange for more work and security. When the No. 1 association resisted an offer of reduced wages, employers simply replaced them with black nonunion labor. The white screwmen, while denying that race was an issue, continued to ignore this division within the ranks of black labor, choosing instead to characterize all black labor as unskilled and untrustworthy.[14]

The racial and economic tensions on the waterfront reached a climax in March 1895. In a series of violent actions over several days, white mobs destroyed tools and assaulted black workers. The riots, which left nine black laborers dead and many more wounded, only ended when Gov. Murphy Foster called in the state militia. The militia's intervention proved a turning point; by the start of the next cotton season few whites found employment along the New Orleans waterfront. With their respective associations split by internal dissent, white screwmen and longshoremen were forced to admit defeat. As Arnesen concludes: "Their repudiation of the interracial alliance led to a rapid decline of all union power, complete loss of control over the labor supply, widespread elimination of work rules, and severe wage reductions."[15]

Galveston's white and black screwmen closely monitored the situation in New Orleans. The SBA's Executive Committee discussed the deteriorating conditions in February 1895 and contacted James Shaw, president of the New Orleans SBA, to offer "him and his organization favors or assistance that it was in our power to convey." By March the committee was discussing the settlement of the labor troubles "at greatly reduced rates of stowing cotton." Anxious to prevent a similar result in Galveston, the committee sent a delegate to New Orleans to gather information. There were already signs, however, that the balance of power between employers and employees in Galveston was tilting in favor of the stevedores and shipping companies.[16]

In the midst of the New Orleans troubles, the SBA asked stevedores to sever their connection as working members of the association. With the commercial pressures growing increasingly heavy on all sides, not all members were prepared to welcome stevedores such as Ben Dolson, John Young, and Charles Suderman to SBA meetings. The purchase of sixty pairs of jackscrews also again came up for discussion, and plans to retain control of the labor supply by allowing apprentices and nonmembers who had worked cotton for only thirty days to join. Despite these and several earlier measures, the SBA felt compelled to allow one other significant concession to the stevedores. With New Orleans in mind, the SBA acknowledged that working rules in other ports allowed cotton to be loaded much cheaper than in Galveston. The bale limit had already been raised to eighty bales, but after two hours of discussion the SBA notified stevedores and ship brokers that they would remove this limit.[17]

The removal of the daily limit was another temporary measure, but it was still a significant one that coincided with a shift in the SBA's attitude toward the Cotton Jammers. As well as sending a delegate to New Orleans, the SBA appointed a committee to meet in secret with the Cotton Jammers to get "the views of the Galveston Negro Screwmen what in their opinion would be the outcome of the settlement of the strike in New Orleans and its effect if any on the future business of Galveston." The committee reported back that the black screwmen had promised "in case of a strike in Galveston that they would stand by us and uphold us." The shift was small, but it was the first time that the SBA sought this level of support from the black screwmen.[18]

The growing understanding between white and black screwmen was soon tested when the unresolved issues surrounding Parr and Company's work resurfaced ahead of the 1895–1896 season. Joe Benson, a stevedore who worked "all the colored gangs of any account," had told the Cotton Jammers that a committee of white screwmen had offered to work for thirty-one cents a bale. When the Cotton Jammers complained, the SBA's Executive Committee assured them of all protection and that they would stand firm and not touch any of Parr's work. The work was offered to the SBA that September, but they stood by the agreement and refused to take it. The incident convinced both sides of the need for a written agreement, and when the black committee was invited to hear the SBA's decision both sides "mutually agreed that an agreement or Covenant be entered into for our mutual benefit and protection."[19]

The covenant had limits, not least that it only ratified the previous understanding that neither side would take the work of the other under any circumstances. Nor did it end the uneasiness of many rank-and-file members at giving such recognition to a black union. The following season, a new SBA resolution prevented any man who had worked with No. 2 from working with SBA members unless he provided a sworn affidavit that he was not member of No. 2. After considerable discussion at the next the meeting, the resolution was overturned, "permitting several members of the No. 2 society to work with our members." This was one of several similar resolutions that raise the possibility that the Cotton Jammers accepted white members. More probably, the resolutions were aimed at stevedores and apprentice workers who had employed or worked alongside the black screwmen. As one petitioner explained, he was now barred from working with SBA men "on account of him being made in his youth to work with the No. 2 Screwmen against his will." After much explanation and discussion, a motion prevailed "to allow all members of the No. 2 Association to work except those who had formerly been members of this Association or who affiliated with it."[20]

Despite the limitations, a written agreement was a step forward in biracial cooperation on Galveston's waterfront. Moreover, the new accord came at a time when racism and Jim Crow was surging to a crest across the South. As C. Vann Woodward pointed out, Jim Crow was not the legacy of the post-Reconstruction Redeemers, but rather paralleled the rise of white democratic movements during the late 1880s and into the 1890s. The rise of movements such as the Farmer's Alliance and segregation laws were, in fact, linked by the economic rivalry at the heart of Jim Crow. As Woodward explained, with white and black labor increasingly competing for meager wages in cotton fields, mines, and wharves, "It took a lot of ritual and Jim Crow to bolster the creed of white supremacy in the bosom of the white man working for black man's wages." Between 1887 and 1891, Florida, Mississippi, Texas, Louisiana, Alabama, Arkansas, Kentucky, and Georgia all enacted the benchmark of Jim Crow, the separate coach law for railroads. This law was, in fact, almost the only Jim Crow law enacted by Southern states before 1900, but such laws usually only codified existing practice in broad range of public and private institutions. Moreover, a series of Supreme Court decisions, culminating in *Plessy* v. *Ferguson* in 1896, were paving the way for further segregation and the political disfranchisement of Southern blacks in the early 1900s. Another feature of the New South, the convict lease system, replaced the penal function of the plantation and turned it into a source of revenue by leasing convict labor to private corporations or individuals. The police and law courts ensured a steady supply of mostly black inmates, with conditions for the convict laborer often worse than slavery.[21]

Like many other Southern cities, Galveston had been largely segregated by the 1880s, but it did not begin to enact Jim Crow laws until after 1900. In fact, the city maintained its reputation for tolerance by building the first black hospital in the state in 1891. In 1895, however, changes in the city charter effectively disfranchised the town's black citizens. Galveston was governed by a mayor and twelve aldermen representing each ward. This system was commonplace and enabled small businessmen, workingmen, and blacks to be elected as aldermen for their ward. Norris Wright Cuney and several longshoremen had served as aldermen. In 1895 the Chamber of Commerce successfully challenged this system of ward politics by proposing to elect alderman at large. The chamber, supported by members of the Cotton Exchange, formed a Good Government Club to run suitable pro-business candidates. Candidates having to court citywide appeal made the election of a working men's slate more difficult, and it virtually ended black participation in city government.[22]

Perhaps the most grievous blow to Galveston's black population was the decline of Norris Wright Cuney. Cuney stood at the height of his power at the beginning of the decade. He was chairman of the state Republican Party and had been appointed inspector of customs for Galveston by President Harrison, the highest federal post awarded to a Southern black in the late nineteenth century. Cuney had always used his position to challenge segregation and he was one of the first blacks to challenge the legality of the separate coach law passed by Texas in 1890 when he was refused a sleeping berth on an interstate train. His appeal failed, and he was equally powerless to prevent the loss of his federal appointment when Grover Cleveland defeated Harrison in 1892. Despite growing opposition from a rising "lily-white" faction, Cuney held on to his position in the Republican party until 1896, when he failed to support William McKinley's nomination as presidential candidate. With his health failing from tuberculosis, Cuney was unable to fight the rising tide of racism within the Republican party and slipped from power. When Cuney died in 1898 Galveston's black community lost its most powerful voice.[23]

The SBA's agreement with the Cotton Jammers did not resolve all problems on the waterfront as the introduction of the round bale brought the SBA into increasing conflict with the white Longshoremen's Benevolent Union, which handled general cargo on deep-sea and some coastwise vessels. The LBU was fighting its own battle against the use of sailors and other nonunion outsiders and the lowering of wages but, as less skilled workers, ordinary longshoremen could not exercise the same degree of control over wages and working conditions as the SBA and were more vulnerable to the growing power of employers. By 1895 stevedores were using longshoremen to stow round bale cotton at their rate of forty cents per hour, two dollars per day less than the SBA rate. The SBA sent a warning letter to the LBU:

> If stowing cotton is permitted to be done at 40c per hour it will inevitably bring disaster to your association as well as ours as there are a great number of your members who are also Screwmen. It is needless to remind you that it is to your interest as well as ours to keep up the established wages of our respective Associations and to prevent if possible any one working at scab wages.

• • •

The LBU responded with its own grievance against screwmen who were also working as longshoremen. The LBU sent a request asking that these men either stop work or apply for LBU membership.[24]

This exchange settled nothing and employers continued to use long-shoremen and black screwmen to load the round bale. Unable to reach agreement with the LBU, the SBA tried to pressure stevedores. When William Morris directed longshoremen to load two hundred round bales aboard the British steamship *Navarro*, seven gangs of screwmen walked out. Morris argued that he was not attempting to reduce wages, but that he was short of screwmen and with longshoremen loading cotton on other wharves he expected the same right. The SBA characteristically offered no explanation for the "misunderstanding," but again the action did nothing to resolve the situation and these demarcation disputes would continue to mar relations between screwmen and long-shoremen for the next decade.[25]

Coastwise longshoremen for the Mallory Line also faced pressure from their employer to lower wages. Mallory had employed only black longshoremen since the 1885 strike, but now these workers found themselves in the same situation as the white workers they had replaced. When Mallory announced a five-cent reduction in the hourly wage to thirty-five cents for days and forty cents for nights in January 1894, workers refused to unload the newly docked steamship *Comal*. One hundred and fifty men were locked out from the Mallory dock and replaced by twenty-five scabs. According to the *Daily News*, Mallory longshoremen in New York received only twenty-five cents an hour and no overtime. The striking men acknowledged that they received three dollars for days and four dollars for nights, but Mallory ran only two lin-ers a week. Since it only took eleven to eleven-and-a-half hours to dis-charge a ship the leading twenty wage earners had averaged only $10.80 a week over the previous month. The next highest gang made $7 a week and the lowest earners only $3.50. As a strike leader explained, "Ten eighty a week don't go far with a man who has house rent to pay and a wife and three or four children to support. I have been on the Mallory pier three or four years and am in debt and can't get out of debt. We have simply struck against a reduction in our already small wages."[26]

The strike continued for the next month, with Mallory ships being loaded and unloaded by their crews and a small number of outsiders. The strikers were generally peaceful, although there were some attempts to intimidate the strikebreakers during the first days of the strike. Police arrested Elias Parker, foreman of the longshoremen, for carrying a pistol, and two strikebreakers were attacked. Sam Warren, a black night watchman, boasted that he would not be intimidated by the strikers but was chased off the job that evening. According to the *Daily News*, the troublemakers were: "young fellows who have only themselves to look out for, and that men who have families and others dependent upon their labor are not inclined to engage in any violent demonstrations." Mallory's agent, Captain Sawyer, upheld the men's right to refrain from work, but added when "a number of men attempt to dissuade others from working by threats or intimidation, I think that they have stepped pretty close to the danger line." No further trouble was reported after police were called in, although they had to escort Sam Warren to his post past a crowd of jeering strikers that included several women.[27]

Over three hundred and fifty black laborers attended a mass meeting in early February to discuss continuing the strike. Leading the meeting, Howard Hill warned that Mallory was preparing to ship laborers from New York as sailors to do work and then ship them home, thus causing Galveston to lose trade to which the city was legitimately entitled. Other speakers said that strikers were suffering hardship, but they would not accept work at the sacrifice of a principle. Almost to a man, those at the meeting favored opposing the introduction of foreign labor and continuing the strike.[28]

Two LBU officials, probably representatives of Galveston's Labor Assembly, also spoke at the meeting. If Hill and the other strike leaders had been hoping for support from the white longshoremen they were disappointed. The following day LBU leader John Dwyer denied supporting the strike at the meeting. He had, in fact, said that he "sincerely regretted the causes that led to the strike and deprecated in strong terms the resorting to these methods as a means of settlement between labor and capital." According to Dwyer, strikes and boycotts had signally failed to help the people in whose interests they were inaugurated, so in order to understand the remedy for the evils in the body politic the working classes must keep themselves thoroughly posted on questions of political economy. The interests of the working classes and retailers were mutual since shopkeepers themselves lost revenue when wages were paid to outsiders. Dwyer's solution, therefore, was to petition the retailers for support in opposing outside labor. He concluded by telling the meeting that he was glad to notice the absence of political heelers and leaders from the meeting and that the only true remedy for the laborers' wrongs was through the intelligent use of the ballot. Enlisting the support of the local business community, where Mallory's hardline attitude to strikes courted unpopularity, was a recurring tactic for Galveston's central labor body. Business leaders, whatever their views on unions or strikes, were willing to press employers for an equitable settlement to restore their lost revenue. Mallory, however, took little more notice of local shopkeepers than it did the demands of unions.[29]

A few days later, Howard Hill told a meeting of more than one hundred strikers that a petition had been sent to retailers, and that a committee had tried to dissuade those few men who were working. Threats uttered against scab labor drew little support at the meeting, but that evening around three hundred men gathered to dissuade the seven men working on the Mallory wharf. One man escaped unnoticed while the other six preferred to remain out of sight on board ship. The strike, however, was effectively over. When the *Comal* arrived without the threatened extra crew, there were plenty of applications for work at the reduced rates.[30]

The strike was over but workers' grievances continued. In September Lucas Luke complained to the *Daily News* that Mallory was employing outsiders instead of Galveston men. Sawyer denied the accusation, reminding everyone that Mallory had no favorites when it came to labor and their only requirement was ability. The strike was thus in many ways a repeat of 1885, with Mallory now using nonunion black workers to replace organized black labor. It took the company another twenty-five years to fully achieve this goal, however, as black longshoremen demonstrated their deep-rooted commitment to the principle of organized labor. Two of the strike's leaders, George and Harvey Patrick, emerged as leaders of a more protracted strike against Mallory in 1898. Harvey, who listed his occupation as drayman, had been associated with unions since at least 1880, when he acted as treasurer of the Longshoremen's Association No. 1. His brother George, along with Howard Hill, had worked on the Mallory docks since the mid-1880s. George's occupation was also listed as screwman, and it is likely he was a member of the Cotton Jammers. And it was as a screwman that George Patrick demonstrated his commitment to unionism during the troubles in New Orleans.[31]

When stevedores and agents in New Orleans began undercutting union rates in 1894, white screwmen responded with their own cost-cutting proposal: they would buy their own tools and negotiate directly with shipping agents, thus eliminating the stevedores. The stevedores, deciding that it was the screwmen who could be bypassed, turned to outside help and Norris Wright Cuney. Cuney sent fifteen screwmen and thirty-five regular longshoremen to New Orleans. The previous success of labor in New Orleans depended, in part, on the reluctance of the city's ruling Democratic ring to antagonize its white labor vote. In this case, the mayor denied Cuney's men police protection. Taken by barge, rather than the usual streetcars, to their ships, Cuney's men began work, but within an hour they downed tools and demanded to be paid at a higher rate. A deputation from the white screwmen had convinced the Galveston men that the situation in New Orleans had been misrepresented to them.

Acting as leading foreman, George Patrick claimed that the stevedore's agent, Charles K. Lincoln, had told them that the rates in New Orleans were five dollars a day for screwmen and four dollars for long-shoremen. This was one dollar less than Galveston rates, but, believing this to be the union rate and that there was a backlog of work, the Galveston men—or at any rate, Cuney—accepted the contract. Patrick accused Lincoln of misrepresenting the situation by telling him and his men that the strike was over and that both white and black screwmen's unions were working at those rates. Finding only nonunion men work-ing at those rates because of the stevedores' attempt to undercut union rates, Patrick refused to work for less than six dollars. Lincoln quickly agreed to pay the higher rates, but Patrick decided upon another meet-ing with the white screwmen. After further consultation that afternoon, he, along with ten other screwmen and a number of longshoremen, accepted the offer of a free ride home. On his return, Patrick explained to the *Galveston Daily News* that the white screwmen "received us most cordially and showed us the injustice of our continuing to work. They offered to pay our way back to Galveston and twenty-one of us accepted." Denying his men had been paid twenty dollars each to return, Patrick continued:

> We had all the money we wanted for eatables, drinks and cigars two bits and half dollars were generously handed round. I want the News to express our heartfelt thanks to James Shaw, the president of the white screwmen's associa-tion and Hillard of the colored association, for their kind and generous treatment and uniform courtesy.

Patrick also countered rumors of intimidation, denying that threats were made against his or his men's lives. The reason for their early return was simple; "I do not believe in interfering in labor troubles of other places. Home men should be all employed before, strangers are sent for."[32]

The *News* report also carried an article from the *New Orleans*

Picayune in which Lincoln claimed the men were aware of conditions before they left Galveston. Given ample protection, fear, rather than class solidarity, made Patrick and his men quit work. Violence was a feature of the dispute. On March 9 a mob had thrown one thousand dollars worth of screwing and loading tools used by nonunion labor into the river. Four days later, two bloody riots were launched against black longshoremen for breaking a work-sharing agreement and undercutting wages. Patrick's version of events is supported by the official police report, which stated that the Galveston men worked at a five- and six-dollar scale for about an hour before Frank Dennis, one of the black foremen, called a halt pending the meeting with the white screwmen's committee. After the meeting, Dennis spoke to a police officer, confirming Patrick's story that the Galveston men had been misled: "Had they known of the trouble here between the white and the black screwmen they would never have come, and as soon as he could get them together they would try and leave for their homes."[33]

Frank Dennis would also be among the leaders of the 1898 Galveston strike. In the meantime, Mallory demonstrated that it had lost none of its competitive edge in the business world. In 1897 the Miami Steamship Company began operating a service between Galveston and New York. Mallory's response to this new competition was unyielding: "there must be no compromise or admission of that line to the Galveston Trade and that its opposition must be met and fought to the end." Thus resolved, Mallory began another rate war that affected rate agreements across the South. Mallory's railroad allies closed ranks against the Miami, charging the company higher rates and asking for prepayment. Miami fought the case in the federal courts but lost and were forced to withdraw from Galveston after only nine months of operation. According to James Baughman, the Miami Company either failed to understand the nature of the competition or was hoping to be bought off. With this threat defeated, however, Mallory then found its own services suspended in April 1898 due to the Spanish American War. When services restarted at the end of August, the company faced a renewed challenge from its own workers. In the ensuing strike, Galveston's black longshoremen would place their class interests above their race consciousness.[34]

Mallory's New York to Galveston service resumed when the *Colorado* berthed at the Mallory dock at about 1 p.m. on August 31. Waiting at the dockside was a crowd of black longshoremen estimated to be more than a thousand strong. This was not, however, a reception committee welcoming the return of the line:

> for the most part it was a crowd of colored longshoremen, who were there to tell the Mallory people that they must employ none but union men, and must pay the scale of wages recently adopted by the recently organized and chartered Colored laborers' union.

Organizing the demonstration, as chairman of the newly formed Colored Labor Protective Union, was George Patrick, accompanied by his brother Harvey, the union president.[35]

George Patrick explained to the *Daily News* that the Colored Labor Protective Union had organized as a benevolent association, with an initiation fee of ten cents and monthly dues of ten cents. These small amounts were perhaps aimed at encouraging as broad a membership as possible. The union was demanding forty cents per hour for day work and fifty for night, against the company's offer of thirty and forty cents. Another central issue was Mallory's use of "country negroes" to undermine the union's standing. The longshoremen, many armed with "billets of wood," formed a complete cordon around the Mallory dock, covering every approach. Some declared they were simply preventing their own men from blocking the gangways, and others suggested there was no intention of preventing men from working but that "we are the men who will unload that ship, and we will get union wages for it." Police on the scene denied witnessing any coercion, but any man attempting to work was quickly surrounded by a small group of strikers and persuaded to reconsider.[36]

Addressing the gathered workers on the first afternoon of the strike, Harvey Patrick told the crowd speaking "to and for every man with an interest in the community and a family at home to support, be he white or black." Accusing the Mallory Line of offering reduced wages, Patrick continued:

> Now the Mallory line is charging 85 cents a hundred for freight, and they refuse to pay us 40 cents an hour for unloading that freight . . . yet they will not pay us a living wage. . . . We have not come here to prevent the Mallory line from working but to ask them to pay us what we pay them through our merchants.

He then declared that scab labor from the country, "which comes here for three or four months every year after making a cotton crop to gobble our work and make stake for Christmas, should not be employed at reduced wages. We stay here all the year round." If the scabs returned to the country, and longshoremen were paid a decent wage, better prices could be paid for farm produce, thus satisfying everyone. Patrick warned against violence, saying the men would retain the sympathy of white labor unions only so long as they remained within the bounds of the law. Cautioning the men to stay away from the Mallory docks for less than forty cents, he added "When they are ready to consent to our terms, union men will do the work at union wages, we don't want scabs to do the work at union wages, but we want union men and union wages."[37]

As Patrick spoke, the Mallory Line's traffic manager, J. B. Denison was complaining of the situation to Mayor Ashley Fly and Deputy Chief of Police Anderson. The police arrived in force during the middle of the afternoon with orders from Mayor Fly to disperse the crowd. Fly, a good politician, was a poor administrator who used city hall as a club for his drinking cronies. Fly had also earned a reputation for being anti-labor. Although pushed back by the police, many men hung around to prevent any attempt to unload the *Colorado*. Denison, not satisfied the crowd was adequately dispersed, again complained to the police. Deputy Chief Anderson arrived to warn the men to disperse and not to return.[38]

Denison told the *Daily News* that he regretted not being allowed to employ his old hands, who had suffered during the suspension of shipping. The rates offered were the same as had been paid for the last five or six years with no complaint; wages were "liberal and which in fact are higher than we can afford." According to Denison, the trouble was caused by men like George Patrick, who had no connection with the Mallory Line. Charles Scrimgeour, superintendent of the Mallory wharf, similarly blamed the trouble on intimidation by the black cotton screwmen. The Cotton Jammers officially denied any involvement in the strike. W. H. Davis, chairman of the Executive Committee, explained that screwmen had ceased to work for Mallory five or six years ago when the company refused to pay the recognized rates. The union was not now trying to raise wages and retake the work although, rumors apart, evidence suggests that this was the goal of at least some rank-and-file members. Certainly the numbers involved in the strike far exceeded the 150 to 250 men regularly employed by Mallory. Strike leaders Patrick and Frank Dennis had worked as screwmen in the past, and Preace Henderson had served on at least one Cotton Jammers delegation to the SBA. Patrick himself admitted that he had not worked for Mallory for several years, claiming instead a "general interest" in preventing Mallory's low wages from depressing wages all round.[39]

Denison, however, refused to concede that Mallory men were purposely paid less than those working on tramp steamers to cut costs, arguing instead that his work had the advantage of a degree of permanency. With at least one ship regularly every week, a man working between thirty-six and fifty hours could make $10.80 to $15 a week. Denison then played the race card, claiming that if he was forced to pay the white scale of wages the work would be opened to white labor, and, at an equal pay scale, white labor was preferable to black. Having implicitly admitted that Mallory was deliberately underpaying its black workers, Denison indulged in an act of verbal legerdemain typical of Mallory managers. Ignoring his own striking workers, Denison claimed that this preference for white labor was "a fact that seems to be tacitly acknowledged by the negroes by their acceptance of lower wages at least so far as loading and unloading of ships is concerned." He was adamant that work would begin at 7 a.m. the next day, with Fly and Anderson promising their support. Mayor Fly's personal supervision of the police the next day would result in the deaths of two men—one white and one black—as well as several wounded.[40]

The day began peacefully with police asking George Patrick to speak to the crowd of strikers. In a "pleasant talk," Patrick warned his men that it was against city ordinances to congregate and recommended that they go to their appointed stations and see that no scabs worked. He warned against violence or creating a disturbance before linking the strike to a broader goal of black manhood:

> We want a larger scale of wages so we can take our women
> from the washtubs and the cook kitchens . . . so we can
> educate and save our daughters from prostitution. The
> white man will not respect you as long as you live as we are
> compelled to do . . . I have, thank God, quit paying rent
> and am now a taxpayer, and that is what you all should be.

The men quietly dispersed as asked, but Denison still remained unsatisfied. Mayor Fly addressed the crowd, telling them they had a right to withdraw their labor but not to prevent others from working. He suggested that "some trifling white man, too indolent to work himself, has caused all this trouble among you colored people for political reasons, and I am sorry your intelligence has not enabled you to discover its full meaning." The end result would be no employment at all for black labor, and it would be their own fault. He finished with a warning that if they used violence, the police would be forced to respond with violence.[41]

The men divided into small squads posted at two-block intervals, but did not interfere as the *Colorado* began unloading. The *Daily News* noted the crew "working along very well—as well as a gang of thirty to forty men could do who were not fully gifted in that line of work." The day passed without incident until 3:40 p.m., when a train arrived carrying sixty-five black laborers from Houston. As these men disembarked, the strikers advanced, and shots were exchanged with the police escort. Thomas Baker, a white screwman there to "see the fun," lay dead, reportedly shot by a "light-skinned negro." Hurrying the scab workers into wharf sheds, the police took up a defensive position. The Galveston men advanced toward the police line, claiming that they only wished to make an attempt to persuade the scabs not to work. Fly advised the longshoremen to leave private property, but when they continued to press forward he gave the order to fire. The men temporarily retreated before police precipitated a further confrontation by attempting to snatch ringleaders from the crowd. Warning volleys were fired before twenty policemen fired into the crowd. Heavy rainfall ended the confrontation, ironically, as firemen prepared to disperse the crowd with water hoses. At nightfall, an armed posse of citizens protected the wharf from behind breastworks of cotton bales.[42]

The next day Frank Robinson, a black longshoreman, died from his wounds, and the Houston Light Artillery arrived with twenty-six men and two Gatling guns. At the wharf, the day passed quietly with no attempt to cross the police line. Behind the scenes, the strike committee asked the Cotton Exchange to intercede on its behalf. Denison flatly refused an offer of compromise and arbitration. Between seven hundred and one thousand men attended a meeting that night where two white screwmen, arguing for "the benefits of unionism," declared that "union labor would stand together regardless of race, creed or color, and that prejudices would be buried." After the meeting, George Patrick told a reporter that the shooting was uncalled for, and that it served to make the men more determined and loyal to the organization. They would continue to rely on moral suasion. Patrick also announced the Protective Union had joined the American Federation of Labor: "In our meeting to-night we signified our intention to stick to the scale of wages we asked for and to hold the union to its duty to aid us. We are members of the American Federation of Labor. Oh, we will stick." Mr. Patrick, the reporter noted, "misuses words occasionally, but on the whole speaks very well, and has no difficulty in giving full expression to his ideas. He says he is not an agitator, but a conservative workingman; he is a grandfather and tries to be a good citizen."[43]

The CLPU joined the AFL as Federal Labor Union No. 7147. Like the Knights of Labor in the previous decade, the AFL's official policy was to organize all working people, "irrespective of creed, color, sex, nationality, or politics." Samuel Gompers expressed his personal opinion in a letter to colleague James H. White:

> Wage workers . . . may not care to socially meet colored
> people, but as working men we are not justified in refusing
> them the right or the opportunity to organize for their
> common protection. . . . We will only make enemies of
> them and of necessity they will be antagonistic to our
> interests.

The AFL held to this policy at first by refusing to affiliate unions that excluded black workers However, the AFL had always favored craft unions over industrial workers and gradually Gompers began to accept the prejudices of skilled workers against unskilled and black labor. The exclusionary practices of all-white unions were simply ignored at first, but by 1900 even the facade of biracial unions had been dropped. Yet, even as Jim Crow laws and racial violence replaced Gompers' earlier vision of the New South, many black workers still turned to the AFL.[44]

In his study of black labor in Richmond, Paul Wortham described federal labor unions as a way for the AFL to circumvent the racism of white unions by organizing Southern black workers into associations directly affiliated to the AFL. As the return to prosperity in 1897 reinvigorated the trade union movement, the AFL financed a nationwide organizing campaign that included the South. Little is known about the number of blacks who belonged to these unions around the turn of the twentieth century but without a national union to bargain for them, and the AFL increasingly retreating from industrial workers, the federal labor unions rapidly failed. However, as Arnesen points out, focusing on white discrimination and racism within the AFL misses the question of how black workers viewed joining federal labor unions or other bodies. As the actions of Galveston's black waterfront workers demonstrated time and again, "It was not integration at the level of the union local but equal rights and equal consideration within the labor movement that topped the black unionist's agenda." These unskilled black laborers— "conservative workingmen" like George Patrick or James Porter, the long-serving secretary for New Orleans' black longshoremen's union— ignored the opposition of Booker T. Washington, local black ministers, and regional industrial employers to unionize and seek the support of the white labor movement. According to Arnesen, Patrick and Porter and their middle-class counterparts drew on a shared language, but these working-class black activists "contributed distinct ideas about the relationship between labor and capital that contrasted sharply with the ideology espoused by middle-class black politicians and journalists of the era."[45]

On the day following the AFL announcement, police arrested George and Harvey Patrick, Lucas Luke, and Frank Dennis on charges of unlawful assembly and inciting riots. The four men were bailed out for $300 each. Earlier that day, Patrick had led a delegation to talk to the Houston men, who remained unmoved. Their agent explained that waterfront wages in Galveston were generally higher than elsewhere; the rates represented a fair wage to the Houston men. Denison hinted that, if the strike continued, white labor would return to the Mallory wharf. Despite this threat, racial strife, much less racial violence, as Obadele-Starks seems to suggest, was not an issue in this strike. There was no evidence, however, of the work being offered to white labor, or of any interest among Galveston's white longshoremen in working for

Mallory. There was, however, an impressive public display of black and white union sympathy.[46]

The funeral of white screwman Thomas Baker was held on September 4. According to the coroner's verdict and that of an SBA investigating committee, Baker was shot by an unknown assailant. No one, however, blamed Patrick's men, and the SBA was determined to make Baker's funeral a public event. Patrick's men and the Cotton Jammers joined with white screwmen and longshoremen and other members of the Trade Assembly in what the *Daily News* described as an "unusual" procession:

> There were 1500 men in line, of which 1000 were negroes.
> The white screwmen and longshoremen, central union,
> composed from all the labor unions in the city, and the col-
> ored screwmen and the new organization marched in
> columns of fours from the hall.

Although white and black marched in separate sections, each headed by their own band, it was indeed an unusual and unprecedented display of labor solidarity.[47]

The next few days passed quietly, but opposition to Mallory's conduct was beginning to surface. Loading on the Mallory wharf continued without interruption, although the strikers continued to pressure the strikebreakers with their constant presence, forcing the Houston men to spend their days and nights confined to their ship and the wharf sheds. A striker who strayed too far received a beating or was thrown into the bay. There were also rumors of men being prevented from returning to work by their fellow strikers. Denison had declared his willingness to meet with any committee, but refused to consider any discussion on wages. The *Daily News* had already pointed out that, despite the determination of both sides, the militia and police could not be expected to keep order indefinitely, nor could strikebreakers be kept in sheds, yet both sides remained determined. Captain Roff, commander of the departing militia, observed that his men "cannot remain here forever, especially in the face of a Mallory management not making any perceptible effort to adjust the differences with the strikers." Police Chief Jones was tired of assigning all his men to the wharf when the rest of the city was entitled to protection. Galveston's merchant community also expressed their concern over the strike. Writing to his uncle George Sealy, John Sealy observed that: "The Mallory strike here has been a very serious one and the situation is not in the least relieved as yet: the negroes are very strong in their Union and will not yield nor will they return to work, from what I can learn, at the old rates."[48]

On September 10 a wholesale dealer's association, "interested parties on the grounds that their freights were being delayed, and that they were otherwise injured," arranged a meeting between Harvey Patrick and Denison. Denison regretted that money was being spent outside of Galveston but refused to alter his position. The *News* reported that Sheriff Henry Thomas was in Houston to persuade men there not to return. According to Thomas, "the best element in Galveston is in favor of sustaining the men in their strike against the Mallory line for better wages." A further report suggested that white longshoremen being paid forty and sixty cents would not work for thirty and fifty cents: their interest was to see black labor paid a decent rate rather than providing cheap competition. On September 13 up to two thousand men tried to attend the meeting of affiliation with the AFL. George Harvey suggested that a ten-cent wage rise would mean $80,000 more a year to be spent among Galveston's merchants. By now, even Mayor Fly was promising to talk to Denison. Denison responded by giving the men one week to return to work.[49]

The *City Times,* Galveston's leading black newspaper, interviewed a prominent union member, "a negro of more than ordinary intelligence, who is recognized as a champion of his race and a man who has many followers in the different negro organizations in the city." The man, who would not be named, declared that, "I am a negro, and am for my race first, last and always. I am with them in their struggle for higher wages, and as a member of the union fully indorse the organization." Condemning the use of violence, he continued: "The union is all right in itself, and organized labor is what the negro needs."[50]

The black union member went on to accuse white politicians of "endeavoring to use the union, or, rather, its members, as a political catspaw." Throughout the strike, vague rumors and accusations had surfaced that "certain" white politicians were manipulating the strikers for their own ends. This informant accused "certain white men, several of them very prominent in commercial and business circles in Galveston," of preying on the many illiterate union members, "for the purpose of feathering their own political ambitions and aspirations, at the sacrifice of men who have stood by the negro, and in politics have received the support of the colored citizens of Galveston." Refusing to publicly name the men involved, he concluded that the struggle for higher wages drew moral support from gold and silver democrats, republicans, and populists:

> But white politicians began to work on the members, and have tried to convince the negroes that certain political friends of theirs have indorsed the actions of certain men, who in politics have lost a good deal of the support of the negro vote.[51]

Strike leader Lucas Luke was more forthcoming in an interview the following week. Luke accused anonymous white politicians of trying to make political capital from the dispute. Two of these men had tried to persuade the strikers that the city's leading white Republican, R. B. Hawley, was using his influence against the strike. Luke denied that this trick would turn black voters away from Hawley, affirming instead that "our people will not be gulled in this way." As Republican congressman for Galveston, Hawley had proved a useful envoy to Washington earlier in the decade when Galveston wanted money from the federal government. Clearly, some local Democratic politicians felt Hawley had outlived his usefulness and were using the strike to turn the traditionally

Republican black voters against him. Hopefully, with no Cuney to orchestrate events, black voters would turn from Hawley because of his failure to support the strike and to appoint blacks to high office.[52]

The strike took a more serious turn when violence flared again on the night of September 22. At 11:15 p.m., forty or fifty masked black men attacked a wharf shed housing the Houston scabs. The "mobbers emptied their pistols," wounding only one man, not seriously. However, a Galveston man, a drayman, not a longshoreman, was discovered dying nearby, the victim of an accidental shooting, according to the *Daily News*. The raid, although clearly intended only to frighten the strikebreakers, gave the forces of law and order an excuse to act. On Friday, September 24, police issued a warrant for George Patrick's arrest. Police searched for Patrick all day and found him that evening at his home, having been notified that Patrick himself had been shot. Patrick claimed he was shot in the thigh that night while visiting the outhouse. He recognized his black assailant but refused to name him. Patrick also refused to be examined or go to a hospital. He was arrested and taken to a hospital, where a doctor declared that the wound had been inflicted between eighteen and twenty-four hours previously.[53]

On Saturday authorities charged Patrick with conspiracy to commit murder and murder. Initially charged only with conspiracy, Patrick was about to pay his $1,000 bail when Mayor Fly appeared in court. After a consultation with judge and counsel, a murder charge was added and bail refused. Patrick claimed to have worked all day Friday as a screwman, so he could not have been wounded on Thursday night. A stevedore confirmed this story, adding that he had not noticed Patrick limping. The stevedore later withdrew his statement, claiming he had been busy when questioned and had mistaken the day. That Saturday night a reporter from the *News* interviewed Patrick in jail. Patrick asked the reporter why he was charged with murder. When the reporter suggested it was because of the shooting incident at Patrick's house, Patrick laughed and replied, "Well. I guess that's it."[54]

Police released Patrick from jail a few days later on $1,000 bail, this time after an appearance in court by Chief Jones. Jones was rewarded for his support the following year when he beat Fly in the mayoral race with support from labor groups and black voters. The strike, however, had lost its momentum. On September 25 the union decided to continue the strike, claiming a near unanimous vote. On Monday, 135 men, many of them reportedly union men, began unloading the *Lampasas*. Support for the strike fell away, despite the union's claims, as the hardship of a prolonged strike forced black longshoreman to return to the Mallory wharf with no gains made. During the strike Daniel Ripley, general agent for the defeated Miami Company's Lone Star Line, had observed: "The Mallory line was very keen to make a combination with the railroads to drive out the Lone Star line. They don't seem so keen to sustain another combination that is trying to make them pay a little more money. Chickens come home to roost. The Mallory line had a little better success in appealing to the law than I had."[55]

On November 26 a grand jury indicted George Patrick, he was again arrested for murder, and released on bail. In December police arrested Roxie Henderson, Ida Rice, and Robert Rice, all neighbors and witnesses of Patrick, on charges of perjury. The following January a court found strike leader Frank Dennis not guilty of stealing a steam whistle. Still awaiting trial, Patrick sat on the first all-black jury to serve in a Galveston courtroom. On May 7, 1900, an appeals court judge acquitted Patrick of the charge of carrying concealed weapons. His trial for conspiracy to commit murder was scheduled for a few days later, but the *Daily News* carried no report of the outcome. Patrick's acquittal on the lesser charge, however, suggests that a conviction would have been difficult, particularly since the police case relied on circumstantial evidence. Moreover, and despite his being wounded at the time of his arrest, there was more than a suggestion of efforts to frame Patrick for the crime. What is known is that instead of going to prison, Patrick and his wife moved to Oklahoma Territory in 1901 and settled in Oklahoma City in 1904.[56]

Migration was a growing option for blacks who wanted to escape

Jim Crow laws and racial violence in Texas. The move to Oklahoma began in the early 1890s when Edwin McCabe, harrassed by the lily-whites in the GOP, like Cuney, began promoting all-black townships such as Langston City. As "Oklahoma fever" struck, Oklahoma Clubs sprang up across the South and blacks continued to move into the territory. Support for emigration came generally from members of the large black lower class who faced greater problems with fewer alternatives than the much smaller black middle class. Migration north involved a more varied group as the *Dallas Express* explained, "This exodus is not by any means confined to the worthless or the ignorant negro. A large per cent of the young negroes in this exodus are rather intelligent. Many of the business houses in Houston, Dallas and Galveston, where the exodus is greatest in Texas, have lost some of their best help." Some of those who left rose to considerable prominence elsewhere, including Cuney's daughter Maud, who moved to Boston to become an accomplished pianist, playwright, lecturer, and author. Patrick returned to visit Galveston in 1904. He gave several speeches at local churches, thus reinforcing the respect that he and other black union leaders garnered from their community.[57]

Not all black workers, however, shared the faith of men like the Patricks in white labor organizations, preferring instead to maintain their independence. Independence meant the ability to secure work by undercutting white labor. But independence could mean no work at all, and it was a devil's bargain that played into the hands of employers. In ports like Galveston, cotton screwing represented one of the few opportunities for black workers to enter a relatively skilled, well paid, and respected occupation. The Cotton Jammers had sought to protect that status by seeking closer links with white labor organizations yet were reluctant to risk jeopardizing the gains they had made with employers by raising their scale of wages to equal that of the SBA. However, some union members were prepared to accept even lower wages to gain work, thus creating a breach in the ranks of the Cotton Jammers. Walter Edmundson was one of several foremen fined ten dollars and expelled from the association in 1898 for working below the forty- and fifty-cents-per-hour scale. Edmundson sued the association in a two-day trial that aroused considerable interest among the black spectators and witnesses crowding the courtroom to hear the jury find in favor of the union. In another case, James Taylor sued the Cotton Jammers for $1,000 after he was expelled from the association for working for the Lone Star line. Taylor, a self-described charter member and active participant in the Cotton Jammers, was then unable to get work because of his nonunion status. The court found in Taylor's favor, but his damages were reduced to $85. Amid these suits, a new black organization appeared on the waterfront sometime before the beginning of the 1898 season.[58]

The disaffected former members of the Cotton Jammers formed the Lone Star Cotton Jammers Association, also known as the No. 3, and began working for Daniel Ripley, former agent of the failed Lone Star line, at rates that undercut both the SBA and the Cotton Jammers. The loss of the Mallory strike may have convinced some that a black worker's best opportunity lay in undercutting the white man's wages. The loss of Cuney's influence after his death that year may also have helped precipitate the division. Perhaps the most important factor was the tremendous growth in cotton exports by more than 1 million bales per season after 1896. Growth offered more opportunities for black workers, but also meant that more employers were willing to exploit the situation. In addition to these local factors, the pressures of racial discrimination created tensions between black Southerners. As Edward Ayers notes in his study of the New South, class issues divided black society against itself. A similar split had occurred among New Orleans's black screwmen during the trouble of 1894–1895, but those two rival bodies had amalgamated by the end of the decade. The Galveston rift was more permanent and lasted until federal courts ordered the desegregation of waterfront unions in 1970s. Relations between Galveston's two black organizations remained acrimonious for at least the next twenty years and seriously hindered attempts to forge biracial cooperation.[59]

The appearance of a second black screwmen's organization, one prepared to undercut the established wage scale, threatened the ability of both the SBA and the Cotton Jammers to maintain wages, particularly in the case of the round bale. At the beginning of the 1898 season, the SBA made a renewed effort to enforce working rules. After a heated debate on the subject of round bales, the SBA resolved to enforce the rule that only screwmen should load cotton. The stevedoring firm of Chase and Smith, who were using longshoremen, were told to obey the SBA rules and were refused gangs until they did so. Chase and Smith offered the work to the Cotton Jammers, but when they refused the stevedores were forced to agree to abide by the rules. This episode demonstrated to all sides that, when combined, the screwmen still held considerable power. The SBA had less success, however, in winning the support of the longshoremen. The LBU's membership more than doubled to three hundred men around this time, perhaps partly by absorbing the coastwise white Longshoremen's Benevolent Association. This increase and the promise of work on the new Southern Pacific docks created a new interest in coastwise work among deep-sea longshoremen. The LBU agreed to prohibit members from stowing cotton on ships bound for foreign ports "but that stowing Cotton without tools on vessels for domestic ports had always been considered longshore work, as the regular lines such as the Mallory and Lone Star are paying now and have been for years paying 40 cents per hour and less, and it would be suicide to their Union if members should refuse work of that kind when offered." This time, it was the SBA who had little option but to accept the decision.[60]

As the *Daily News* noted the following year, the round bale was gaining favor in the industry, meaning that its use would only increase. With black labor loading the round bale at forty cents an hour, or four dollars a day, compared to the six dollars earned by white screwmen, employers who used white labor were at a disadvantage. As a group of seven ship's brokers explained in an appeal to the SBA:

we are not in favor of reducing the laborer's pay, were it not
for the fact that our opponents who are working colored
stevedores will eventually drive you and us out of business
unless some remedy is applied and very quickly to equal
matters.

The SBA's executive committee called a meeting with the two black
locals, hoping to reach an agreement on joint rates for the round bale.
Stevedores had offered ten cents per bale, but the SBA wanted its usual
rate of five and six dollars per day. Several meetings failed to produce
any results. The Lone Stars at first appeared willing to work with the
other two associations, but at the last minute they refused to ratify an
agreement, claiming that they had already made a contract for that year.
They considered hand-loading to be longshore work and therefore
resolved to continue working for forty cents an hour. Committees from
the SBA and the Cotton Jammers made repeated attempts over the next
nine months to persuade the Lone Star Association to fall into step, to
no avail. The SBA continued trying to persuade the Lone Stars even
after the Cotton Jammers had concluded that it would be "useless to
humble ourselves any further." By June 1900, the Cotton Jammers were
forced to accept forty cents an hour for loading round bales or risk losing the work to the Lone Star Association.[61]

• • •

The completion of Galveston's deep-sea harbor was both a fulfillment
and the beginning of a new era. Galveston now rivaled New Orleans
and New York as one of the leading ports in the nation, a position it held
for the next thirty years. On the waterfront, it was not a new beginning,
but was definitely a significant change in direction. The SBA began the
decade by again rejecting contact with the Cotton Jammers, yet within
three years the association had instigated the first official negotiations
with its black rival. Three factors influenced this change, beginning in
1893 when Cuney and the Cotton Jammers won a new contract and

greater share of cotton work. In addition, the balance of power between employee and employer was shifting as the increased cargo capacity of modern steamships and the introduction of high density cotton compresses began to make the screwmen's skills redundant. Finally, New Orleans provided a timely example of the consequences of a racially divided workforce when facing the growing power of larger, foreign owned lines. These factors convinced at least some in the SBA to explore biracial cooperation in the name of self-interest. The Cotton Jammers reacted with caution, balancing their desire for recognition with their need to protect the gains they had already made.

Elsewhere on the waterfront, black coastwise longshoremen began their long struggle for union recognition from the Mallory company. Mallory responded by reviving tactics from 1885, introducing cheap black labor to undercut union strength. The irony here was that black workers, who previously had benefited from this tactic, were now themselves its victim. The strike's leaders, men with a long record of union activity, sought support from the white union movement during the 1898 strike by amalgamating with the AFL. Such was their commitment that the most serious of the rare outbreaks of violence in the history of the waterfront occurred in 1898. A commitment to union principles alone, however, was not enough against an employer with the resources and determination to wait out a strike.

Many rank-and-file workers on both sides of the color line did not share this belief in the benefits of biracial cooperation, a point driven home by the split in the Cotton Jammers in 1898. As the Cotton Jammers and the SBA began to explore the possibility of a joint agreement, some members of the black association preferred to maintain their one advantage over white workers—being cheap labor in order to secure work. This rift between black workers surfaced in several court cases and resulted in the formation of the Lone Star Association. There was a similar short-lived division among black screwmen in New Orleans, but the presence of rival black associations became a permanent feature of Galveston's waterfront. With both black and white workers facing similar challenges from changes within the industry, the Lone Stars threatened to bring a halt to the progress made toward biracial cooperation. The debate on how best to meet that challenge and reconcile the interests of all waterfront organizations occupied the next fourteen years.

CHAPTER FOUR

"Amalgamation regardless of color or race"

The New Orleans Plan

A
fter thirty-five years of uninterrupted growth the new decade started disastrously for Galveston when a devastating hurricane hit the city at the beginning of the new cotton season. The hurricane caused great loss of life and massive structural damage and could have destroyed a less determined community. Galveston, however, disposed of its dead and rebuilt the city to withstand the strongest storm. Cotton was moving on the waterfront just weeks after the storm, and Galveston was soon restored as the nation's leading cotton port. As trade resumed so too did the problems facing Galveston's waterfront workers. Changes in the shipping industry and technology meant that speed, rather than skill, was now the most important economic factor when loading cargo, thus allowing ordinary white and black longshoremen to encroach upon the SBA's dominance of cotton work. Employers also were increasingly prepared to play one race against the other in their efforts to wrest control over wages and working conditions from the unions. Faced with these challenges, the SBA increasingly sought to bolster its waning power through closer ties with other labor associations at local, state, and national levels.

The International Longshoremen's Association was the most

important of these affiliations and would provide the organizational framework for resolving local disputes and working toward biracial unionism over the next twenty-five years. As always, New Orleans proved to be several steps ahead of Galveston in setting an example as the racial divisions of the previous decade were laid to rest. At a time when racial segregation was becoming more absolute than it had ever been under slavery, New Orleans's black and white screwmen agreed to work side by side aboard ship. For Galveston's Cotton Jammers, this New Orleans plan—or amalgamation, as it was also known—quickly became the precondition for reaching any substantive agreement with the SBA. The Cotton Jammers recognized biracial unionism as an opportunity to press for equal rights, at least within the union movement. While white and black labor leaders took care to rule out any desire for social equality, both sides acknowledged the necessity for an industrial equality. Yet, while leaders on both sides appeared ready to countenance amalgamation, rank-and-file members appeared, as they had in the previous decade, more reluctant to set aside their racial antipathy and take such a radical step. Moreover, while the Cotton Jammers saw biracial unionism as the means to push both their class and race interests, the Lone Stars continued to take a more narrow view in undercutting the other two associations. The Lone Stars' presence thus impeded the cause of biracial unionism, as demonstrated by an abortive attempt to reach a three-way agreement based upon the New Orleans plan in 1908. As wages and working conditions continued to deteriorate, however, the Cotton Jammers joined the ILA and finally signed a wages and work-sharing agreement with the SBA. This amalgamation contract of 1912 was the high point of biracial unionism on Galveston's waterfront.

• • •

Galveston entered the new century as the nation's leading cotton shipping port, surpassed only by New York and New Orleans in the total value of its trade. Galveston also was one of the nation's richest cities, second only to Providence, Rhode Island, in per capita income. Yet the zenith of Galveston's commercial triumph quickly turned into an act of hubris. Hurricanes were a recurring danger on the Gulf Coast, and Galveston had been struck by major storms in 1818, 1837, 1867, 1875, and 1886. On September 8, 1900, the "Queen of the Gulf" was torn apart by the worst natural disaster ever to hit North America. The hurricane and ensuing flood claimed more than six thousand lives, leaving another four thousand people homeless and eight thousand destitute. One third of the island's property, valued at up to $30 million and including the partly constructed Southern Pacific facilities and much of the waterfront, was destroyed or badly damaged. The port of Indianola, an earlier rival of Galveston's, had never recovered from the storms of 1875 and 1886 as its citizens chose to abandon their enterprise rather than rebuild. Indianola, however, had already lost the battle with the railroads for its major export of cattle. As many as two thousand citizens left Galveston after 1900, but the port still had its cotton exports and the expanding market of the western states it had worked so hard to secure.[1]

Galveston's leading businessmen led the recovery effort. With the city government paralyzed in the aftermath of the storm, members of the Deep Water Commission took control, forming a Central Relief Committee to oversee relief operations. This committee supervised the disposal of bodies, clearing of debris, sanitation, humanitarian aid, and, before the arrival of the state militia, policing against looters. After the initial clean up, Galveston's citizens began to rebuild their shattered city. The relief committee, backed by the Deep Water Commission and the Galveston Wharf Company, began by instituting a new form of city government with five commissioners replacing the inefficient and allegedly corrupt structure of a mayor and twelve aldermen. The strong links between these several bodies—Isaac H. Kempner, for instance served on the deep water and relief committees and as city treasurer in the new government—placed control of the city even more firmly in the hands of a commercial oligarchy. By placing local government on a more businesslike footing, however, the commission government helped restore confidence and raise the funding for three great engineering projects to protect the city against future hurricanes. The most impressive of these projects, completed in 1911, was raising the level of the island's populated area by an average of eight feet. Entire buildings, from small family dwellings to large churches, were lifted by hydraulic jacks, and the ground beneath was filled in and elevated using silt pumped from a canal built for that purpose. The second project was the building of a seventeen-feet-high seawall, completed in 1908, to protect the coast against waves and abnormally high tides. Finally, in 1912, a new multipurpose, weatherproof causeway stretched two miles across the bay to connect the island to the mainland. In addition, the commission undertook the rebuilding and improvement of the urban infrastructure, adding new schools and water and sewer systems as well as resurfacing commercial and residential streets and modernizing the police and fire departments. The success of the commission government in rebuilding the city made this "Galveston Plan" a model for other progressive cities across America, with archrival Houston among the first cities to adopt the new form.[2]

Galveston's remarkable physical recovery was matched by a swift revival of commercial activity. The first load of cotton left the port just three weeks after the storm. Within six weeks the waterfront was operating near normally with the sounds of reconstruction adding to the regular scene of noise and commotion. The port ranked second in cotton exports by the next season, regaining its leading position in 1903–1904 as well as topping the nation in wheat exports for that year. Despite the potential danger from future storms, Southern Pacific rebuilt its facilities, and the Mallory Line also made improvements. The deepwater harbor continued to attract trade to the port, including new commodities such as lumber and bananas. As continued growth attracted more large shipping companies, such as the Lykes line, to the port, Galveston quickly regained the air of a prosperous city. With the planned building of the Panama Canal on the horizon, the city looked to have a bright future.[3]

As always, however, booming trade figures belied the underlying limitations of the Island City. New Orleans was no longer Galveston's only Gulf Coast rival as ports such as Houston, Beaumont, and Port Arthur also sought and received federal aid for harbor improvements. Texas City, just a few miles directly east across Galveston Bay, received its first deepwater vessel in 1904. According to Wharf Company historian Thomas Barker, unlike the tightly held monopoly of the "Octopus of the Gulf" these competitors were "invariably municipally-owned corporations which enjoyed tax exemptions and capital improvements funded by public taxation." Moreover, although the hurricane did not define Galveston's future, the threat of future storms also favored the development of these newer ports. When the Spindletop gusher signaled a new era in the Texas economy in 1901, investors preferred to build their oil pipelines and refineries in more sheltered locations than Galveston.[4]

Outsiders were not the only people unwilling to invest in the island's future. The storm ended the era of building ornate private homes and commercial buildings that gave the city its unique air of prosperity and grandeur. Of more tangible economic significance was the failure to develop a diverse industrial base. Between 1899 and 1909, the number of manufacturers in Galveston fell from one hundred to eighty-one. In that same period, Houston grew from 145 to 249 places of manufacturing and increased the value of its manufactured goods by four times more than Galveston. The growth of tourism on the island was one of the few industries supported by local money, as both Isaac H. Kempner and John Sealy invested in Hotel Galvez, completed in 1911. Despite its increasing importance over the next several decades, tourism was no substitute for the economic importance of the port. Some historians have blamed Galveston's business oligarchy for failing to invest in the city's industrial base with the Wharf Company and the island's three leading families, the Sealys, Moodys, and Kempners as particular targets. However, according to Kempner family historian Harold Hyman, this "Fly in Amber" thesis of the insularity and control of a business oligarchy has been overemphasized. The most decisive factors, David

McComb points out, were the limitations of the island location and the forces of urban development that were beyond anyone's control.[5]

Although Galveston's physical and economic recovery typified its citizens' will to succeed, the immediate aftermath of the storm revealed the limitations of their racial attitudes. While some black and white citizens had sought shelter together during the storm, racial anxieties quickly resurfaced in its wake as reports of blacks looting and robbing the dead immediately circulated. These stories and claims of the summary executions of seventy-five "ghouls" were largely unfounded but persisted in press reports and later accounts of the storm. Many men of both races were reluctant to perform the awful task of recovering bodies, but a party of fifty black men was forced at gunpoint to load seven hundred bodies onto barges for burial at sea. Yet black workers were among the first to volunteer to join the clean up, including men from the Cotton Jammers. The SBA also immediately volunteered to assist in any way they could and donated one thousand dollars to the Central Relief Committee, and the *Daily News* praised the spirit of both organizations. But while at first the SBA men were armed and put to work policing the streets, white fears of armed blacks meant that the black screwmen were given the task of clearing debris. However, the appalling conditions quickly necessitated men from both groups working side by side at the funeral pyres and clearing the debris. In the months following the storm, the black community continued to receive uneven treatment in the distribution of relief, despite the supervision and best intentions of Clara Barton and the Red Cross.[6]

Such discrimination was a part of the broader pattern of Jim Crow laws enacted at state level since 1890 and, after 1900, by local city policies. In the 1890s the South had experienced a bitter split between conservatives and the radical Populist movement. White supremacy served to heal that division, beginning with the disfranchisement of blacks. Property or literary qualifications for voting were enacted by seven Southern states between 1895 and 1910. These states and four others, including Texas, also adopted the poll tax. Texas adopted the poll tax in 1902 and the following year instituted the all-white primary system, a recognition of Texas's one-party status, which had prevailed since the demise of the Populists in 1896. Between 1896 and 1915, nine other Southern states adopted this final bulwark of the disfranchisement policy. In Louisiana the number of blacks qualified to vote fell by 96 percent. In Texas, figures dropped from the peak of one hundred thousand in the 1890s to five thousand in 1906; in Galveston, only five hundred blacks could vote out of the city's total population of thirty-six thousand.[7]

By the early 1900s local authorities were beginning to enact their own segregation laws. In Galveston, housing was becoming increasingly segregated by 1900, a trend aided by the storm damage that year. Moreover, black home ownership figures compared poorly against state and national levels. Only 8 percent of black homes in Galveston were owned; 87 percent were rented. Comparable figures for white homes were 36 percent owned and 60 percent rented. The storm also increased overcrowding, although reform groups such as the Women's Protective Health Association did try to improve some of the worst conditions. Another legacy of the storm, the commission government elected at large rather than by district, completed the removal of blacks from the local political process that had begun in 1895. In 1906 the city passed a law requiring blacks to sit at the rear of streetcars. In fairness, not all of Galveston's citizens supported these new laws or the unrest they caused among the black population. As one citizen complained to the *Daily News*, resentment at the streetcar law was causing black servants to quit work. Agreeing with the writer, the *News* concluded, "The negroes here are the most orderly, and at the same time the highest toned, of any place in the South. It is a notorious fact that the jim crow law was passed to appease excursionists." As C. Vann Woodward pointed out in his study of the rise of Jim Crow, patronizing the local black community while placing the blame for segregation elsewhere, usually on poor whites, was a common response from Southern authorities. However, while Southern conservatives could once make exceptions for the "better" element of the black race—men such as Norris Wright Cuney—Jim Crow made no such distinctions.[8]

Galveston's black citizens protested against these new indignities. In newspaper editorials and appeals to the commission, Galveston's black community vigorously fought against the streetcar law and the decision to make the new Rosenberg public library an all-white institution. As the *City Times* argued, the black citizen was not seeking social equality "but he does insist upon being treated as an American citizen in all manner due him as such which is tendered to others." In reality, however, Galveston's black community lacked political power or an influential leader such as Norris Wright Cuney and was increasingly forced inward on its own community and institutions. Among the more successful of these institutions were the two waterfront unions, the Cotton Jammers and the Lone Stars.[9]

· · ·

In the first years of the new century, the *City Times* celebrated the number of black workers on Galveston's docks and the wages they earned. In 1903 more than one thousand black laborers on the waterfront earned more than $332,514, which was less than pre-storm but still an encouraging figure. Three hundred and fifty Cotton Jammers worked for the William Parr Company while a similar number of Lone Stars worked for Daniel Ripley. In addition, one hundred and fifty men worked for the Mallory Line and more than one hundred on the Southern Pacific docks. For the *Times*, the waterfront was a shining example of what equal treatment could achieve:

> we cite the fact that at any place where both the whites and
> the blacks get their share of the labor, that place is a com-
> munity wherein lives peace between the laboring classes of
> both the white and the black races. And such action of such
> a people does a great deal toward the general uplift of one
> another and the community in which they labor.

To the *Times*, as long as there was enough work for all, the waterfront, at least, appeared to be one place where there was no racial friction. This view was substantially correct: Galveston's waterfront was largely free of the large-scale labor conflict and racial antagonism experienced in New Orleans. There were, however, ripples of tension on this calm surface.[10]

Employers who had failed to win any reduction in SBA wage rates in the previous decade were now devising ways to cut costs by circumventing established working practices. In February 1900 employers asked the SBA to lower their loading charges or allow longshoremen to load cotton. The executive committee recommended the compromise of allowing LBU men to truck cotton to the gangways and load it into the slings, thus taking over the work of one SBA gang. After much debate, a full meeting of the SBA instructed the committee to consult with the Cotton Jammers. The black screwmen opposed the measure, fearing that since they were paid by the bale it would be used to compel them to reduce their rates. The SBA accepted this decision and notified the brokers that no changes would be made. The following November, the SBA and Cotton Jammers renewed their wage-and-work-sharing agreement. SBA rates were set at six dollars per day for hand stowing and seven dollars for using tools, while the Cotton Jammers worked for the slightly lower piecework rates of ten cents and thirty-five cents per bale. The two sides renewed their agreement not to take each other's work and established a joint committee to investigate grievances. Rumors occasionally surfaced that an employer was prepared to switch his labor force from white to black, or vice versa, or that one group of workers were preparing to bid for the work of another. The new committee successfully negotiated such disputes and misunderstandings over wages and working rules that arose between the two associations. However, despite the persuasive efforts of both the SBA and Cotton Jammers, the Lone Stars continued to reject a joint agreement and the Cotton Jammers were still forced to load round bales at forty cents per hour or risk losing their work to the Lone Stars.[11]

The Lone Star Association was not the only divisive influence on the waterfront in the first years of the new century. The SBA and LBU had to contend with a new general longshoremen's union, Local 155, which was organized in March 1900 with seven hundred members. Evidence suggests that the new local was organized to work on the Southern Pacific docks, then still under construction. The LBU, a deep-sea union, also laid claim to the promise of regular coastwise work, and even some SBA members sought work on the new docks. The LBU and SBA opposed the new union and refused to work with members of the new local, who were rumored to be working below scale. Even some SBA members were accused of working for scab wages. The new local sought protection by joining the International Longshoremen's Association, which had been trying to organize in Galveston for several years. Formed in the early 1890s in the Great Lakes area by Daniel Keefe, an Irish tugboat captain, the ILA had around fifty thousand members by 1900. The ILA affiliated with the AFL in 1902, but, unlike the craft orientation of the latter, the ILA took on the character of an industrial union as Keefe aggressively sought to recruit any class of workers connected to marine transport. Like the AFL, however, Keefe and T. V. O'Connor, his successor as ILA president, adopted a conservative policy of anti-radicalism and maintaining good working relationships with employers.[12]

According to ILA historian Maud Russell, the dispute in Galveston was caused by independent unions opposing the ILA in order to maintain their own power. The ensuing "bitter and bloody" strike led to the "undoubted" murder of Local 155 secretary L. R. Taylor by other longshoremen or "hired killers of the shipping company." Taylor suddenly disappeared while working aboard ship, and, according to the ILA investigation, "His body was discovered after he was missed about three days in an almost unrecognizable state. No one can account for this particular mystery, and some are of the opinion that he must have fallen overboard while going from one vessel to another." Russell's account, which favors the ILA, ignores the fact that it was the new local that was the usurper against the long-established SBA and LBU. There was no record of a strike or violence in the *Daily News* and the charge of murder, while melodramatic, lacks a clear motive and is uncharacteristic of Galveston. Taylor's untimely death was not wholly unusual in a hazardous industry without any legal safety standards. In 1890, for instance, screwmen Charles Cox went missing after falling through the hatch of a lighter. His body was found seventeen days later "in a high state of decomposition." A few weeks later, John Burke died from his injuries after being hit by a cotton bale. Nor were employers or union officials exempt from these hazards. In January 1901 stevedore John Young was nearly killed when he fell into a ship's hold. In 1907 Local 310 president Harry Michlousky was literally cut to pieces when caught in a steam winch cable and pinned against the winch.[13]

The dispute did, however, generate ill-feeling on all sides. Before his death, Secretary Taylor had written to Samuel Gompers, accusing the SBA of working contrary to the principles of the AFL and the Galveston Labor Council of encouraging "a lot of unscrupulous non-union men in their work." The LBU and SBA had enlisted the support of the Labor Council and opposed the new local's application to join the council. The dispute was not simply a local power struggle or a fight against the ILA, which both the SBA and LBU joined within two years. The fundamental issues were the right to jobs and the maintenance of wage standards. The Labor Council made repeated efforts to resolve the conflict over the next year, inviting both Gompers and Keefe to Galveston to settle the dispute. Agreement was finally reached in March 1902, when LBU members agreed to disband their organization and reorganize with their rival as ILA Local 310. The SBA quickly followed suit by joining the ILA the following month.[14]

The SBA's traditional policy of isolationism had been softening over the past decade and joining the ILA was not the SBA's first step into the broader labor movement. In 1891 the SBA had sent delegates to the Texas Labor Conference organized in Galveston. The Labor Conference was the central body of the Knights of Labor and Farmers' Alliance and included more than twenty of Galveston's white trade unions. This movement received further momentum when Populists sought to further the alliance between farmers and workingmen. However, the effectiveness of these early state organizations was limited because individual unions adamantly refused to consider political matters. As one contemporary newspaper explained:

> A trades union is simply a voluntary assembly of artisans formed for the express purpose of limiting the competition in the labor market and thereby maintaining as favorable conditions as any governmental policy, religious truth, or even moral conduct. And no one is more bitterly opposed to the introduction of such questions into trades union meetings than the member.

The result, according to one historian, was that conventions would be called only to "announce they were nonpartisan, issue a set of demands, and disappear." The conference was, however, a forerunner for a more effective organization, the Texas State Federation of Labor, which was formed in 1900.[15]

The state federation was composed of delegates from local labor councils and Galveston's three delegates to the first convention represented some eighteen hundred workers, numerically the largest delegation. The federation was affiliated to the American Federation of Labor, but, according to historian Grady Mullenix's account, its principles were closer to the Knights. The state federation's main purpose was to pursue legislative action and its declaration of principles supported such current concerns as the eight-hour day and child labor laws. Opinions, however, were divided when contemplating any more overtly political action. The first convention did pass resolutions encouraging worker interest in political issues, but some delegates were reluctant to go even this far.

The federation's reluctance to engage in political debate reflected the staunchly nonpartisan stance of its constituents. In Galveston, the poll tax and new commission government were the only political issues to arouse any action. In 1903 the Labor Council passed a resolution urging union members to pay their poll tax. The introduction of any political topic was guaranteed to lead to a prolonged and fierce debate, but this resolution did pass by a two-to-one majority. The next year Local 310 resolved to pay the poll tax for members who could not afford to, allowing them three months to repay. Although passed, this resolution was withdrawn at the next meeting. In 1906 the Labor Council discussed raising subscriptions to start a labor journal. According to a longshoremen's delegate, many of his men could not read but "when they get married they would get their wives to read for them and that possibly they would subscribe." Literate or not, at least one longshoreman used the new journal to rouse support for political action, arguing that the day was past when trade unionism was nonpolitical: "It is our duty to elect men to all offices who have the interests of the working man at heart. . . . The forthcoming election will be a great opportunity to show the capitalist class what organized labor can do when it stands shoulder to shoulder for its rights." Thereafter, the council did make efforts to propose labor candidates for the commission, a move the SBA and Local 310 supported. However, while the two locals could support labor candidates at the local level, they firmly opposed any attempt at forming a working-class political party. Local 310 even prohibited its members from using the name of the local in any campaign for political office. However, at least some of the longshoremen leaders, including O. A. Anderson and J. Gahagahan, did try to start a Progressive Labor Party. Anderson brought this issue before the state federation in 1910, proposing "to get control of the lawmaking body of the state and the several municipalities." SBA President Fricke opposed the idea, and the federation endorsed a declaration of principles supporting wage earners' political participation but denouncing "the practice of indorsing political parties or candidates or indulging in partisan agitation, leaving each voter to act as a free citizen in these matters."[16]

Although political action was forestalled, local unions did use the state federation to pursue legislative action of direct concern. In the SBA's case, this meant the Spider Bill. "Spiders" were the exposed ends of metal bands, buckles and rivets that bound a compressed bale of cotton. Screwmen wore a "handleather" to protect the back of the hand from cuts when using a cotton hook to hook and roll a bale, but injuries from improperly bound bales were common. The Spider Bill passed in 1910, despite strong opposition from the cotton compress owners, who were made responsible for ensuring that bales were safely bound.[17]

The state federation also followed local practices on the issue of race, rather than pressing for a more progressive course of action, but by this time the AFL itself was retreating from its earlier promise of organizing black workers. Gompers and the AFL leadership were themselves racist or, at best, unwilling to challenge the prevailing mood of the times and particularly in the South. Moreover, the AFL was becoming almost exclusively a craft union and most black workers were unskilled. Efforts to recruit black workers faded and the question of integration was left to be decided at the local level. In private, Gompers continued to acknowledge the necessity of organizing black workers. In practice, federal labor unions fell from 7 percent of AFL membership in 1897 to only 1.3 percent by 1910. The International Workers of the World was the only labor organization to fully live up to its rhetoric of racial equality, but this radical organization had little impact in conservative Galveston.[18]

The Texas federation supported separate black unions, recognizing that practicality and even a sense of justice dictated accepting the black worker "and moulding him to purposes of honor and advancement along parallel lines with the white worker." The first black delegate to the conference was seated in 1904, although the following year Galveston's black laborers were still being represented by O. A. Anderson, a white longshoreman's union official. The 1911 convention rejected a resolution to exclude blacks from the federation by forming a separate black federation. Still, the federation's black organizers were reminded of the need for great discretion:

and that in all his work he should teach his people the
principles of unionism in their own color and crafts, and let
them know that the sympathy and aid of the white man
will be extended to them only so long as they retain their
own self-respect and maintain their proper position in our
society and government.[19]

If black delegates were resigned to accept their place in society, they
were less ready to accept second-class status within the union movement. Yet some local trade assemblies still refused to accept black
unions. In 1914 two black delegates, one from Waco and the other a
member of Galveston's Lone Stars, sought to change federation policy
by allowing the amalgamation of white and black unions. These delegates demanded the full benefits of unionism and a reform of the rank
and file to suppress the evil that divided the races:

and is continually giving capital the advantage of both
races, it is absolutely necessary for us to cement our great
labor forces together for this one explicit purpose . . . and
forget the question of color, which has been a stumbling
block. This reform cannot bring about its best results simply by affiliation, but amalgamation instead.

Rather than face the issue head-on, the federation substituted a
counter-resolution that endorsed the organization of black workers but
left the question of amalgamation to be decided at the local level. Later
that year the federation asked for the enforcement of the law requiring
the provision of equal facilities for blacks on trains and streetcars. In
1919 they called for the abolition of discrimination, which, despite being
against the AFL constitution, existed in Texas. These resolutions
aroused opposition, and nothing practical was done to carry them out.[20]

At the local level, the SBA's attitude to the Galveston Labor Council had always been, and continued to be, ambivalent. The SBA's periodic withdrawals from the council suggested that membership was as much a matter of convenience as conscience. There were, however, signs of a greater willingness to become involved in local issues away from the waterfront. The SBA offered financial support to a striking Carpenters and Painters local in 1900, adding that "we firmly believe the fight of one or more unions is the concern of all labor organizations when arrayed against organized capital." The growing number of appeals for aid from labor unions across the nation and even abroad also met with a favorable response. In 1902 the SBA petitioned the County Commissioners Court to employ local labor on the seawall project at a minimum wage of two dollars for an eight-hour day. Public works no doubt provided a much needed source of income for its members during the off season, but, as the SBA pointed out, a five-thousand-dollar subscription to the seawall bond issue and a one-thousand-dollar donation to the storm relief fund gave the association a right to speak on behalf of all Galveston's manual laborers:

> Experience has shown . . . that men never fail to work at
> their full capacity when the wage and time is reasonable.
> There is no just reason why a private contractor should reap
> a profit from the construction of the seawall: we do not
> object to a just profit . . . but public works should not be
> private spoil.[21]

Rhetoric aside, the SBA's involvement in a broader labor movement was motivated as much by the struggle to maintain its own declining strength as genuine class consciousness.

Despite the growing awareness of a broader labor movement, there were signs that the SBA's internal strength was weakening as it grew in numbers. Changing attitudes toward cultural functions such as Labor Day provide one telling indication. In Galveston, Labor Day was usually celebrated with a morning parade followed by a picnic, speeches, games, and dancing. Both the SBA and LBU placed such significance on this holiday that attendance at the parade was mandatory. Fines were levied for drunkenness and nonattendance, and members had to be absent from the city for a week on either side of Labor Day to escape the fine. Members of both associations purchased a specially selected suit of clothes to wear on the day. The day was still an important demonstration of craft pride and a social event for Galveston's organized workers at the turn of the century. An estimated 2,300 men lined up for the 1900 parade, making it one of the largest ever witnessed in Galveston. The parade included ladies auxiliaries, alderman, and other local dignitaries, and many trades and several merchants entered decorated floats. The SBA's float won third prize that year and, as usual, the marching ranks of some five hundred cotton screwmen made one of the more impressive displays. The men had discarded their traditional working uniform of blue flannel shirts and dark trousers in favor of more versatile brown linen suits with matching hats. In 1902 between 3,500 and 4,000 people attended the picnic, held at Wollams Lake, to hear a speech on behalf of the eight-hour movement and a longer speech by governor-elect Col. S. W. T. Latham. Latham's theme, the common interests of labor and capital, was standard fare for the occasion. In 1910 Galveston's Mayor Lewis Fisher urged the assembled union men to reassure employers:

> that you believe that the interests of capital are the same as those of labor, and that the contract you, as a union, enter into with your employers will be carried out both in the spirit and the letter. When your organization reaches that status there will be no more friction between capital and labor.

Such oratory, as always, received "hearty applause."[22]

By the middle of the decade, however, rank-and-file members were beginning to demonstrate a waning enthusiasm for the event, particularly the parade. In 1907 the SBA decided to parade in Houston, and Local 310 and several other locals did not parade at all. As one GLC delegate explained, Labor Day harmed the organization because it lost members due to fines and failure to pay for uniforms. The fine for nonattendance had risen to ten dollars by 1905, and Local 310's uniform of black serge pants, flannel shirt, black necktie, belt, and gray fedora hat cost $6.40. Loans were given to those who could not afford the new clothes, but the total cost of uniforms was $1,181 plus another $130 to hire a band. In 1909 a motion to parade on Labor Day passed by a narrow margin only after the fine for nonattendance was dropped to $5 and members were allowed to wear any suit "providing it was respectable." The SBA and Southern Pacific workers did not parade at all that year, leaving the deep-sea longshoremen to make one of the most impressive displays: "This organization had the greatest number in line by far and they were a fine body of men—muscular and healthy looking . . . the large number of private vehicles in this section was frequently remarked upon. The men showed prosperity in every line." Despite the show of prosperity, there was no parade at all for the next several years, a failing the *Labor Herald* attributed to the apathy of younger members.[23]

Juneteenth, the annual celebration of the first official reading of the Emancipation Proclamation in Galveston and Texas on June 19, 1865, was the most important annual cultural event for Galveston's black citizens. This event was also celebrated with a parade and speeches but, by the early 1900s, there were signs that this too was becoming less popular as many chose to go on all-day picnic excursions arranged for the occasion. In 1902 a committee of black women decided to organize the parade because their men had allowed the occasion to drift into disuse: "The women . . . propose to celebrate the day in a becoming manner, as is done elsewhere. They will be supported in the matter by the white citizens who have pledged themselves to assist them if they get up creditable displays like the colored people of Houston, San Antonio and Austin." The 1904 parade, while not as large as previous years, was still judged "quite creditable" with more than thirty carriages, traps, and other vehicles stretching for eight or ten blocks. Labor Day was also an important celebration, particularly for the black longshoremen, who held their own parade and picnic. In 1900 around 150 members of the Cotton Jammers and Lone Stars marched through the business district to Douglass Park for speeches, games, and prize contests, with dancing that lasted until a late hour. After 1900 the animosity between the two black associations caused them to hold separate celebrations, thus turning Galveston's day of labor solidarity into a three-cornered affair. Nevertheless, the event remained important to black labor. In 1904 more than three hundred people, including a ladies auxiliary, joined the Cotton Jammers in a parade followed by a picnic at Lincoln Hall. In 1909 between five and seven hundred black people marched to a celebration held at the Cotton Jammers' own hall and park on Thirty-seventh Street and Avenue S.[24]

The SBA was still far from powerless in 1900. Savings stood at $47,000 and other assets included sixty-five jackscrews and the Screwmen's Hall that stood on the corner of Market Street and Twenty-first Street. Although 47 men were lost to the storm, SBA membership grew from 464 in 1900 to 556 by mid-decade and was still over 500 in 1909. Moreover, although stevedores continued to win concessions from the SBA, such as a no-strike agreement in 1903, many employers still preferred to work with the SBA rather than against them. Despite the pressure from employers, some SBA members still believed they could do without affiliation with other associations. In 1901 the executive committee heard a motion to withdraw from the Labor Council on the basis that "we are a purely local organization we deem it not necessary to have representation." The majority of the committee, however, recognized that the SBA could no longer stand alone. Labor organizations in other Southern cotton ports had failed to uphold their wages because they stood without affiliation to a national or international body. To avoid the same fate, the committee now believed that the best interests of the SBA lay in joining the ILA. A general meeting accepted the committee's recommendation and the SBA received its charter as ILA Local 317 in April 1902.[25]

ILA membership did little in the short term to settle differences between the screwmen and deep-sea longshoremen's Local 310, formerly the LBU. The Morgan Line was about to begin a service to New York from the now completed Southern Pacific docks. The stevedoring firm of Suderman and Dolson claimed to have the necessary six hundred men willing to take on the work at thirty cents for days and forty cents for nights, the same rates Mallory paid. According to the stevedores, Local 310 seemed to believe the work was theirs by right, yet the organization only had three hundred members. Local 310 President L. G. Koen replied that his union was willing to accept the offered rates but wanted an additional sixty cents for Sunday work since "the men do not care to work Sundays if they can avoid it." Moreover, the union not only had the six hundred men but, "We would rather do the work for nothing than to put one thing in the way of this traffic for Galveston." Or, of course, risk losing the work altogether.[26]

This wrangling over wages was further complicated by the SBA, which also claimed a share of the Southern Pacific work. Some screwmen had always supplemented their wages with longshore work, but this was the first time the association itself had actively sought coastwise work. Local 310 accused the screwmen of overstepping their bounds by claiming mixed cargo work in violation of local protocol and ILA rules, which bound each local to a specific class of work. Koen declared that his men would not be driven from what was rightfully theirs and threatened to retaliate by contracting for cotton. Suderman and Dolson, both former screwmen, asked SBA president Fricke to find a solution. Fricke was warned that the stevedores wanted to employ white labor, but they had made their best possible offer: if no compromise was reached the work would go to black labor.[27]

The stevedores' warning had the desired effect. Faced with the threat of losing the work to black labor, the two ILA locals agreed on a compromise by forming a new organization, the Southern Pacific Transport Workers Local 385. Stevedores agreed to employ the new all-white local, paying thirty cents for a ten-hour day and forty-five cents for overtime and Sundays. Local 851 had more than 1,700 members, three times the number of any other waterfront union, but only seven to eight hundred men found regular work. Clearly, many casual laborers as well as screwmen and longshoremen joined the new union in the hope of picking up extra work. Size, however, was no indication of strength, particularly in the coastwise trade. With such a large labor pool, it would be difficult to earn a sufficient regular wage, and, when it came to a strike, the white Southern Pacific workers found themselves in a no better position than their black counterparts at Mallory.[28]

The poor average wage was the central issue when Southern Pacific dockworkers struck for higher wages in September 1907. O. A. Anderson, president of Local 385, claimed the men earned an average of eight dollars a week. Many union members worked elsewhere, and the strikers could do no worse by trying to do the same. "We have everything to gain and nothing to lose," explained Anderson, "It is simply impossible for a man and his family to live even in the coarsest manner on the wages earned in this work. The strike is a necessity. It is a demand for the actual necessities that life may be sustained in the workers and their wives and children." Suderman and Dolson responded to the union's claim for a five-cent-per-hour pay raise by offering the work to the two black locals. The Cotton Jammers responded by offering to consider the work but only for a higher rate than sought by Local 385. Lone Star leader William Porter visited the *Daily News* office to publicly state that his association was not interested in taking the work and that their sympathies lay with the strikers. Porter also appeared before 385's executive committee to offer his association's moral and financial support, and both black locals promised to make every effort to prevent the use of black strikebreakers. The strike was also threatening to spread to the black workers on Mallory's docks, who had not been organized since their defeat in 1898.[29]

With the stevedores' attempt to exploit racial divisions stalled, Southern Pacific officials took over the handling of the strike by bringing in forty black strikebreakers from Houston protected by private armed guards. A delegation of white and black union representatives persuaded some of those enlisted to quit, and the company found it difficult to recruit other nonunion laborers despite a widespread search. When sixty more black workers were brought in, some claimed not to have known of the strike and asked the union for their fare home. Dockside checkers refused to work with the strikebreakers, although it is unclear if this was because they were nonunion, because they were black, or both. The strike, however, was taken out of the hands of union officials when a Citizen's Committee met with Southern Pacific. Galveston's merchants were always concerned when trouble flared on the docks, both because of the delay in shipments and the loss of their revenue from workers' wages. This time, another and perhaps greater fear surfaced with the possible loss of one thousand white jobs to black labor and the consequent increase of Galveston's black population by several thousand. The danger, explained the *News*, lay "with a possible shifting of political conditions, always more or less uncertain where the irresponsible negro voter and the scheming white man are afforded an opportunity for bargaining." Addressing a rank-and-file meeting of Local 385, the Citizen's Committee stated that they were convinced that Southern Pacific would not change their position. After just nine days, the strike ended with a few small concessions, but no pay raise.[30]

The Galveston *Labor Journal* hailed the strike as a victory but made it clear that the threat of an influx of black labor had been decisive. The concessions, though small, were important and indicated both the fragility of a longshoreman's earnings and the ability of a company to gouge more out of its workforce. The company agreed to no longer charge a 10 percent levy when workers were forced by exigent circumstances to take a part of their pay before the official Thursday payday. The insecurity of dockwork made such advances a necessity, the only alternative being the loan sharks that plagued the waterfront. Workers would also no longer be charged ten cents a week for ice but could provide their own. The *Journal* calculated that this weekly levy had amounted to far more than the cost of ice supplied to the men. Other practices whereby men lost time, including losing a full fifteen minutes when starting a job a few minutes late or finishing early, also ended. The *Journal* praised the dockworkers' loyalty to Galveston and the stand taken by the black unions: they, unlike the Southern Pacific, had the city's best interests in mind. Continuing the strike would have meant: the displacement of more than 2500 white people, good law-abiding citizens, many property owners and the acceptance of a bunch of blacks who can be bought body and soul for a few paltry dollars. It would mean the political upheaval of city and county government, to the detriment and everlasting disgrace of their citizenship.

• • •

The *Labor Journal* and President Anderson tried to make the best of the settlement by representing the strike as an important first step in a longer struggle. However, the strike again exposed the weakness of coastwise workers when faced with an obdurate employer. It would be another thirteen years before Local 385 again challenged Southern Pacific.[31]

The formation of Local 385 had settled the initial Southern Pacific dispute in 1902 but did not end the wrangling between the screwmen and longshoremen. With job competition intensifying, each association became more determined to protect against encroachment by the other, and the long-accepted practice of joint membership in both unions became a contentious issue. The dispute escalated when 310 expelled thirty-one members for belonging to the screwmen's local. Attempts to resolve the problem failed, although ILA rules forced 310 to reinstate the expelled members. In addition, both black locals remained outside the ILA with the Lone Star Association resisting even a local agreement.[32]

New Orleans's screwmen and other waterfront workers faced similar pressures to their Galveston counterparts. In addition, employers and businessmen worried about the increasing cotton trade through Galveston played up the strong managerial control and high productivity of the rival port. According to the *New Orleans Picayune*, cotton in Galveston was "rushed from the cars across the docks into the ships at a rate that would make an old-timer screwman's hair turn grey." According to Arnesen, New Orleans employers continually made these unfavorable comparisons with Texas ports and making exaggerated claims as to their work rate. Whether accurate or not, employers used the rallying cry of "parity with Galveston" to introduce a new "shoot the chute" system for loading cotton. This system, where one gang was expected to load between four hundred and seven hundred bales a day, was dangerous and threatened the screwmen's control over the work process.[33]

Mindful of the lessons provided by the bitter racial troubles of 1894–1895, New Orleans's screwmen responded to this new system by forming a new Dock and Cotton Council in October 1901. Black unions were particularly strong in New Orleans, forming their own Central Labor Union and parading an estimated ten thousand men from twenty different unions on Labor Day in 1903. Many black dock unions affiliated with the newly formed ILA early in the new century, often before their white counterparts. James Porter, a tireless worker and organizer, led the black screwmen, and, under his guidance, black waterfront unions remained committed not only to their own organizations but to the national labor movement as well. White and black screwmen first agreed to abide by a uniform wage scale and then in October 1902 entered into an agreement on what they termed "amalgamation." More than simply a work-sharing agreement, amalgamation meant blacks and whites working side by side, or "abreast" one another, in gangs headed by either a white or black foreman. According to Arnesen, this unprecedented agreement resulted in the screwmen reaffirming their control over the labor supply and working conditions and regaining their position as the aristocrats of the levee. The New Orleans screwmen successfully shifted their struggle from one between black and white labor to one between labor and capital.[34]

Having reached their local agreement on amalgamation, the New Orleans screwmen tried to further strengthen their hand by renewing the call for an alliance of all Gulf Coast organizations. Setting industry-wide standards for wages and working rules would prevent employers from playing race against race and port against port. The SBA and Cotton Jammers sent a joint delegation to New Orleans to discuss setting up a Cotton Council for all Southern ports. On returning to Galveston, the black screwmen agreed to adopt the recommendations of the New Orleans convention, which included, among other things, amalgamation with an equal division of work and white gangs to work abreast black gangs. The SBA made a counterproposal that included lower bale limits but rejected any consideration of amalgamation. The Cotton Jammers clearly felt that any meaningful agreement would have to include amalgamation; they rejected the counterproposal, thus laying the issue to rest for the next several years.[35]

With a formal alliance with the two black associations stalled, the SBA pursued the idea of forming a local association with other white locals. In November 1905 the SBA approached Locals 310 and 385 with the idea of forming a Marine Council in Galveston. Despite an apparent willingness on the part of all three organizations, little came of the idea. The following season was a relatively good year for the screwmen, which perhaps lessened the drive for a joint association. By 1908, however, there were again signs of increasing pressure. SBA members expressed concern about expenditure exceeding income and recommended a reduction in the salaries of union officers, although the executive committee reported that union funds had in fact increased by $4,000 over the last five years. Cost may have been a factor in the decisions not to parade on Labor Day or to send delegates to the annual ILA conference. In June stevedore John Young asked for a change in work rules to allow gangs to make up time lost due to bad weather so that ships would be loaded and men would not lose pay. Young had sought concessions before and claimed that this system, which operated in New Orleans, was of the "utmost importance to his firm" in competing with black labor. That October the executive committee reported that screwmen were working at an "even gait," but work was short for that time of year because most ships were loading loose cotton rather than screwing it.[36]

A more exact picture of conditions on the waterfront came from members of the New Orleans Port Investigating Commission who visited Galveston the previous January. The commission was gathering evidence on working practices and labor and shipping costs in Southern ports competing with New Orleans by interviewing white screwmen's and longshoremen's leaders and their employers. Two facts emerged from the commission's findings in Galveston: the growing dominance of large foreign-owned shipping lines and the consequently increasingly precarious position of skilled, white screwmen. Gentry Waldo, freight manager for Southern Pacific, summed up the new economic imperative for employers: "there is not much advantage in screwing cotton, unless the boat is waiting for cargo . . . but if she has all of her cargo waiting, it is better to hand stow and get out as soon as possible. It is more profitable and less expensive."[37]

Charles Suderman of Suderman and Dolson spoke for Galveston's stevedores. His career followed a familiar pattern—he had worked as an SBA foreman for twelve years before becoming a stevedore in the early 1890s. Suderman still paid his SBA dues but took no active part in the association's affairs. Most of Suderman's work came from Southern Pacific, but he also employed one hundred screwmen in twenty gangs. His weekly payroll from September to February averaged from $15,000 to $25,000, but this dropped by about 50 percent during the offseason when only Southern Pacific had any work during the months of July and August. Suderman estimated that in the previous season, an "extraordinary year," each of his gangs made two hundred days of work. That year, gangs were averaging four days per week, which would yield an annual wage of $900 to $1,200. Suderman himself cleared around five dollars per gang per day. Each gang stowed 200 to 210 bales per day by hand and 85 to 87 using screws. Of the 300,000 bales Suderman's men loaded in a season, a little over half were screwed although a gang received the same wage, thirty-one dollars, for hand stowing. Those 300,000 bales were less than one tenth of the port's total cotton shipment.[38]

Suderman acknowledged that all the cotton shipped by the large companies such as Leyland, Harrison, and Booth and Hogan was hand stowed as were three quarters of the 4 million bales leaving Galveston the previous year. Other interviewees confirmed the division between the large and small shipping lines. A Mr. Lengbehn, an independent agent who chartered ships rather than working for a particular line, estimated that 90 to 95 percent of his cotton was screwed. His men were mostly Scandinavians, some of whom had worked for him for twenty years, and averaged 120 days per year or $720 to $750 in six months. Lengbehn estimated that one third of the vessels entering port were tramp steamers, which offered much-needed competition for the regular services the large lines provided. Lengbehn also conceded that "I do know that competition drives the employers down to lower wages."[39]

The commission interviewed three SBA officials, Vice President William Garland, President J. H. Fricke, and Financial Secretary Julius Schilke, as well as a recent president of Local 310, A. Harry. All four agreed that property values on the island were high and that the already high cost of living in Galveston was rising at an "alarming rate"; property values were high, with house rent costing between twelve to fifteen dollars per month. A report published in 1912 by the *Daily News* confirmed the high cost of housing and the problems of overcrowding and poor sanitation caused by the alley system where houses were situated at the rear of streetfront properties. According to the report, conditions for the white working class were generally good. There was little overcrowding in the homes of working people except from the inflow of itinerant laborers during the height of the shipping season. There was a comparative lack of poverty in the city, and wages on the docks, where the majority found employment, were adequate to meet the cost of living. Wages were high enough to even allow savings, so workers could not only afford the relatively high rents without complaint, but, in time, the majority became homeowners. The report recognized that waterfront wages were seasonal and the part played by "the good women" of Galveston:

They are as a class frugal, thrifty women and take care of

their homes with diligent pride. They have as a rule mastered the economy of the home and have assisted their husbands to put by for the hard times or investment definite portions of their annual incomes.

The one exception to these relatively high standards was, of course, believed to be the black workers, who "crowd into their houses without regard for sanitation, ventilation, or decency." The *Daily News* itself at least acknowledged that, like their white counterparts, black women played an important role in the household economy, working in the summertime to feed their men while in the wintertime the situation was reversed.[40]

The report was overly optimistic and underestimated the growing problem of irregular work on the waterfront. According to the three interviewees, perhaps as few as 3 or 4 percent of longshoremen owned their own homes. Even allowing for error, this was well below the 1910 census figure for white home ownership. Home ownership was higher among screwmen but even Garland, a foreman for much of his twenty-six years, still rented a house. He estimated that he had worked 130 to 140 days the previous season while Fricke gave 100 days as an average. Schilke estimated 90 days as his lowest ever figure with a rarely attained high of 150 days. Longshoreman averaged little better as only the coast-wise lines had work all year round. Both screwmen and longshoremen had to seek alternative work during the summer. Some found employment on public works projects such as grade-raising or digging water mains. Many screwmen worked as painters and carpenters; Schilke himself worked regularly during the summer months as a house carpenter. Many of Lengbhen's Scandinavians owned fishing boats. According to Fricke, fully half the membership, particularly single men, went north for the summer months to work as crew for private owners during the yachting season. Perhaps 25 percent of the longshoremen left town for the summer. Behind these facts and figures, however, lay a more telling statistic. The white screwmen worked all tramp steamers but held contracts with only two big lines, the North German Lloyd Company and the Hamburg-American. All the other companies running a regular service employed only black labor. The longshoremen were in a similar position, handling all tramp steamers but working for only one large line, Elder-Dempster.[41]

The commission was also anxious to know the state of labor and race relations in the port. Employers and employees alike agreed that their relations were cordial. Each side met at the beginning of the season, and any differences were settled in an amicable manner. There had been no strikes since the early 1880s. Like most of Galveston's six or seven other stevedores, Suderman hired only white labor, but the members were keen to solicit his opinion about whether blacks were likely to do more work than white men if paid by the piece? Suderman felt that white labor paid by the day was more dependable even though he personally "could make more money out of the negroes." According to Arnesen, the influence of black workers on the waterfront was more important to the commission than broad issues of class conflict. The commission was looking for ammunition it could use against the large shipping lines in New Orleans, where the alliance between black and white workers was being blamed for a recent bout of labor militancy. According to one New Orleans agent interviewed, the system of amalgamation meant that "we are practically under negro government." The blame for this threat to white supremacy fell on two British-owned lines who had exploited racial divisions in past years, thus creating the impetus for amalgamation. The commissioners found what they were looking for in the strict division of black and white labor in Galveston. As Fricke assured them, "You know we do not associate with those fellows. It ain't like they do in New Orleans. We don't associate with them at all."[42]

Fricke's assessment, while glossing over events of the previous fifteen years, did point to a major difference between the two ports. In New Orleans, the labor market was highly competitive, while in Galveston, black and white labor each kept to their particular sectors. Coastwise shipping lines in both ports employed a regular force of either white or black labor, thus eliminating racial competition. In Galveston the Mallory Line employed only black labor while the Southern Pacific employed only white, and, although there were no formal agreements, each side refused to take the work of the other. This tacit understanding was evident during the strikes of 1898 and 1907, although in 1898 white longshoremen were perhaps motivated by their unwillingness to work for black wages. The deep-sea sector, where contractors hired gangs from job to job, was highly competitive; in New Orleans it was far larger than the coastwise trade or Galveston's deep-sea trade. It was here that the intense competition among different unions and white and black workers made cooperation vital to maintaining wages and working standards. According to Arnesen, one of the major differences between the employment structures in New Orleans and Galveston was one of scale. Between ten and fifteen thousand men worked on and around the docks in New Orleans while only about three thousand were employed in Galveston. Galveston's deep-sea work also was dominated by cotton, with employment relations more settled in spite of the emergence of competition from the Cotton Jammers and Lone Stars over the previous decade. As the commission discovered, the large, foreign-owned lines preferred to hire black labor—with the two black unions working exclusively for separate agents—while independent stevedores and agents stuck by the SBA and Local 310.[43]

While it was true that Galveston was not New Orleans, no one knew better than Fricke that, however gradually, race relations on the waterfront were moving in a similar direction. Galveston's waterfront was largely free from racial tension, but it was not wholly free from competition and interunion rivalry. Employers, mindful of the growing competition from other ports, continued to press the SBA for concessions in wages and working rules, thus forcing the SBA to continue trying to maintain a working relationship with the Cotton Jammers and Lone Stars. The presence of rival black unions in Galveston, a significant difference from conditions in New Orleans, had been a major stumbling block in reaching a joint accord, but Fricke soon would be leading fresh efforts to forge an agreement between the major black and white unions. At the beginning of the 1908 season the SBA renewed its efforts to form a local dock and marine council, but the committee appointed for this purpose again met with little response from the other white organizations. Undeterred, the SBA turned to the Cotton Jammers, inviting a nine-man committee to meet with the executive committee on September 23. Chairman John Hall of the Cotton Jammers sat on the speakers' platform while the remainder of the two committees occupied opposite sides of the aisle.[44]

Fricke led the meeting with a twenty-minute speech on the conditions existing between employers and those employed on Galveston's waterfront. Stevedores and agents had wrung enough concessions from the screwmen, he said, and now it was time for all the wharf front associations to work together. Fricke, in fact, went so far as to propose some sort of amalgamation for the common interest of both races in resisting the brokers and stevedores:

> As conditions are at present, the stevedores attempt to dictate to us how we shall work & when we shall work but if we could form some sort of amalgamation regardless of color or race, we would reverse the conditions and instead would be in a position to tell Mr. Agent and Stevedore how we will work and when we will work.

• • •

Working together would prevent stevedores and agents from playing one race against another, using each association as a lash against the other. Fricke's comments were echoed by William Manning, whose forceful speech argued for the absolute necessity of a definite working agreement between the white and black associations as the only solution from "becoming the mere slaves of the employers in future."[45]

The Cotton Jammers reacted with a mixture of surprise, welcome, and suspicion. Sam Williams confessed his initial surprise at the SBA's invitation had turned to delight on hearing their proposition, which he supported heart and soul. Closer ties between the two associations would bring greater understanding and "kill the effect of false rumors spread by our enemies for the purpose of stirring ill feeling." Sam McCormick agreed with Williams but argued that the only successful plan of amalgamation was to adopt the New Orleans plan and for white and black to work abreast one another in a ship's hold. Daniel Baxter reacted more cautiously, asking whether the SBA had some grievance with the employers or the Cotton Jammers. Fricke replied that there was no hidden motive; they were planning for the future, taking care to prepare for war in a time of peace. Thus placated, Baxter joined with the other members of his committee in endorsing the proposition.[46]

John Hall addressed the meeting last. Born and raised in Galveston, he said he had experienced all the ups and downs of his association, but the present conditions were as bad as they had ever been. At the present time, Hall continued, we never know when we go home at night if our work will be there in the morning. With work seeming to change hands at a moments notice, it has been "a regular game of hide and seek this last two years." Screwmen had been asked to give up their lunch time and quartering time and to make up for lost time on rainy days. The black screwmen were "down to their last ditch" and could not last much longer under present conditions; if white and black were to end the uncertainty and better their conditions they must "stand together as one unit." Hall then purposefully buried any connection between amalgamation and social equality:

> We are content to live as we do at present, socially apart
> from each other, but when it comes to our meat and bread
> . . . it is necessary that the white and black races should
> stand by one another and if you white folks are earnest and
> sincere in this matter, you will find that us colored folks are
> as true as steel and will follow you anywhere you lead, be it
> into the bay. If you rise we will rise too, and if you fall we
> will fall with you.[47]

The meeting ended with a round of applause for Hall, but at the next meeting the Cotton Jammers again voiced suspicions of a hidden motive, forcing Fricke to repeat his earlier assurances. Hall then raised the more troublesome issue of the Lone Star Association. The whites were competitors, but it was the Lone Stars that gave him the most trouble and anxiety. Hall considered his black rivals as "not much better than scabs," having broken a scale agreement between the two organizations. He also thought that they were prepared to take work from the Cotton Jammers in a case of trouble with the agents. Caught between the SBA and the Lone Stars, his association was in the worst position of all three. The two associations could not proceed without the Lone Star organization, but the SBA would have to make the invitation because of the bad feelings between the two black unions. The SBA wanted to first reach an agreement with the Cotton Jammers since this would make it easier to bring the Lone Stars and the other white associations into line. Hall, however, insisted that they should waste no time in approaching the Lone Stars.[48]

The Cotton Jammers failed to appear at the next meeting, but a meeting was held two days later at their association's hall. Each committee, having consulted its respective members, was to present ideas for closer ties for joint discussion. SBA members had watered down a motion indicating their willingness to discuss amalgamation. Their priority was an agreement on wage scales. The Cotton Jammers preferred payment by the bale while the SBA worked to a flat daily rate and bale limit. One system favored younger, stronger men while the other was fairer to all members by stretching out the work. The resulting proposal was long on the principles of mutuality, harmony, and joint security but contained no concrete suggestions beyond "yearly agreements which will guarantee our individual and collective protection and welfare and satisfactory to our respective organizations." However, the committee was authorized to discuss this and any proposal, including amalgamation, from the other side. The black committee members were disappointed at the lack of a clear proposal but admitted that they had nothing to offer, although George McCormick reiterated that the New Orleans plan offered the best chance for a lasting agreement. He also indicated that they should try to include all the Gulf and southern ports in their consolidation. Other committee members were more cautious, believing it best to start small. One delegate from the Cotton Jammers suggested that the two associations should become better acquainted first in order to form closer ties until the time was ripe for complete amalgamation. It had, after all, taken many years of trouble and strife in New Orleans before workers there recognized amalgamation as their only salvation.[49]

The Lone Star Association attended the next meeting on October 26, but the Cotton Jammers again failed to appear. The Lone Star committee welcomed the SBA's move as long overdue, and they were willing to meet "on any proposition that will give us bread and meat." Regretting the Cotton Jammers' absence, Edward Wiggins challenged anybody to prove that his organization had at any time acted unfairly. Despite accusations, the previous year's Southern Pacific strike, when his men had turned down an approach from Southern Pacific officials to take the work, demonstrated that his men were not scabs. Another member also emphasized his association's sincerity, adding that an agreement would give them more independence:

> In our present conditions our employers want to bring us
> down less and less, they like to handle us as brutes instead
> of as men. We must come together and unite else we will
> run down like a clock, men working against each other can
> not stand and hold their own against organized capital.[50]

Committees from all three associations sat down together the following week. Flanked by his fellow chairmen from the two black committees, the SBA's Garland asked them to forget their past differences and to work in harmony. Discussions then turned to wage scales. Fricke argued for the flat rate wage scale, pointing out that under the 12.5 cents per bale scale a black gang had to stow 248 bales for the same money a white gang received for a day's work of nine hours. Both black associations agreed they would all have to work to the same scale, but the Cotton Jammers repeated that amalgamation was a precondition for success. At least some of the Lone Star committee, including its president, Edward Wiggins, concurred, although Chairman William Porter voiced the earlier suspicion of some hidden grievance being behind all the talk. The meeting finally agreed to set up a joint subcommittee with five members from each organization to continue discussions. Before going any further, the subcommittee decided to sound out their respective organizations, particularly on the central issue of amalgamation.[51]

The executive committee informed the next full SBA meeting that, although they had no definite proposition, the black locals were likely to accept nothing less than amalgamation. After some discussion, the meeting concluded that they would accept amalgamation if there was no alternative. By early January the joint subcommittee formally recommended that "the only reliable and satisfactory solution was to adopt the old and tried plan of amalgamation." Fricke informed his members that, after much hard work and considering all possibilities, the only way to create a better understanding and "give equal and positive assurance for the betterment of the conditions of all who are employed in the handling of cotton on the wharf" was to adopt the New Orleans plan. Only after amalgamation could the three associations move forward with agreements on working rules, wage scales, and work sharing. After a lengthy debate at their next meeting, the SBA voted to accept amalgamation by 135 votes to 9. Members of the two black locals, however, seemed more reluctant to follow the advice of their committees.[52]

At the next joint meeting, both black locals reported they had not reached a decision yet. For the Cotton Jammers, Chairman Hall explained that his association needed more time because many of his people were slow to grasp a new proposition: "the white folks seems to understand problems quicker and is able to act on and decide a question as soon as it is brought before them, a thing his people could not do." Hall then revealed a more concrete reason for failing to act: he had been told by their agent, William Parr, that a white screwmen's representative had offered to do his work for one cent less per bale. Hall suspected an agent's trick to prevent amalgamation, but he wanted confirmation. Amused at such a transparent agent's ploy, Fricke confirmed that it was a pure fabrication manufactured to stir up trouble. Parr, it seemed, had been hoping to convince the Cotton Jammers to sign a five-year contract. Since the Lone Stars also had failed to reach a decision, and the SBA would not reveal its decision prematurely, nothing more came of the meeting. When only Hall appeared to represent the Cotton Jammers at the next meeting, the SBA sent a delegation to urge the association's president, George Harris, to take action, but the momentum had clearly been lost, and amalgamation had run its course for the moment. Why the two black associations failed to respond more positively to the SBA's proposal is unclear, although a lingering suspicion as to the white association's motive appears to have played a part. With their leaders in favor of amalgamation, it seems certain that the rank and file of black workers were not ready to give up their independence and meet white labor on equal terms.[53]

As hopes of reaching an agreement with the black associations faded, the SBA renewed efforts to persuade Locals 310 and 385 to form a council of ILA locals. These plans had been put on hold in the hope of first reaching an agreement with the two black associations. Both ILA locals were initially reluctant, but by the following year Local 385 was pressing the SBA for action. Finally, on August 25, 1909, the three white locals formed the Galveston Dock and Marine Council. From the outset, the council sought to include black associations. Perhaps much of the impetus for this came from J. H. Fricke. From his position as SBA president, Fricke became involved in a network of labor organizations. As well as his SBA role, Fricke at various times served as head of the Texas State Federation of Labor and the Dock and Marine Council, and he later led a Gulf Coast district association of ILA locals. He was at the heart of the amalgamation negotiations, and that same year organized black teamsters into a federal labor union. When questioned by the Labor Council about the latter action, Fricke explained that "he thought the time had come when it was advisable to organize the negro, for the white man's protection if anything was to be accomplished." A committee visited the black organizations to impress upon them the importance of affiliation, and efforts were made to organize new associations among groups such as the Mallory Line workers. At the same time as reaching out to black labor, the white locals made every effort to ensure that any new work went to white labor.[54]

Despite the Dock Council's efforts, the black locals remained reluctant to give up their independence and throw in their lot with a white labor organization. The council's pressure finally paid off in March 1911, when the leadership of the Cotton Jammers announced that they were ready to change their rules and wage scales to correspond with those of the white organizations and join the ILA. The following month, the Cotton Jammers joined the ILA as Local 329, taking their seats on the Dock and Marine Council soon after. Their delegates' attendance was poor in the first few months, however, and many rank-and-file members still appeared reluctant to accept these new affiliations. By August some Cotton Jammers were negotiating a contract with a nonunion stevedore despite the continued efforts of the leadership. The council enlisted the help of Thomas Woodland, president of the black screwmen in New Orleans and organizer for the ILA's Southern District. By November Woodland had successfully persuaded the remainder of the Cotton Jammers to affiliate. Fricke was able to report that at a meeting of the black screwmen, 110 of the 114 men present had agreed to join the ILA. Woodland and leaders of the Cotton Jammers were confident that all of Galveston's black workers, including the Lone Star men, would be organized by June the next year. Woodland's confidence was misplaced, although the round of organizing continued with the formation of the long-heralded Gulf Coast Association.[55]

Where the SBA had once been reluctant, it now led the way by getting the Dock Council to pass a resolution recommending the formation of a Gulf Coast branch of the ILA. When southern locals met at a convention in New Orleans in September 1911, J. H. Fricke was chosen as president of the new association. The Gulf Coast District Association ensured local autonomy—the Pacific Coast already had its own association—and provided the means to equalize wage rates and working conditions and organize the unorganized. In his convention address, ILA President T. V. O'Connor hailed the dawning of a new era. O'Connor's speech made clear that race was the central issue for the new association by speaking directly to black workers:

> The black man has got to play fair with the white man and
> the white man has got to play fair with the black man. We
> are not going to attempt social equality, but we can, if
> properly and thoroughly organized, bring about industrial
> equality. The white man is ready to assist you to get the
> same wages and working conditions which they enjoy but
> you colored workers must stand ready to assist yourselves.

O'Connor carefully delineated the extent of the ILA's ambitions, and, while uniting black and white locals in their demands for better working conditions was the first priority, the particular biracial arrangement was to be worked out at local level. Not all black associations were immediately ready to take up this invitation, however. Delegates at the convention drew particular attention to the absence of any colored locals from Galveston, where the Cotton Jammers were still divided over the issue of ILA membership and the Lone Stars remained completely outside the fold. The following year, however, was very different.[56]

The Cotton Jammers, as ILA Local 329, not only attended the second annual convention but they used the occasion to push the associa-

tion into taking a stand on amalgamation. Delegates Smith and Bow-
dre introduced a resolution calling for two locals in the same port working at the same craft to work to the New Orleans plan of half and half
at each hatch. After lengthy discussion, the convention instructed
Locals 317 and 329 to appoint committees and devise a plan for amalgamation. Both locals accepted the instruction, and the two reached an
agreement after many meetings. At the start of the 1912 season, stevedores and ship agents were presented with a joint contract that included
the principle of amalgamation.[57]

The contract immediately aroused strong opposition from the
employers, who offered their counterproposal to sign the previous year's
contract for a term of from two to five years with the SBA only. When
the white screwmen rejected this offer and stood firm by the joint contract, employers turned to the Lone Star Association. Agents Daniel
Ripley and S. Sgitovich and stevedores Young and Suderman and I.
Heffron offered the Lone Stars all their cotton and longshore work for
a term of one year at a lesser rate than was paid the white screwmen the
previous year. This contract covered about 60 percent of the entire work
done on Galveston's wharves. The SBA and Cotton Jammers, joined by
Local 310, now considered themselves locked out and refused to perform any work or go near the wharves until a satisfactory contract had
been agreed on. After several days of negotiations between the three
ILA locals and shipping interests, the employers agreed to drop their
opposition to amalgamation. Young and Suderman and the Lone Stars
were persuaded to void their contract "in the best interests of the port."
The screwmen returned to work on September 7, having signed a one-
year contract with five companies that placed the Cotton Jammers on
an equal footing with the SBA.[58]

According to the Daily News, all parties to the dispute had behaved
amicably although outsiders had tried to stir up racial antagonism. The
newspaper reported threats of race troubles "and the extraordinary sale
of guns and ammunition to laboring men, especially to the negroes."
The rumors were groundless, however, and all sides were reported to be

happy to sign the new contract. The majority of screwmen were well pleased with the terms of the new contract, and any problems with the new system would be resolved over the next few weeks. Overall, there was much satisfaction that no cotton had been diverted to other ports. The *News* did offer one caveat; apparently some white screwmen were not pleased with the equal division of work, or at the prospect of working side by side in a hold with black labor.[59]

• • •

Galveston's remarkable recovery after the 1900 hurricane demonstrated the possibilities of the Progressive movement. The commission form of government enabled Galveston's citizens to undertake an ambitious series of public works projects to resurrect the city's infrastructure and economy. On a lesser scale, and with a much less idealistic vision, the port's waterfront unions also looked to new institutions and policies to restore their fading power. While the city exemplified progressive reform, organized labor's approach ran counter to the conspicuous blind spot in the progressive vision, segregation. As the South enacted the letter if not the spirit of the separate but equal doctrine, Galveston's waterfront unions felt their way toward biracial unionism. The ILA, the most important of the waterfront's new institutions, set a standard of biracial unionism at a time when Samuel Gompers and the AFL were retreating from their former high principles. New Orleans, as always, demonstrated how effective a biracial policy could be in combating the growing influence of technology on the waterfront and the power of the big shipping lines. The "New Orleans plan" of amalgamation became the standard for others to follow. In Galveston, however, the limitations of the ILA's policy become apparent. Self-interest, rather than any feeling for racial equality, was the clear motivation for both black and white labor. With the ILA and other state and national labor organizations prepared to allow local organizations to pursue their own inclinations regarding biracial unionism, self-interest had to reach a critical level in order to overcome the racial divide.

Galveston's SBA had reached that critical level by 1908. Work for skilled screwmen was becoming increasingly scarce and the Southern Pacific strike of 1907 confirmed how easily employers could exploit racial divisions to their advantage. The SBA finally acknowledged that workers had a common interest in uniting against their employers irrespective of color and agreed to accept amalgamation. For the Cotton Jammers, amalgamation had become the starting point for any negotiations, but, when this opportunity came in 1908, both the Cotton Jammers and the Lone Star Association rejected it. Rank-and-file workers on both sides of the color line appeared reluctant to abandon their racial position. In 1912 ILA President O'Connor had hailed the formation of the biracial Gulf Coast District branch of the ILA as the dawning of a new era and that now also seemed true for Galveston. The Cotton Jammers joined the ILA and immediately used the forum of the district association to press for amalgamation. After a brief skirmish with employers, the SBA and Cotton Jammers began the 1912 season working side by side. The 1912 agreement was a high point for race relations on Galveston's waterfront, but it was short-lived. There was lingering discontent among some rank-and-file screwmen, the amalgamation contract was only for one year, and the Lone Star Association remained outside the ILA fold. Second, as a condition of receiving an ILA charter, the Cotton Jammers had undertaken the task of recruiting members of the Lone Star Association or driving them out of town, which they failed to do. The Lone Stars had considered joining the ILA just six weeks after the signing of the amalgamation agreement. Left to compete against the combined strength of the two ILA associations, the Lone Stars petitioned Local 310 to support their application for an ILA charter, but were told that there was no room in Galveston for another local. The Lone Stars were told to amalgamate with the Cotton Jammers, a move they refused to make. The Lone Stars continued to provide employers with a ready source of alternative labor and, if necessary, a wedge to drive between the other two associations.[60]

CHAPTER FIVE

"The benefits of organization have been lost sight of"

The Decline of Union Power

Galveston's economic prospects burned bright on the eve of World War I as the opening of the Panama Canal in 1914 seemed to confirm the port's future prosperity. That same year, however, the Houston Ship Channel opened, thus shifting the economic balance of power in favor of Galveston's longtime rival. By 1925 it was clear that Houston, not Galveston, was to be Texas's major port. Matters also were coming to a head on the waterfront, where employers had slowly been winning the struggle between capital and labor since the mid 1890s, abetted by the occasional excessive number of workers. Black waterfront workers had benefited from this struggle as employers turned to black labor organizations to circumvent the power of white unions such as the SBA. These changes had forced the SBA and other white unions to seek the protection of the ILA and to abandon their policy of exclusion in favor of biracial unionism. Biracial unionism had enabled waterfront workers in New Orleans to reestablish their control over wages and working conditions as black and white workers violated the tenets of Jim Crow to work abreast one another aboard ships. Conditions in Galveston, however, created a more tentative biracial movement that only cautiously moved toward the climax of

Despite the decline of the craft of cotton screwing, loading continued to rely on strength and experience in handling unwieldy cotton bales. *Courtesy of the Rosenberg Library, Galveston, Texas.*

an amalgamation agreement between the SBA and the Cotton Jammers in 1912. The following year Galveston's Labor Day parade included a black section for the first time. Four black ILA locals joined the parade, including a newly formed Mallory workers Local 807 and three hundred men under the banner of the Cotton Jammers Local 329. The parade also included Locals 385 and 310 but, ominously, not the SBA. The joint contract of the previous year was already falling apart.[1]

The racial balance on the waterfront had been tilting in favor of black longshoremen for over a decade, but from 1910 they began to make up a majority of the workforce in Texas ports. White unions, which once had fought to exclude black labor entirely, now struggled just to maintain their decreasing share of work. In Galveston this growing imbalance caused the SBA to abrogate the amalgamation agreement after just one season. The decision led to a bitter dispute during which the port's other ILA unions took the Cotton Jammers' side against the SBA. Despite this support, the SBA's unilateral abandonment of amalgamation left the Cotton Jammers, formerly receptive to biracial unionism, disillusioned and more prepared to pursue the group's individual interest. This shift of former roles was completed as the once independent Lone Stars entered the ILA as Local 851.

War in Europe brought an uneasy peace to the docks as a shortage of foreign shipping brought widespread unemployment to the industry. War also brought federal oversight to the industry and efforts to equalize the pay rates of deep-sea and coastwise workers. The end of the war sparked off a round of pay claims in both sectors, but a wave of anti-radicalism was sweeping the country. Employers exploited the Red Scare of 1919 to 1920 by pushing their version of industrial democracy, the open shop. In Galveston this antiunion campaign led to a prolonged strike of coastwise workers on the Mallory and Southern Pacific docks. With both white and black workers on strike, employers brought in strikebreakers, including Mexican immigrant labor, and open shop campaigners enlisted the support of Gov. William Hobby and the state government. Although there was little evidence of civil disorder during the strike, Governor Hobby declared martial law in Galveston and sent one thousand troops to the city. The 1920 strike ended in a decisive victory for the employers and led to the collapse of ILA power on the coastwise docks for more than a decade.

By 1920 Galveston's deep-sea locals also were reaching a critical point in their history as hand-loading all but replaced cotton screwing and black labor replaced white. Moreover, employers, who in the past

often had been in competition against one another, formed a trade association, thus strengthening their negotiating position. With skill differentials fading and employers pressing for an end to what they saw as the
restrictive practices of the white screwmen, it became increasingly
inevitable that the SBA would have to give up its independent identity
and merge with the white deep-sea Local 310. The new local also would
have to reach a work-sharing agreement with the Cotton Jammers and
Lone Stars that granted white labor its rightful share of work. The two
white locals amalgamated to form Local 307 in 1924 in a deal that
included a fifty-fifty work-sharing agreement with the Lone Star Association. The Cotton Jammers, who had been expelled from the ILA the
previous year, continued as an independent organization. The 1924 contract set the pattern of biracial unionism on Galveston's waterfront for
the next fifty years but where once the SBA had, however haltingly,
sought to forge biracial understanding, it now became its victim.

• • •

Galveston was still one of the nation's top three ports at the beginning
of the decade, second only to New York in 1913. The opening of the
Panama Canal the following year promised to bring new trade; as the
nearest major port to the canal, Galveston would be the natural conduit
for trade with Asia and South America. The Houston Ship Channel
also opened in 1914, but this had little immediate effect on Galveston's
trade since shipping firms were reluctant to use the new channel for fear
of running aground. The onset of war in Europe, however, proved disastrous in the short term. A shortage of foreign shipping brought some
ports, including Galveston, almost to a standstill. Revolution in Mexico
also proved detrimental to Galveston's imports. According to ILA President O'Connor, the assumption that war in Europe would have little
effect on working people was wrong; no other class of worker was as
much affected as longshoremen, he claimed. Even after the end of the
war, J. H. Fricke reported that commerce and shipping were still at a
standstill in many Southern ports, leaving many men unemployed. One
consequence of the scarcity of tonnage was an increased demand for

high density bales, particularly on foreign-bound ships. A new compress plant with high density presses had opened in Galveston in 1913, and the outbreak of war hastened the conversion of all presses to high density. Another important consequence of the war for labor was an increase in the cost of living. With longshore wages already badly affected, the rise in prices during the war only augmented the distress.[2]

Despite these setbacks, Galveston recovered fairly quickly after the war despite being hit by another potentially devastating hurricane in 1915. Thanks to the protection given by the grade-raising and seawall projects, the city survived with relatively little loss of life or property damage, although the renewed threat further tarnished Galveston's future. In the short term, however, the port still carried its long history of success coupled with modern facilities and a deserved reputation as the "Port of Quickest Dispatch." By 1924 Galveston was the second port in the nation in the value of its foreign commerce for the first time since 1913 and the fourth since 1900. Figures, however, once again revealed the enormous imbalance in Galveston's trade. Exports totaled $530,539,863 with cotton alone accounting for $485,723,468. Imports, although up from the previous year, totaled only $32,962,180. That same year, the port of Houston celebrated the loading of its millionth cotton bale, having begun a major campaign in 1918 to challenge Galveston's dominance of Texas's shipping business. Houston held a crucial advantage in intrastate rail freight rates, which increasingly forced Galveston to rely on cotton and other produce from out of state. When the Texas Railroad Commission upheld this differential in the mid-1920s, Houston began to overtake Galveston, becoming the nation's second cotton port behind Galveston in 1925. The commission equalized rates in 1930, but the damage had already been done; Houston continued to win more markets from Galveston and became the nation's leading cotton port that same year. Aided by the railroad commission's decision, Galveston regained first place the following year and continued to compete successfully for many more years, but its days as Texas's leading port were over.[3]

The 1913–1914 cotton season began with the waterfront in turmoil as the groundbreaking amalgamation agreement of the previous season proved all too fragile. The first hint of trouble came that May at a meeting of the Dock and Marine Council, where the white Texas City screwmen charged the SBA with signing a five-year contract without consulting them. Following this unilateral action, the Texas City men had signed their own three-year contract. The Cotton Jammers voiced a similar grievance, adding that the Lone Star men had predicted that "the white men of 317 would stick them and that they would trick the Negro in the end and now that that prediction had come true they did not know how to proceed in organizing any more colored men or how to hold those that were organized."[4]

SBA president Fricke had opposed his local's decision but was not able to overcome grievances nurtured by the rank and file since the first agreement with the Cotton Jammers back in 1895. The two black associations were blamed for failing to respond to the SBA's repeated attempts since then to negotiate a permanent joint agreement. More particularly, members blamed the joint committee on amalgamation for two failings. First, the contract had not set a new wage scale. Second, the Cotton Jammers had failed to recruit members of the Lone Star Association. According to the SBA, the Cotton Jammers had 200 members in 1912 while the SBA had 450. After amalgamation, the Cotton Jammers began recruiting men "right and left" irrespective of their ability to do the work. They now had more than four hundred men but, despite assurances to the contrary, had done nothing to recruit Lone Star members. Before amalgamation, the Cotton Jammers had averaged 60 days work in a season, but under amalgamation they received 160 days work. The vast majority of their new men "did not know how to get aboard ship, much less use a cotton screw." Whole gangs of such men were sent to work abreast of gangs of experienced white men, leaving the white men to do nearly all the work or risk losing money. In their defense, the Cotton Jammers claimed to have recruited forty Lone

Star men but argued it was impossible to do more because the Lone Star leadership was firmly against amalgamation. The Lone Star association refused to even discuss the issue with a committee from the Cotton Jammers. Talking on the street, Lone Star members professed to be "perfectly satisfied" with their situation. The association not only had all the work it could handle but was promised more if it steered clear of organized labor. Since the Lone Stars refused to meet with them, the Cotton Jammers asked the SBA to take the initiative. The SBA's action not only confirmed the Lone Stars' belief that they would not stick to amalgamation, it threatened to damage the whole ILA movement.[5]

The SBA's five-year contract with the three stevedoring firms of Richard P. Williamson, Young and Suderman, and the Galveston Stevedore Company covered nearly three-quarters of the cotton shipped over Galveston's wharves. The contract not only excluded the Cotton Jammers, it broke agreements with white cotton men in Texas City and Port Bolivar. The dispute involved three thousand white screwmen and four hundred black in all. With the new contract due to go into effect on September 1, ILA President O'Connor, accompanied by Thomas Harrison from New Orleans, visited Galveston in mid August in an effort to persuade the SBA to maintain the integrity of the Gulf Coast Association and renew the amalgamated contract. The New Orleans screwmen also had signed a five-year contract, but it was a joint contract that maintained the principles of amalgamation, putting them in a strong position. According to one union official, "The International Longshoremen's Association views a man as a union man, whether he is white or black, once he has been affiliated with the ILA. The controversy will doubtless be decided on that basis."[6]

The ILA acknowledged that the SBA had legitimate grievances and was not asking for a renewal of last year's contract but a revision of the new contract in order to accommodate the black screwmen on an equitable percentage basis. Pressured by the ILA executive, the SBA agreed to confer with Locals 310 and 385 but still refused to budge despite indications that two of the three stevedores were willing to make some provision for the Cotton Jammers. Local 310 supported the committee's view that the dispute was not a matter of color but concerned union principles and upholding an ILA charter. Despite a warning that they risked forfeiting their ILA charter, the SBA began working under the new contract. After just four days they were forced to quit work when Galveston's other ILA locals refused to recognize the SBA or to deliver cotton. After a brief return to work pending a settlement, work again stopped on September 15.[7]

The contract was no longer the main issue. According to O'Connor, the affiliation of the Lone Stars would all but settle the dispute, and fresh efforts were made to persuade them to amalgamate with the Cotton Jammers. The Lone Stars clung to their independence, denying that they were the sole cause of the present conditions, or that they had played any part in the dispute between the other two associations. A few days later, however, the Lone Star Association agreed to join the ILA under its own charter as Local 851. Under a new agreement, the three screwmen's locals agreed to maintain a uniform union wage scale. Amalgamation appeared to be a dead issue for the moment. The Lone Star Association was finally an official party to biracial unionism, and membership lists for 1914 gave a clear indication of why it was so important to the SBA to bring the independent black association under the jurisdiction of the ILA. Membership in the SBA and Local 310 stood at 406 and 341 respectively. Figures for the Cotton Jammers and Lone Star Association were 400 and 385. Since the two white locals handled only cotton or general cargo while the black locals handled both classes of work, the black locals not only held an overall majority but heavily outnumbered the individual white locals in either class. The biracial mechanism now offered perhaps the only chance for the white locals to negotiate what they considered to be a fair division of work.[8]

The settlement shook the Cotton Jammers' faith in the ILA, particularly since they felt that they were the losers. They did not give up on the idea of amalgamation, however, and the following year the Cotton Jammers and the Lone Stars placed a joint resolution before the Gulf

Coast District calling for all locals to "to try to accomplish amalgamation of the white and colored organizations at the earliest time possible." The resolution passed but, in Galveston at least, went no further. Instead, a new dispute arose when the Cotton Jammers applied for an ILA charter to take on coastwise work in Texas City for the firm of J. H. Steele, stevedores for the Mallory company. Mallory had been absorbed by the Atlantic, Gulf Coast and West Indies group that controlled shipping between New York and Gulf Coast ports. Steele may have been acting under the direction of this New York–based association when he locked out the white longshoremen's Local 636 of Texas City and replaced them with nonunion black labor supplied by Mallory. Since the Cotton Jammers believed they had lost work because of the previous year's settlement, they felt justified in taking on this work. Both Local 636 and 310 of Galveston opposed the charter at the annual ILA convention in 1915. Local 636 paraded all the accusations brought up against the Cotton Jammers during the amalgamation dispute, accusing its officials of opposing amalgamation with the Lone Star Association for good measure. Speaking for the Cotton Jammers, W. H. Davis denied the accusations, adding that they received the work because they had gone after it. Black laborers were in Texas City to stay, and either the Cotton Jammers could do the work or lose it to nonunion blacks.[9]

O'Connor again was forced to urge compromise on the Galveston locals, either by extending the Cotton Jammers' charter or creating a new local. Local 310, however, opposed any settlement that threatened to replace white labor with black, which it claimed was just a ruse by Steele to get rid of organized white labor. According to Local 310 delegate Dorman, the stevedore would soon find reason to replace Local 329 with nonunion labor. He ended by noting the irony of the current dispute: "329 have been just as loyal union men as could be desired, but lately they have become a little shaky . . . and recently the members of Local 851 have proven that they are the better union men than the members of Local 329." O'Connor reminded the convention of the consequences of failing to reach a compromise with black labor. Savannah, once an all-white port with the highest cotton wages in the South, had opposed black labor. That port was now all black laborers who hardly made a living wage, and the same thing had happened in Mobile. New Orleans had learned to compromise, making that port the example to follow. Other delegates supported O'Connor, arguing that black labor was here to stay and should be organized since blacks made as good union men as any. Dorman repeated 310's opposition, but the convention agreed to grant the Cotton Jammers a new charter for coastwise work.[10]

Other labor leaders shared Dorman's belief that employers were exploiting racial divisions to introduce nonunion labor. One employer even went so far as to tell a delegate to Galveston's Dock and Marine Council that they wanted black men on the wharf so "that they could get better results by having a big bonehead of a white man on one side and a big nigger on the other side so that he could drive them by using one over the other as a club." This tactic was hardly new, but Mallory, in particular, was becoming more insistent in its antiunion policy. In 1915 Steele locked out the white screwmen's Local 704 in Texas City despite being in the middle of a five-year contract. The following year Steele also locked out Local 864 of Westwego, Louisiana. In Galveston Mallory workers had been struggling to maintain their union status in the face of company opposition since the defeat in 1898. In 1903 Mallory Line workers appealed to the other dockside unions for moral and financial aid. Although Mallory officials agreed not to discriminate against union members, the company continued to find other reasons to lay off men it considered unsuitable. Mallory workers joined the ILA around 1912 as Local 807, but this did nothing to improve their circumstances. The company refused to recognize the new local and continued to discriminate against union members, forcing 807 to disband by 1915. That year, sixty Mallory workers petitioned the ILA convention for help. Most of Mallory's 350 workers were afraid of losing their jobs, yet many were forced to work for twenty cents an hour and to work extra time without meal breaks or overtime pay. Mallory had no need to exploit racial divisions as long as its discriminatory policies were successful. In Houston, though, the company faced a very different situation.[11]

Black longshoremen were the first to organize in the Port of Houston when fifteen men organized ILA Local 872 in 1913, the year before Houston became a deepwater port. These men, who worked for thirty cents for days and forty cents for nights, were sent to Galveston to learn cotton screwing. The following year, Local 872 agreed to the formation of a white local, Local 896, and screwmen were brought in from Galveston to train the new men. The two locals agreed upon a ninety-nine-year contract to share work and to work abreast one another according to the New Orleans system. White and black foreman alternated, taking charge of all gangs irrespective of color. This biracial agreement was quickly put to the test. In 1915, when members of Local 872 celebrated Labor Day, their union president, Bob Roberts, led a group of nonunion men to work. Violence flared when the union men returned to reclaim their jobs. Ernest Williams, who was almost stabbed to death during this struggle, replaced Roberts as union president. Some time after this confrontation, nonunion black workers formed an independent group known as the "Buffaloes."[12]

The appearance of this independent group gave Mallory the leverage to try to pry apart the biracial agreement. The Mallory-controlled Southern Steamship Company refused to continue with the fifty-fifty working agreement, offering instead to work Local 872 and nonunion black labor but not the white Local 896. Local 872 refused to accept an offer that excluded the white local and went on strike, resulting in the lock-out of both locals. With only two locals the ILA had little power in the port, and, despite repeated appeals, the District Association was unwilling to risk calling a general strike to support the Houston men. The strike lasted for four years, during which time the "Buffaloes" took on Mallory's work. The dispute was settled in 1919 with the formation of a new coastwise local, while 872 and 896 became deep-sea locals. Mallory, however, had succeeded in enforcing the open shop in Houston. In 1916 Gulf Coast District president Fricke had recognized that this antiunion offensive by employers was becoming more organized and insistent:

> Big corporations, wealthy firms and individuals are com-
> bined in the crusade against our members in several parts,
> and nothing will satisfy their greed for power and money
> but the disruption of some of our locals and the reduction
> of the workers to a state of peonage.

Mallory's actions were only a prelude, however, to the full-scale offensive that hit Galveston with full force after World War I.[13]

In contrast to the solidarity displayed by the two Houston locals, the gains made in Galveston over the past few years threatened to evaporate. A delegate to the ILA conference in 1915 conceded that in Galveston "the benefits of organization and the protection it affords our members has to a great extent been lost sight of." This situation was made worse by the presence of up to one thousand nonunion black workers. Repeated appeals from officials of Locals 329 and 851 for the ILA to send a black organizer met with little response. After the Texas City controversy, however, there was no further serious dispute over the next few years as locals struggled to find what work they could. The effects of the war in Europe were felt on Galveston's waterfront as early as the beginning of the 1914 season. A committee from the Labor Council met with city commissioners in an effort to secure employment for the men who lost work due to the war. The work shortage did nothing to bring about an agreement between the white and black screwmen. According to the Galveston *Union Review,* deep-sea longshoremen averaged as little as 2.3 days of work per week while coastwise men fared little better with an average of 3.3 days. With war looming on the horizon, Galveston had reestablished at least a minimum of fraternal cooperation by the beginning of 1917. Locals agreed not to take each other's work, and, despite several disputes, matters were settled at local level.

Even the Cotton Jammers had reestablished themselves as "true and faithful union men."[14]

When the United States entered the European war in April 1917, the ILA, the U.S. Shipping Board and employers agreed to set up a National Adjustment Commission with twenty-four local boards to arbitrate wages and working conditions for the duration. Industrial unrest had been disrupting the country during the war years and this three-way agreement was designed to ensure stability in the transportation industry during wartime. The adjustment boards had no powers of enforcement, although participants were expected to abide by their decisions. In Galveston, as elsewhere, federal control of the industry prompted a series of wage claims. In September 1917 the National Adjustment Commission awarded Local 310 a wage raise to fifty cents per hour with seventy-five cents for nights and one dollar for Sundays and holidays. Screwmen and deep-sea longshoremen were given their raises without having to appeal to the national board. The coastwise workers, however, had greater trouble securing their raises.[15]

Coastwise lines came under the supervision of the U.S. Railroad Administration, and, while some efforts were made to equalize wages between the coastwise and deep-sea longshoremen, the board generally accepted the existing dock hierarchy. Local 807, perhaps encouraged by the promise of federal oversight, had reorganized by 1917 and claimed to represent 95 percent of Mallory's workers. In September Local 807 made a wage claim for a scale of forty, sixty, and eighty cents, which Mallory turned down. Local 807 called a strike but quickly returned to work when the local Adjustment Commission set an hourly rate of thirty-five cents for a ten-hour day. The commission, however, had no power to enforce its decisions in the coastwise trade. After working a few days under the new agreement, the local struck again, claiming discrimination in favor of new employees. This charge was then withdrawn, but the union demanded recognition of its business agent to see that working agreements were carried out. The waterfront locals each employed one of their members as a business agent, or walking foreman, as their on-the-job representative. The business agent could quickly settle disputes and ensure that both workers and employers met their contractual obligations. To employers, however, the business agent was a very visible manifestation of workers' control. When Southern Pacific granted Local 385 a raise in January 1918, Mallory agreed to pay the same rates but still refused to recognize Local 807.[16]

As the war in Europe came to an end, the federal government's priority shifted from maintaining industrial stability to controlling the cost of living. Federal arbitration in the deep-sea sector proved so successful that the system was renewed in September 1919. Coastwise lines, however, were to be returned to private control. In October coastwise workers were refused a pay raise while deep-sea longshoremen were awarded the same raise the following month, thus restoring the wage differential and creating dissatisfaction among coastwise workers. Wage parity between the two sectors now became a central goal for the ILA, but employers and the National Adjustment Commission dragged out negotiations until all coastwise lines had been returned to private hands by the spring of 1920. Having regained full control of the industry, coastwise employers launched a concerted effort to break the power of the ILA—an assault that was part of a broad campaign against radicalism and organized labor in the 1920s.[17]

The end of the war brought a period of economic uncertainty to the country along with social and political upheaval. Wartime production ceased, demobilization led to rising unemployment, and inflation kept the cost of living high. In addition, the Great Migration of blacks from the rural South to the industrial North had begun during the war years. Political radicalism also was on the rise following the Bolshevik revolution of 1917. The country was rocked by a series of bombings during 1919, including one aimed at Attorney General A. Mitchell Palmer. More than 4 million workers were involved in a series of strikes as unions sought to build on the small gains made during wartime. Federal troops were sent to Seattle to end a peaceful five-day general strike, and race riots erupted in Northern cities during the summer of 1920. In the heightened patriotic atmosphere of the immediate postwar period, radicalism provided a ready-made explanation and scapegoat for social unrest. Radicals, blacks, and organized labor all found themselves stigmatized as anti-American Bolshevik revolutionaries and targets for federal repression. During the Red Scare, or Palmer raids, that were at their height from February 1919 to January 1920, police carried out a series of mass arrests of suspected communists and other radicals, leading to the deportation of many.[18]

Employers capitalized on this anti-radical fervor in their bid to end the wartime experiment in industrial democracy and roll back the gains unions had made under federal arbitration. The employers' main strategy was to establish the open shop, which supposedly represented American values of democracy and equality and, so business leaders claimed, was open to all workers, union and nonunion alike. By contrast, the union or closed shop was branded as un-American. Numerous local and state open-shop associations had sprung up by 1920 and, early in 1921, twenty-two state associations met to officially adopt their "American Plan." Despite the seemingly patriotic title, the employers' goal was to eliminate the gains trade unions had made during the war, or even to eliminate unions altogether by imposing open shop conditions. While employers professed to uphold the principles of democracy and equality, they used a variety of legal and extralegal coercive measures to enforce their plan. These measures included firing or refusing to hire union members and circulating blacklists of union men. Many nonunion employees were forced to sign "yellow dog" contracts agreeing to have nothing to do with organized labor. Employers also could look to friendly courts for labor injunctions that prohibited union activity in or near the workplace. Among the less democratic methods used were the planting of company spies and the employment of private detective agencies and private armies as strikebreakers. The use of what were essentially hired thugs often led to violence.[19]

Organized labor had made only small gains under federal arbitration and still sought further improvements in wages and working policy. The key to achieving this goal was the right to organize and bargain collectively, and unions recognized that the open shop movement deliberately threatened these rights. As AFL secretary Frank Morrison argued, it was the union shop that represented democracy by allowing workers to bargain collectively and have a voice in their working conditions. In the so-called "open" shop, an employer might provide a system of corporate welfare, but he retained absolute control over wages, hours of work and working conditions. For Morrison, there was no difference between the nonunion employer and the antebellum slave owner:

> Both provided amusement for their workers. The slave owner prided himself on being "a good master." The nonunion employer says: "I protect my employees." In neither case was the slave or is the employee permitted to protect themselves.

Like the industrialists, union officials used the rhetoric of patriotism as each side staked its claim to be the upholders of true "Americanism." As J. H. Fricke declared in his address to the 1921 Gulf Coast District Convention, "Labor ... speaks from the standpoint of American citizenship." Moreover, he continued, American labor was battling to preserve American democracy and institutions against reactionary employers. The open shop movement was solely intended to destroy trade unions and eliminate collective bargaining. Yet Fricke recognized that labor was caught between two converging forces, "the conscienceless autocrats of industry and the followers of European fanaticism." He was speaking from experience: these forces had converged on Galveston in 1920.[20]

The cause of the 1920 coastwise strike lay with the failure to achieve wage parity in 1919. Despite four months of further talks in Washington, the issue was still unresolved when private companies resumed control of coastwise shipping. According to the ILA, these companies immediately changed their attitude by refusing to recognize the union: "our members were advised to throw their buttons overboard; failing to do so, they had to submit to abuse, threats and many other unlawful acts." There was more than a little justification to this charge. Mallory always had been antiunion, despite denials to the contrary, but the Southern Pacific company now was displaying a similar attitude. In Galveston Southern Pacific took control over its own stevedoring work for the Morgan Line, thus giving the company direct control over its workforce. In Houston black Local 872 found itself locked out of the Southern Pacific dock after the 1919 settlement. With Southern Pacific refusing to allow ILA men on the wharf, there was a clear threat of nonunion men taking over the port. With no arbitration in sight, nine hundred Southern Pacific workers in Galveston struck on February 4 for a wage increase from 60 to 90 cents per hour for ordinary time, and from 80 cents to $1.20 for Sundays and overtime.[21]

The men returned to work two weeks later and, according to President Anderson, were "well contented" with the prospect of further talks and arbitration. A few days earlier, a strike by coastwise longshoreman and freight handlers in New Orleans also had ended pending arbitration. In March, however, strikes erupted all along the Atlantic and Gulf coasts after coastwise workers in New York struck for wage parity with deep-sea workers. On March 19 ILA members in Galveston refused to load a vessel that had already been partly loaded by nonunion labor at Port Arthur. The following day the black Mallory workers joined the white Southern Pacific workers in a strike in support of parity. Business interests in Galveston feared the strike would jeopardize the expected development of trade with Cuba and the West Indies. Attempts to reach a settlement stalled by early April; shippers refused to raise wages unless their application to the interstate commerce commission to raise freight rates was granted.[22]

The stalemate held through April, although Mallory announced that at least one vessel a week would sail for New York. In spite of statewide newspaper advertisements, however, Mallory was having trouble securing and holding on to willing strikebreakers even though the company brought in armed guards for protection. When only a small force of nonunion labor began unloading the strikebound *Alamo*, local merchants suggested that a "volunteer" force should unload the vessel. The merchants were careful to point out that their suggestion was not meant as a "slap" at union labor or as an attempt to help Mallory break the strike. The unions regarded the use of armed guards as a provocative move designed to place them in a bad light. There had been no violence, but union officials, concerned that the sight of armed company men could provoke trouble, passed a resolution emphasizing the need for peace and law and promising that union men would act like good citizens.[23]

Unable for the moment to secure a workforce in Galveston, Mallory began to reroute vessels to Port Arthur, where a stevedore was ready with three hundred nonunion workers. The position of both sides began to harden as J. B. Denison, now in New York as Mallory's general manager and vice president, announced that the line might permanently move its business to Port Arthur. While this announcement alarmed Galveston's merchants, the frustration of the strikers also began to show. Angry strikers harassed scabs as they boarded a streetcar at the docks after unloading the *Alamo*. Later that same day, a Houston–Galveston interurban car was fired on, although it was not carrying strikebreakers, with a bullet narrowly missing the conductor. Several more shots were fired at a second car that carried sixty-five strikebreakers. The *Daily News*, always quick in the past to condemn any threat of labor violence, revealed that there was no evidence that striking longshoremen had been involved in either incident. With the *Alamo* finally unloaded, Mallory announced the cessation of its Galveston operations and gave no assurance that the line would return at the end of the dispute. As the Southern Pacific began to import strikebreakers, Galveston's Mayor Sappington appealed to Governor Hobby for help in maintaining order, and four Texas Rangers were sent to Galveston. On May 19 black longshoremen in Port Arthur stopped a streetcar carrying black strikebreakers, who were shot at and beaten. Rumors suggested that Galveston blacks had a hand in the attack. Back in Galveston, Anderson addressed a mass meeting of one thousand from the courthouse steps. He predictably laid the blame for the strike on Morgan and Mallory, singling out Mallory as "that running sore of Galveston." With Mallory now hiring white labor and Morgan black, a reversal of previous policy, both lines were guilty of trying to exploit racial divisions.[24]

With no end to the six-week-old strike in sight, representatives from the Texas Chamber of Commerce and the Galveston Commercial Association called on Gov. William Hobby to provide protection for the strikebreakers in Galveston. Texas had acquired a reputation for progressive reform in the 1890s when Gov. James S. Hogg had used reform to ward off the Populist threat to the Democratic party. Although Hogg was motivated by political expediency rather than conviction, he did establish the principle of an active state government. This tradition continued into the second decade of the new century, broadening into a broad range of reforms including prohibition, women's suffrage, and business regulation. Governor Hobby upheld this legacy, but national fears of militant workers and strikes found a receptive audience in Texas.[25]

The open shop movement first appeared in Texas between 1903 and 1904 when Citizen's Alliance groups formed in Houston, San Antonio, Waco, and Beaumont. These organizations successfully enforced open shop principles against opposition from streetcar and typographical unions by provoking a strike, having previously arranged to have a force of strikebreakers on hand. The movement resurfaced in 1919 with the formation of the Southwestern Open Shop Association to coordinate activities throughout the Southwest. According to F. O. Thompson, general manager of the Southwestern Association, "It is not the purpose of the open shop to discriminate against the union man or any other persons, but to give all a chance to enjoy the privileges delegated them under the constitution." Businessmen like Thompson found powerful political allies willing to use the power of the state to impose their version of labor relations on the workforce. Gubernatorial candidate Joseph Weldon Bailey played on these fears during the 1920 campaign, making support for the open shop movement a major part of his platform. Although Hobby was not seeking reelection, the open shop was a major political issue.[26]

When open shop advocates met Governor Hobby, they exploited the few minor incidents of violence for all they were worth, claiming that no protection could be expected from the Galveston police because "practically 100 per cent" are union men. They also voiced support for Mallory's open shop drive, arguing that it was useless to make contracts with Galveston's waterfront unions: "they violate them as fast as they are made. The unions have no property interests of moment, they can not or will not make contracts that are enforceable and it is folly to temporize with them. Only from the state can we expect such measure of protection as will allow us to operate." The pro-business lobby then threw in the race card for good measure, claiming that the Dock and Marine Council that controlled the waterfront was composed of five black men and four white men. In fact, the council was composed of around fifty delegates, not nine, and the majority was white. Nevertheless, Hobby accepted these exaggerated or specious claims at face value. As his biographer recorded many years later, Hobby regarded the Galveston situation as out of control:

> A strike that had started on orders from a New York union, largely in sympathy with New York port workers, had become a bitter gang-type war on the freight-clogged docks. It was reported that Galveston authorities, concerned over the political power of the unions, were slow to interfere even when physical violence was used against the strikebreakers.

• • •

Other reports carried ominous warnings of vigilante groups and imminent race riots. Whatever the source of these reports, they did not come from authorities in Galveston and bore little connection to the real situation.[27]

Hobby immediately sent Adjutant General W. D. Cope to Galveston to investigate conditions, with the authority to take any action necessary to enforce state law. Twenty-nine units of the Texas National Guard, including three machine gun companies, were assembled to await further orders, and an emergency appropriations bill for $100,000 was presented to the state legislature. Galveston's city commissioners protested to Hobby and called for a mass meeting of citizens. According to the commissioners, not only had the governor been misinformed, but his action in calling for the militia was unwarranted. With few exceptions, the strikers were law abiding and peaceful, and, considering the duration of the strike and the number of men involved, there was less disorder and violence than had occurred elsewhere. The police department was coping and had not refused protection to strikebreakers. I. M. Barb, president of the Galveston Labor Council, further pointed out that Mallory had no ships, and the Morgan Line men were working behind a high fence, which prevented the strikers from getting within half a mile of the docks. With the docks also protected by Texas Rangers and a strong force of armed guards, it was impossible for the men to cause trouble even if they so desired. Even the Morgan Line's general agent admitted that there was "scarcely any difficulty" obtaining labor. H. H. Haines, manager of the Galveston Commercial Association and party to the Texas Chamber of Commerce appeal, deflected Galveston's resentment to outside parties by suggesting that Hobby was not responding to the Chamber of Commerce's appeal but to "numerous telegrams of complaint sent to Austin from merchants and bankers throughout the state."[28]

Cope met with all sides in the dispute, telling them that his only purpose was to ensure the movement of freight. With nonunion labor loading freight from the *Alamo* into railway cars, union leaders claimed that they were not preventing shipments. However, the *Daily News* estimated that Morgan had only shipped four cargoes since the beginning of the strike, instead of its normal sixty-six for a similar time period. Some loads were diverted to New Orleans or sent by rail, but freight was being held up by strike. Despite the earlier protests from officials in Galveston, Hobby declared martial law in Galveston on June 6, and more than one thousand troops, led by Brig. Gen. Jacob F. Wolters, entered the town. City commissioners renewed their protests, describing Hobby's decision as "the biggest outrage ever perpetrated on a peaceful community. . . . your action plays into the hands of those who desire to establish the open shop in Galveston and use military force to accomplish that end." Despite the vehemence of their protest, the commissioners could do little else except prevent the troops from billeting on city property in Menard Park.[29]

F. O. Thompson triumphantly declared that an open shop association would be organized in Galveston. According to the head of the Southwestern Association, "The only solution to the strike is the establishment of the open shop. . . . Give us law and order and we can bring in the open shop and put it into successful operation." Thompson was unwilling to reveal the names of the new association's members, but membership in the open shop movement and in the local Chamber of Commerce were often the same, and he undoubtedly found plenty of support among Galveston's business community. The current city government had been elected the previous year on a "City Party" platform that advocated tax reform favoring workers' interests at the expense of business and the well-off. Voters approved these reforms in a referendum in May 1920, despite strong opposition from business groups such as the Young Men's Progressive League, the Galveston Commercial Association, and the Galveston Merchants' Association. Now the commissioners appeared to be favoring the cause of strikers who were holding up freight and disrupting local and state commerce. Moreover, Mallory, which had already threatened to move its operations to Texas City, was being courted by Houston interests, thus adding to the list of grievances.[30]

The policy of the coastwise locals had been to wait out the strike, and the declaration of martial law strengthened that resolve. The Labor and Marine Councils sent Hobby a joint resolution condemning martial law, but they did not call a general strike as some observers had been expecting. Despite continuous rumors that deep-sea locals would join the strike, the coastwise workers insisted that a general strike was not in their best interests. The purpose of the troops was to break the strike and establish the open shop, but the striking locals would not be frightened into returning to work, nor would they escalate the dispute by involving other waterfront locals. Since escalation would play into the hands of the open shop movement, labor leaders believed that their only choice was to remain peaceful and expect the troops to be removed sooner rather than later. The longshoremen claimed that practically all of the men out on strike were already working at other jobs and earning as much as they ordinarily made in longshore work. Many were finding work with the deep-sea lines in Galveston and Houston, or working on the causeway and seawall extension in addition to the usual recourse to work in other trades.[31]

With no immediate end to the strike in sight, the Mallory company again began to exploit racial divisions. Mayor Sappington, while expressing his support for the strikers, had already suggested that some shipping interests believed that white labor leaders saw the Mallory strike as an opportunity to expand the white labor force: "The number of negroes on the Galveston waterfront has been increasing rapidly and white labor leaders are understood to be tactfully trying to swing the balance of power further towards whites. It is for the reason that white organized labor is generally more intelligent and considered more dependable as to their labor affiliations." Such rumors had surfaced before during strikes, but now Mallory increased the stakes by throwing a new element into the racial mix. On June 10 two hundred Mexican laborers began work unloading the *Comal*.[32]

Immigration from Mexico had been increasing since 1900, particularly following the revolution of 1910. Demand for labor also increased as railroads and irrigation fed the growth of agriculture. The European war created a further labor shortage. As cheap Mexican labor became vital to agriculture, immigration into Texas more than trebled between 1900 and 1920 from 71,000 to almost 252,000. These official figures took no account of the number of illegal immigrants crossing the border. A 1917 Immigration Act tried to limit immigration by imposing a tax and literacy test, but Texas agricultural and industrial employers won an exemption for Mexican laborers despite opposition from organized labor, Southern nativists, and eugenicists. By 1930 the number of Mexican immigrants in the state was approaching 684,000.[33]

Although one local resident recalled many Mexicans in Galveston during the 1880s and 1890s, the 1900 census recorded only 156 foreign-born residents from Latin America in the city. However, the grade-raising and other public works projects offered increased opportunities for unskilled labor in the early decades of the new century. Galveston's waterfront workers undoubtedly took advantage of these opportunities but employers also took advantage of alternative sources of cheap labor. In 1908 Local 385 president Anderson complained to the Labor Council that the street railway company was using imported Mexican labor. The large casual component of Anderson's union was most at threat from this and he wanted the company to use local white labor. Another delegate rather pointedly remarked that, despite all the complaints about Mexican labor, "when you wanted an able-bodied white man to do the work of the Mexican—that of wading in water knee deep—they were invariably suffering from sciatic or some other 'attic.'" Undeterred, Anderson introduced a resolution opposing the influx of Mexican labor at the 1911 ILA convention, one of several such resolutions introduced during the decade. There was no evidence, however, that immigrant labor was providing a direct threat to longshoremen until 1918, when the Mallory company began to use Mexican labor in Texas City and Galveston. Local 807 had immediately recognized the potential threat: "The danger lies in the future, in the event there comes a disagreement . . . it is probable that the broker will employ these Mexicans." This prediction proved to be accurate.[34]

The introduction of immigrant labor gave a new basis for black and white solidarity on the waterfront. Just as the open shop movement wrapped itself in the rhetoric of Americanism, Galveston's white and black dockworkers used the language of nationalism to separate themselves from immigrant labor. Local 807, for instance, accused Mexican immigrants of un-American cowardice by returning to Mexico during the war to avoid the draft. Union leaders also claimed that it took up to five Mexican laborers to equal one white or black man. The Dock and Marine Council appealed to the U.S. secretary of labor to investigate the practice of employers using Mexican immigrant laborers, who had been brought into the United States under the pretext that their labor was needed for agriculture, to colonize industrial centers, break strikes, and lower wages. Governor Hobby's office declared that there was no evidence of immigrant labor being used in Galveston, yet at the same time Morgan and Mallory were declaring their right to "employ men of any race, color or nationality." A union official responded in terms that made explicit the boundary between the American worker and immigrant labor:

> I, for one, will never agree to any such un-American terms
> as those submitted by the steamship companies, which
> would displace American citizens in favor of alien peons
> who are absolutely without any desire for a decent standard
> of living, and who pass their lives huddled together under
> their filthy ponchos when they are not at work.[35]

Immigrant labor was not the only threat to citizenship, as martial law and National Guard troops replaced the city commissioners and the regular police force. One consequence of martial law was that military police began to close down the gambling dens, bawdy houses, and bootlegging operations that had troubled military authorities since the stationing of regular troops at Fort Crockett in 1897. By 1913 there were seven thousand soldiers in Galveston and another eight thousand in Texas City, all with money to spend in Galveston's notorious red-light district. Soldiers frequently fought with blacks and Mexicans among the brothels and bars of the segregated district, and the army itself had to quell one major disturbance in April 1917. Besides these affronts to military discipline, health was another concern. War brought a new urgency to these concerns, and military officials tried, unsuccessfully, to close down Galveston's brothels that same year. Under the authority of martial law, the army again tried to make the city safe for respectable soldiers by closing brothels and enforcing prohibition. Martial law also was used to coerce local citizens, particularly those who supported the strikers. A general order prevented local shopkeepers, restaurateurs, and hotelkeepers from refusing to serve strikebreakers. General Wolters halted a protest meeting called by the city commissioners and banned all political meetings. Military police also broke up a regular meeting of the Labor Council. Wolters also fueled rumors by claiming that there had been a sudden demand for ammunition, especially among the black population. The most egregious excess of authority came at the end of August, when Col. Billie Mayfield and five military policemen dressed in civilian clothes attempted to arrest G. V. Sanders, editor of the *Houston Press*, at a dinner in Houston. Wolters had given verbal instructions for Sanders's arrest if he came to Galveston because the *Press* ran articles criticizing the stationing of troops in Galveston. The illegal arrest was only prevented when friends of Sanders came to his aid. Despite such high-handed action, some of Galveston's citizens refused to be cowed. A tailor was arrested for refusing to sew a chevron on a soldier's shirt because he did not care to do work for "scab protectors." A few days later, a motorman was arrested for running his streetcar through a detachment of cavalry. Similarly, local blacks refused to help black strikebreakers, who had to be housed on the Morgan wharf.[36]

Ironically, the only casualties suffered by the occupying troops were self-inflicted. One guardsman accidentally shot himself while showing his pistol to his sister-in-law, and an officer who failed to stop his automobile when challenged at night was shot and killed by the sentry. Injuries aside, it cost the state $4,000 a month to maintain five hundred troops in Galveston while the city was paying $7,000 for an idle police force. Hobby came to town in late July to meet with business and judicial leaders but not the mayor or city commissioners. Hobby declared that he must have an "absolute demonstration" that local forces could ensure the uninterrupted movement of freight before withdrawing the troops. The city appealed to the courts to end martial law, claiming that Hobby had acted unconstitutionally by sending troops to stop trouble where none existed. The commissioners' accusation that the whole affair was an excuse to enforce the open shop failed to convince the court.[37]

By mid-August there were signs that the strike was weakening. Following the lead of longshoremen in New York, a joint meeting of Galveston's striking locals agreed to return to work pending arbitration if the companies agreed to dismiss their strikebreakers. While these terms were accepted in New York, in Galveston Morgan and Mallory stipulated that "no discrimination will be made in the employment of labor as to union or nonunion." Furthermore, no union officials or walking delegates would be allowed on the piers of either company. The companies stood by their right to employ any man, regardless of race, color, or nationality. The strikers unanimously rejected these terms, withdrew their offer of arbitration, and renewed their original wage demands. With martial law in place to protect their strikebreakers, employers saw little need to make concessions. Meanwhile, a Citizen's Committee, which included white union officials, was working with the city commissioners to persuade Hobby to end martial law. A proposal for a force of Texas Rangers to oversee the local police finally convinced the governor, and martial law ended on September 30, when a force of thirty-five Texas Rangers replaced five hundred National Guardsmen.[38]

The end of martial law did not signal a softening of the state's militant anti-labor policy. Galveston, the most unionized city in the state, undoubtedly represented a major prize for the open shop movement, but the movement's goal was always much larger than one strike or city. On September 22 Hobby introduced an open port bill to a special session of the legislature. The bill confirmed the governor's right to use the full power of the state whenever a strike disrupted a port's commerce and set punishments for anyone violating the right to work. Despite the protests of organized labor, the legislature enlarged the act to include all common carriers such as railroads, streetcars, and pipelines. The act effectively prevented unions from picketing or otherwise interfering with nonstriking workers. As one Senate supporter explained: "If you refuse to pass this bill, you are pandering to the worst element in Texas. You are framing conditions so that we may soon have Lenines and Trotszkys among us. This is not a political matter, but a matter on which the good government of the State of Texas is at stake." Stigmatizing Galveston's conservative waterfront unions as potential revolutionaries clearly had more to do with the virulently anti-radical mood of the time than reality, but, nevertheless, the bill was passed by an overwhelming majority the following month.[39]

Local 807 finally capitulated in early December, settling the strike on Mallory's terms. One hundred and twenty-six men went back to work alongside nonunion labor. No walking delegates or stewards were allowed on the docks except as longshoremen, and the company chose its foremen and clerks. Workers were given a raise from sixty to sixty-seven cents for eight hours and one dollar for overtime, the same terms offered in other Atlantic and Gulf Coast ports. Mallory also agreed to supply free ice water. More significantly, the company agreed to employ only black longshoremen. Southern Pacific, however, insisted on employing both white and black labor, thus prolonging the strike on its docks until February 1, 1921. However, many Local 385 men still had not been reemployed by the following June. Weakened and demoralized by the strike's failure, Locals 385 and 807 gave up their ILA charters in 1922 to be replaced by company unions in 1924.[40]

Governor Hobby was considered a progressive, but his actions in 1920 set a pattern of anti-unionism for later, more reactionary, governors to follow. Hobby's successor, Gov. Pat Neff, would use the open port bill to break a strike by railroad workers just two years later. In 1925 the State Federation of Labor successfully challenged the constitutionality of the bill in the test case *Ratliff v. State*. In 1929 a federal court ruled the open port bill a violation of both the Texas and United States constitutions.

During the 1920 strike the Galveston Open Shop Association had declared: "Our opposition is not against the unions, but against autocracy of any source, whether labor or capital. We heartily commend the action of the governor in the sending of troops here." Governor Hobby had willingly colluded with business interests, who misrepresented conditions in Galveston, to use the overwhelming repressive power of the state to break a largely peaceful strike and enforce the open shop in Texas ports. Whatever other qualities the open shop movement possessed, a sense of irony was not among them.[41]

While the coastwise lines overwhelmingly won the 1920 strike, the struggle between capital and labor on the deep-sea docks had been moving to its less dramatic conclusion. Black and white screwmen had been fighting a rear guard action against changes in the industry since the 1890s, although black workers also benefited from these changes. As employers turned to the Cotton Jammers, and later the Lone Stars, to circumvent the SBA's control over wages and working conditions, the numbers of black workers in the industry rose. By 1910 blacks accounted for 35 percent of all longshoremen in Texas; by 1920, that figure was over 54 percent. This increase in the number of black longshoremen played a central role in the SBA's decision to end the amalgamation experiment in 1913. The issue resurfaced in early 1917, when longshoremen's Local 310 appointed a committee to investigate a more equal division of work on the waterfront. The committee was discharged and then reappointed a few months later without result. In 1919 the SBA sought the backing of the deep-sea longshoremen on the question of taking on cotton work done by the Lone Stars. The ILA locals had agreed in 1917 not to take each other's work and, after much discussion, at a joint meeting the two white locals decided not to break this agreement for the time being. There were other signs of the waning power of the white screwmen. In late 1919 the SBA appeared to be suffering financially as dues were raised and benefits and some salaries cut. By 1922 membership had fallen from a peak of nearly six hundred to 371. The following year the SBA sent no delegates to the ILA and state conventions, and the initiation fee was reduced in an effort to boost membership. Most tellingly, the issue of taking work from the Lone Stars resurfaced, although the SBA also discussed reducing the number of its gangs by ten.[42]

Labor relations in New Orleans had been relatively settled since the troubles of 1907 to 1908, when labor leaders shifted to a conservative policy more akin to that of Galveston's unions. The port's unions reached a new understanding with employers based upon the mutual advantages of cooperation between labor and capital. The cornerstone of this new understanding was the five-year contract that guaranteed stability and continuity to both sides. As in much of the country, however, this situation changed in the immediate postwar years as a series of strikes hit New Orleans. Neither labor nor employers were able to gain the upper hand during this volatile period between late 1918 and early 1920. In 1920, however, there was a decisive shift in the political balance, which, as in Texas, turned the open shop into a campaign issue. The Democratic machine in New Orleans had always relied on the support of white working-class voters and so had not interfered in biracial agreements or labor troubles, but this changed in 1920, when anti-labor politicians were elected at local and state level. The end of high wartime production also brought an economic downturn, which in 1921 forced the ILA to advise black and white longshoremen to accept a voluntary reduction in wages rather than risk more serious cuts. With plenty of willing strikebreakers, including many ex-servicemen, and a favorable political climate, the New Orleans Steamship Association of employers was prepared to challenge the port's screwmen for the first time since 1907.[43]

In September 1923 the habitual round of contract wrangles broke out along the South Atlantic and Gulf coasts. In New Orleans four thousand black and white screwmen and longshoremen went on strike demanding an increase from eighteen to twenty-one cents per bale for hand-stowed cotton. The Steamship Association claimed that such an increase would place the port at a further disadvantage to its rivals, particularly Galveston. The association also wanted to end restrictive practices, particularly the traditional distinction between screwmen and longshoremen, which meant that when a ship finished loading cotton, gangs of screwmen would have to be replaced by ordinary longshoremen to load general cargo, or vice versa, a time-consuming arrangement. The solution to these problems was to eliminate the unions by imposing the open shop. The Steamship Association recruited armed police to protect its nonunion labor, which led to a waterfront riot of strikers against police and strikebreakers. The strike ended after the U.S. Shipping Board, which operated four lines accounting for 30 to 35 percent of the port's tonnage, reached a settlement with the white and black screwmen's associations. The two unions continued the strike against the Steamship Association, but eventually men were forced to return to work on the employers' terms or find jobs elsewhere. The strike was the first major defeat for New Orleans's black and white screwmen and for biracial unionism. Solidarity was no longer enough to counter a combination of determined employers backed by political and judicial allies. The two screwmen's associations and biracial cooperation all continued after the strike but with greatly reduced power: two-thirds of the port's tonnage was being handled by the open shop labor of the Steamship Association.[44]

Contract negotiations on the Gulf Coast began in earnest a week after the beginning of the New Orleans dispute. In Texas waterfront workers now had to negotiate with a new trade association, the Master Stevedores' Association of Texas, rather than with individual stevedore firms. Galveston stevedores had formed an association in 1918 that quickly expanded into a larger statewide body. The Stevedores' Association denied that it was anti-labor, but the organization did enable employers to present a united front and negotiate agreements that bound several ports to the same conditions. ILA locals asked the Stevedores' Association for a 20 percent increase for longshoremen from 65 to 80 cents per hour for ordinary time and from $1 to $1.20 for all overtime. Screwmen were after a 23 percent increase from twenty to twenty-four cents per hand-stowed bale. Despite a rumor that all Texas locals would strike if an agreement was not reached by the time the old contact expired on September 30, work continued beyond that date, while locals further along the Gulf in Mobile and Gulfport struck in early October.[45]

On October 11 Galveston, Houston, and Texas City appeared to have reached a settlement when the Stevedores' Association agreed to the longshoremen's wage increase. The screwmen were not granted an increase. While negotiators in Galveston worked out the details of the new contract, the New Orleans strike continued, which raised the question of whether the Galveston locals should handle diverted vessels, including those loaded by scab labor. ILA president Anthony Chopek ordered all locals not to handle vessels loaded in New Orleans by nonunion labor. Galveston's SBA and Local 310 were prepared to follow this directive, but the two black locals were reported to have worked two such ships. White and black locals held a six-hour joint meeting to settle the matter, and, after further meetings of the individual locals, the two white locals and the Lone Stars announced that they would not work on vessels from New Orleans. The Cotton Jammers, however, only agreed to not work on vessels that were usually handled by the other locals. Vessels consigned to their regular agents would be worked as usual. One Houston local, probably the Buffaloes, was also prepared to continue normal working. The previous year, the Cotton Jammers had argued against a rise in ILA dues because they were suffering from a shortage of work. Up to eighty Cotton Jammers had to find work in Houston that year, and conditions had not changed. Still suffering from a severe shortage of work, the Cotton Jammers felt they had no alternative but to disobey President Chopek's order.[46]

In October the Cotton Jammers compounded their breach of ILA discipline by signing a one-year contract with R. P. Williamson, a stevedoring firm that had been employing the two white locals. Nine gangs were put to work on a prohibited vessel, the S.S. Jolee, as the other locals scrambled to reach an agreement with the Stevedores' Association. The joint negotiating committee had tried to insert a clause in the new contract allowing for sympathy strikes. The stevedores, having previously won an agreement for no strikes under any circumstances, refused to sign. The contract with Williamson threatened the permanent loss of this work to the black local, forcing negotiators to drop the sympathy strike clause as long as all work was restored to former workers. The Stevedores' Association agreed to employ only union labor, but they reserved the right to decide which union labor. After a token half-day stoppage in Galveston, locals in Houston and Galveston conceded the stevedores' terms. The final contract included the previous year's clause that: "there shall be no stoppage of work or lockout under any circumstances."[47]

Having lost to the Stevedores' Association, the white locals tried another tactic to regain the lost work. In November the Dock and Marine Council found the Cotton Jammers guilty of violating Article 15 of the ILA Constitution. The council also affirmed that the 1917 agreement whereby locals would not touch each other's work would be readopted and enforced. The SBA, having retreated from cooperation after the failure of amalgamation, had only reluctantly adopted the 1917 agreement and now opposed its renewal. The Gulf Coast District confirmed the Galveston verdict the following month, finding the Cotton Jammers guilty of taking work from the SBA and Local 310. The Cotton Jammers were suspended and fined $500, and then had their ILA charter revoked in March 1924. The SBA immediately reminded the Stevedores' Association of their agreement to hire only union labor. The stevedores, however, insisted that they would continue to use the banned local, thus forcing the Dock and Marine Council to seek a court injunction to enforce the agreement. Such wrangling did little to solve the problems of the waterfront. The solution would depend on new variants of two old remedies, the fifty-fifty system and amalgamation.[48]

The Stevedores' Association made its ideas public that August, ahead of the coming cotton season and contract negotiations. In a *Daily News* interview Walter Terry Smith, president of the ship agent's Daniel Ripley Company, recommended that longshoremen and screwmen should perform the same work. The crux of the interview, however, was Smith's suggestion for a fairer division of labor. Galveston possessed the

best-equipped wharves and boasted the quickest dispatch of any southern port, but was the hundreds of thousands of dollars paid out to labor
reaching the "proper channels" so as to benefit the city as a whole? By
"proper channels," Smith meant the city's white merchants. According
to him, the proportion of black labor on Galveston's waterfront had
risen to 65 percent in recent years with a corresponding rise in wages:
wages that were being spent in the stores of black shopkeepers. Smith
allowed that black labor performed well but acknowledged the white
employers' preference for white labor, though his argument for racial
preference was coded in economic terms. By introducing the fifty-fifty
system, "merchants east of Twenty-fifth street should be greatly benefited and the merchants west of Twenty-fifth street would also retain
their present advantage."[49]

Despite Smith's public support for the new system, demand for the
fifty-fifty system seems to have come from the white locals and merchants rather than the employers, and still less from the black locals as
in former times. Where once the white locals had fought to exclude
black labor, they and the local white shopkeepers now had much to gain
from accepting an equal division of work. Stevedores had always
insisted on employing who they chose and had wanted to continue
employing the barred Cotton Jammers. The Stevedores' Association
agreed in principle to the white locals receiving a larger portion of work
but only on "a percentage basis to be left to the judgment of the MSAT."
Furthermore, this acceptance was conditional upon two points, one
being the recognition of the Cotton Jammers. The other condition was
more far-reaching: the amalgamation of the white locals so that "the
water front work should be done entirely by two locals, one colored and
one white; that the locals do all work, whether longshore or cotton."[50]

The erosion of the screwmen's skill differential made the elimination
of job distinctions an inescapable choice, and the idea of amalgamating
the screwmen and longshoremen's locals had circulated in Galveston for
several years. The proportion of general cargo was small compared to
cotton, but the traditional division of labor on the waterfront had long

been a thorn in the side of the ship operators. During contract negotiations in 1922 stevedores asked the SBA to allow longshoremen to load cotton aboard general cargo ships when the amount was less than fifty bales, but the request was turned down. That same year Local 310 revived an old grievance by claiming that they were unjustly levied a percentage by the SBA for working cotton when they had a standing rule giving preference to SBA men. The SBA again refused to grant any concessions. In early 1923 Local 310 took the matter a stage further by inviting the SBA to discuss the issue of amalgamation, and committees from the four deep-sea locals met in February to discuss a more equal division of work between the races. The talks came to nothing, and the SBA voted against amalgamation in early May. In November Local 310 voted unanimously not to pay a percentage when employed by the SBA to work cotton. The SBA was further pressured by the fact that both the Cotton Jammers and Lone Stars had agreed to change their working practices some time before. Black gangs loaded general cargo and then divided into gangs of five to work cotton. Moreover, in New Orleans, white and black longshoremen had agreed to eliminate the distinction between screwmen and longshoremen in an effort to resolve their long-running dispute.[51]

Finally, in 1924, the SBA was ready to accept the inevitable. The association met to discuss the stevedores' proposal on August 27 and by September 19 had reached agreement with Local 310 to ratify amalgamation effective October 1. The screwmen would join the deep-sea longshoremen to form Local 307. The only remaining barrier was to reach an agreement with the two black locals. On October 1 a joint meeting between Local 307 and the Lone Star Association agreed on a fifty-year contract to split work on a fifty-fifty basis. White and black gangs would work on the same ship but alternating between the fore and aft hatches rather than working side by side as in the New Orleans plan. ILA president Chopek backed the plans, declaring the fifty-fifty system "a wonderful idea [that] will benefit everybody."[52]

The Cotton Jammers, however, were less convinced by amalgamation and the fifty-fifty system than the other locals or their erstwhile ILA president. The Cotton Jammers insisted on maintaining their "individual recognition and organization," and all efforts to persuade them to accept amalgamation with the Lone Stars failed. Obadele-Starks asserts that the Cotton Jammers preferred to align with nonunion labor rather than recognize the fifty-fifty plan. Nonunion labor was not the issue; the Cotton Jammers had pursued work-sharing agreements and the New Orleans plan for at least twenty years. The rejection of a fifty-fifty system was not simply the tactic of "aggressive black longshoremen" but rather the consequence of years of frustration and failure. On October 11 the Lone Stars and Local 307 signed a new contract with the Stevedores' Association, the U.S. Shipping Board, and the Deep Sea Steamship Agents, which also covered Houston and Texas City. Stevedores had wanted to do away with the bale limit, but a joint committee negotiated an agreement that set bale limits at 240 by hand and 105 with tools. The stevedores also agreed to hire only ILA labor, although the contract included a no-strike clause and gave stevedores more control over the choice of foremen and walking delegates and over the working of gangs. Working rules still set the number of men or gangs depending on the type of work and also settled lesser grievances on both sides, including an anti-pilfering clause and an injunction against employers using sarcastic or abusive language. The new system went into effect on October 20 when 870 men, half white and half black, began work on thirteen ships.[53]

The Cotton Jammers, who had once led the way in seeking full recognition from white labor, now found themselves outsiders. They remained with Williamson, who won a new contract with the U.S. Shipping Board that November. The rewards for independence, however, were small. Williamson's contract was worth $600,000 over the next year compared to the total wharf payroll of the same amount just for the month of November. The six largest stevedoring companies alone paid out $300,000 that month. H. Levy, a former president of the Galveston Merchants' Association, praised the "unusually loyal and commendable" concessions the black longshoremen made. Levy was sure that the black laborers would have as much work as they could do while giving the white men of the city their rightful share. However, a *Daily News* editorial made it clear that money, not loyalty, underpinned the new agreement. According to the *News*, the black longshoremen's sacrifice was not a condition imposed by the employers but one dictated by the general public interest:

> No question of relative efficiency was involved. It was sim-
> ply a matter of bringing about a more equitable distribution
> of the enormous pay roll controlled by the employers of
> wharf labor. So important is this source of local income . . .
> that it reaches back into every channel of retail trade.

Whether the equal division of work was a concession won from the stevedores by the white longshoremen in exchange for amalgamation, or a condition urged upon stevedores by local merchants, the result clearly favored both these parties rather than the "general public inter-est." White longshoremen and merchants gained at the expense of the black longshoremen, but as Levy explained, "The general conse-quences of the new arrangement are too well understood to require detailed discussion."[54]

With a fifty-fifty work-sharing agreement with the Lone Star Asso-ciation also in place, the now independent Cotton Jammers were the one remaining threat to long-term stability on the waterfront. Although expelled from the ILA in 1923, the Cotton Jammers continued to work at union scale until 1925, when the association offered two companies a reduction in rates. The port's other employers informed Local 307 that, although they were unwilling to see a general reduction in wages, they could not afford to operate at such a disadvantage. Employers made the reinstatement of the Cotton Jammers a condition for maintaining the current wage scale, and they and the ILA officials worked to persuade the Cotton Jammers to rejoin the ILA. For their part, the Cotton Jammers insisted on receiving their former number of Local 329 and of working exclusively for two companies, the Harrison-Leyland line and the J. H. Steele Steamship Company. The problem was resolved in October, when the Cotton Jammers accepted an invitation to rejoin the ILA, thus binding them to collective wage agreements. Unlike the two white locals, however, the Cotton Jammers and Lone Stars did not amalgamate. Moreover, the Cotton Jammers maintained a further measure of autonomy by continuing to contract for all the work of their two companies while all other work was split fifty-fifty between Local 307 and Lone Star Local 851.[55]

• • •

Biracial unionism on Galveston's waterfront had developed along with the port's economic success since 1865. In 1914 that success seemed destined to continue as the opening of the Panama Canal promised to attract new trade. The opening of the Houston Ship Channel that same year all but assured that much of that trade would eventually find its way to the piers of Galveston's longtime rival. Galveston's trade suffered badly during the war, but the port quickly recovered to again become one of the nation's leading ports. By 1925, however, Galveston's halcyon days were drawing to a close. Although the port remained central to the city's economy for many more decades, Galveston became more notorious for its reputation as a wide-open city for bootleg liquor and illegal gambling than renowned for its port facilities. The ossification so perceptively described by Edna Ferber in 1940 had begun. Biracial unionism had similarly reached its limit.

The SBA and the Cotton Jammers began 1913 working side by side, but their groundbreaking amalgamation agreement did not survive its first year. For the past two decades, the SBA had tried to enlist the support of the Cotton Jammers and Lone Stars in the struggle to maintain wages and working conditions in the face of changes in technology and the employment structure. These changes brought new opportunities for black laborers, and after 1910 they were beginning to make up the majority of the labor force in the deep-sea sector. When the Cotton

Jammers finally agreed to join the SBA as members of the ILA, the black association quickly pressed the Gulf Coast District Branch to implement its policy of amalgamation. Despite opposition from employers, the SBA agreed to share work with the Cotton Jammers on a fifty-fifty basis provided the black association absorb the Lone Star Association. This stipulation reflected a new concern among the white screwmen of being outnumbered by the two black associations. The Cotton Jammers began to take on new hands, but the Lone Stars refused to give up their independence. Rank-and-file SBA members, fearful of being swamped by unskilled black labor, brought the amalgamation agreement to an early end. The SBA's action created mistrust and threatened to drive a permanent wedge between biracial cooperation, but the three organizations reached a settlement when the Lone Stars also joined the ILA. However, this settlement did not include the renewal of the fifty-fifty agreement. Instead, the three locals simply agreed to maintain the status quo by agreeing not to take work from each other. The agreement did mark a significant switch in the position of the two black associations. With the Lone Stars finally within a biracial structure, the Cotton Jammers had become less willing participants.

Federal involvement during the war maintained this status quo as the government, employers, and unions entered into a three-way arbitration agreement. Organized labor saw the slight gains made during this period as a stepping stone to further improvements in wages and working conditions. When a new mood of anti-radicalism gripped the country in the immediate postwar years, employers exploited it to attack organized labor and impose their version of industrial democracy, the open shop. When Galveston's coastwise unions, the white Southern Pacific workers' Local 385 and black Mallory workers' Local 807, struck for a long-delayed wage raise in 1920, the coastwise companies seized their chance. When strikebreakers and armed guards proved insufficient to break the first biracial strike on the port's coastwise docks, open shop advocates easily persuaded Governor Hobby to declare martial law in Galveston. The sending of troops to Galveston was unwarranted but effective. Coastwise employers successfully forced through the open shop on their piers and shattered the two unions.

Employers in New Orleans also used the postwar period to launch their assault against the biracial Dock and Cotton Council, particularly the screwmen and deep-sea longshoremen. As in Galveston, employers in New Orleans won a decisive victory, largely because of political support at state and local level. As always, events in Galveston's deep-sea sector followed a more moderate path toward compromise. The employers' main concern was to end restrictive practices rather than break union power, which required the SBA to accept the inevitable and amalgamate with the deep-sea longshoremen. As a part of the same agreement the new local entered into a fifty-fifty work-sharing agreement with the Lone Star Association. The white screwmen lost their independence while ordinary longshoremen gained regular access to cotton work. The new Local 307 agreed to raise the daily bale limit, but maintained the union scale of wages. The white local also gained a disproportionate share of work under the fifty-fifty system at the expense of the Lone Star Association, which had apparently gained little from joining the biracial structure. The Cotton Jammers remained within the ILA but preferred to work independently rather than enter the work-sharing agreement. Where once this association had identified its class and race interests with biracial cooperation, it now chose to distance itself from joint agreements. The two black locals gained little from the arrangement other than a recognized and regular share of work, but in the segregated South this was in itself something of a gain. After forty years of struggle between the two races, within the two races, and among management and labor, this final compromise fixed the pattern of biracial unionism on Galveston's waterfront for the next fifty years.

"A standing they could not otherwise have attained"

Waterfront workers in New Orleans had provided the model for biracial unionism since the formation of the Cotton Men's Executive Council in 1880. Except for a period during the severe depression of the 1890s, black and white screwmen in that port had successfully controlled wages and working conditions by maintaining a united front against employers. The screwmen reinforced this front in 1903 when they agreed upon a fifty-fifty division of work with white gangs working side by side with black gangs. This biracial agreement left employers virtually powerless to exploit racial divisions at a time when Jim Crow was legalizing the segregation of the races across the South. The power of this biracial alliance fell away before the open shop movement of the early 1920s as employers launched a final assault on what they perceived as the restrictive practices of the waterfront unions. This employers' assault left screwmen and deep-sea longshoremen with their unions intact, but the biracial Dock Council was stripped of its former power. Wages for nonunion workers fell, and, as unions lost their control over the hiring process, the bane of casualization, the shape-up, appeared on the waterfront by the late 1920s. According to Arnesen, the biracial alliance between white and black unions survived this new order, but the former power of the

Cotton Men's Executive Council and the Dock and Cotton Council vanished forever. As Arnesen notes:

> The commercial elite's victory, in imposing the open shop and destroying the waterfront labor movement, buried one of the few significant exceptions to the rule of white supremacy in the Deep South.[1]

Biracial unionism in New Orleans grew out of intense competition among waterfront workers and its strength led to an often adversarial relationship with employers. The less competitive atmosphere of Galveston generated a more tentative biracial alliance and a greater willingness on the part of both workers and employers to maintain stability through compromise. Nevertheless, like Arnesen's work, the history of Galveston's waterfront provides a study of black and white workers' consciousness and how the conflicts between race and class were worked out in practice. This study thus adds to our knowledge of race and the labor movement and the course of biracial unionism in the South, as well as Texas labor history. What this study adds to Arnesen's work is a more detailed examination of this dual consciousness, particularly from the viewpoint of the black worker. As Arnesen acknowledged, no union records were available to him and he, rightly, was not prepared to indulge in "historical ventriloquism."[2] Manuscript records for Galveston's white unions are extensive, although we still receive only a partial glimpse into this workers' world since the details of speeches and arguments were not recorded nearly often enough. Nevertheless, individual voices, including those of black union officials, did appear in these records, and in the proceedings of the ILA and Gulf Coast District and local newspapers. Through these voices, and the decisions made by each union, we can more fully comprehend the particular course taken by biracial unions on Galveston's waterfront.

Like New Orleans, Galveston's waterfront was dominated by white labor, particularly by the Screwmen's Benevolent Association, which from its formation in 1865 was at the forefront of organized labor in the port. Because they held particular skills in a specialized industry, white cotton screwmen played a key part in the overall profitability of cotton shipping; they earned the highest wages and stood at the head of the occupational hierarchy in southern ports. The screwmen's skill in loading the maximum amount of cotton into a vessel enabled the SBA to establish a high degree of control over wages and working conditions and to become the most powerful union on Galveston's waterfront. One aspect of that control was the exclusion of black workers from membership in the association and from working as screwmen on Galveston's piers. This policy was partly a matter of job protection—the union wanted to control the labor supply by excluding all nonunion labor—but also of racial ideology. Many early SBA members were not native southerners, but the working-class foreign immigrants and native-born northerners who joined the association shared many of the South's racial assumptions. Nevertheless, southern white unions such as the SBA were pulled by two contradictory impulses when faced with the challenge of black competition: either exclude the black worker entirely from competition in the labor market, or include him as an ally against employers in the union movement. Since exclusion was not always possible given the number of unskilled black workers in the postwar South, white unions in certain industries such as longshoring were forced toward the latter policy. Moreover, many black workers themselves were not prepared to accept exclusion, and for some, like their white counterparts, organized labor offered the means to achieve better wages and working conditions. Organized labor also offered black workers a means to achieve status within their own community and to compete against white labor in the job market. And, when given the opportunity, unions also were a means to fight with white labor for economic equality in a world that increasingly denied black people social and political equality.

Black labor unions first appeared on Galveston's waterfront in the early 1870s, although black workers made little headway at first in an

industry dominated by white labor. Formed in 1879, the Cotton Jammers broke this dominance with the help of Norris Wright Cuney, one
of the state's leading black Republican politicians and a member of
Galveston's black elite. Despite his race, Cuney's abilities also earned
him respect and acceptance among Galveston's white business community. Because much of their wealth depended upon cotton, merchants
were concerned about what they regarded as the high shipping costs,
which they blamed on the SBA's high wages and working restrictions.
Cuney seized his chance in 1883, and used his influence with the business community to win a contract for the Cotton Jammers to load cotton. The SBA immediately responded with a strike against the use of
black labor. The strike was short-lived, however, as internal dissension
forced the SBA to accept that black labor had won a place on Galveston's docks. In truth, it was little more than a foothold, since Cuney was
the only black stevedore and the white stevedores, many of whom were
SBA members, continued to hire only white labor.

In 1885 Cuney also was instrumental in having black laborers replace
white workers on the coastwise docks of the Mallory company. When a
white union struck in support of a promised restoration of wages, the
Mallory company immediately turned to Cuney to provide black workers at the old rate of pay. Cuney had secured his contract for the Cotton
Jammers by undercutting the SBA's wage rates, a tactic largely forced on
black workers because of the exclusionary practices of white labor. Nevertheless, lower wage rates were a key economic advantage for black
labor in securing work. Employers could exploit this situation by threatening to replace one group of workers with the other and driving down
wages for both races. For the staunchly antiunion Mallory Line, black
workers provided a cheaper alternative to unionized white labor. Faced
with losing jobs, the white union offered a work agreement that Cuney
was prepared to accept. His workers, however, having been promised
regular employment, rejected the offer. The displaced white workers
turned to the Knights of Labor, an order dedicated to the principle of
organizing all workers irrespective of race, skill, or gender. The Knights'

influence could be seen in the formation of Galveston's first biracial Labor Council in 1884, but the Mallory strike exposed the limitations of the southern order. The Knights made race the central issue of the dispute, but, despite the general boycott by KOL locals in Galveston, black workers became Mallory's permanent workforce.

Black workers had made significant inroads against white exclusion, but they were not content to remain outside of the labor movement or to continue as cheap labor. In the deep-sea sector, the Cotton Jammers sought recognition from the SBA and LBU in the late 1880s, although the white unions had firmly rejected this overture. During the 1890s black workers in the coastwise trade began their long campaign for union recognition and higher wages against the Mallory Line. In 1898 a four-week strike by Mallory workers drew a large number of blacks into organized labor. The strike's leaders, several of whom had long been at the forefront of organized black labor, affiliated their union with the AFL, the first of the port's waterfront unions to make such a move. The strikers further demonstrated their commitment to class rather than racial interests by attacking black strikebreakers brought in to replace them. This clash led to the killing of several bystanders, including a white screwman, and, although Galveston's other waterfront unions had little involvement in the strike, the screwman's funeral became a demonstration of biracial support as black and white unions paraded together. Despite such support and commitment, the strikers did not have the financial strength to overcome the determined antiunion stance of the Mallory company.

The 1890s also saw changes in the industry that weakened the power of the deep-sea unions, particularly the SBA. High-density cotton bales and the larger capacity of modern steamers were making the screwmen's skills obsolete. In addition, larger foreign-owned shipping firms were breaking the traditional ties between white screwmen and stevedores. These companies were willing to use ordinary longshoremen, particularly black workers, to hand-load cotton at lesser rates than the white screwmen. The threats of lost work and lower wages convinced the

SBA's leadership to approach its black rival, the Cotton Jammers, with a view to equalizing wage rates. The black association reacted cautiously, agreeing that the two associations should not compete for work, but declined to give up its economic advantage by refusing to raise its wages to the level of the white screwmen. Both organizations faced increasing pressure from employers to lower rates and increase production, thus making biracial cooperation the only effective means to prevent an employer from forcing concessions in wages and working conditions by playing one race against the other. By 1898 the Cotton Jammers agreed to raise their wage rates to a level similar to the SBA's. This decision split the Cotton Jammers in two when members who were unwilling to compete on equal terms with white labor left to form a new Lone Star Association. While self-interest had subsumed race for Galveston's white screwmen, black screwmen were now permanently, often bitterly, divided. Despite all efforts of the Cotton Jammers and the SBA, the Lone Stars refused to enter into a biracial agreement and continued to work below scale.

In the first years of the new century, the SBA sought support in their struggle against the growing power of employers by joining the Texas State Federation of Labor and the ILA, but a biracial agreement with the two black unions remained a key goal. Although prepared to cooperate, the Cotton Jammers were not willing to simply throw in their lot with the white association. Any agreement had to be on certain terms, and after 1903 those terms included the adoption of the New Orleans plan of amalgamation. The SBA was not yet ready to accept the idea of work-sharing, particularly if an agreement did not include both black associations. However, white screwmen and deep-sea longshoremen were increasingly confined to working for those independent stevedores or agents who still maintained an ideological allegiance to white labor. With black labor gaining more and more work, the SBA was forced to reconsider its position. In 1908 the SBA leadership overcame internal opposition from rank-and-file members to broker a deal with both the Cotton Jammers and Lone Stars based upon the New Orleans plan.

Despite initial enthusiasm from the leadership of the two black unions, they were unable to convince their members of the SBA's sincerity, and the deal fell apart. All parties, in fact, appeared torn between the willingness of leaders to recognize the necessity of a biracial alliance for mutual protection and the racial hostilities of rank-and-file members.

The next phase of biracial unionism came with the formation of the Gulf Coast District Branch of the International Longshoremen's Association. The Gulf Coast district advocated a policy of biracial unionism at a time when the AFL had long since fallen from its earlier ideal of recruiting black workers. This policy had clear limits: white unions sought self-protection by offering black workers industrial equality through separate unions. Both white and black union leaders made it clear that social equality was not the goal. The Cotton Jammers joined the ILA in 1911 and immediately pressed the district branch to implement its policy of amalgamation in Galveston. Despite opposition from employers, the SBA and the Cotton Jammers reached a work-sharing agreement based upon the New Orleans plan and began the 1912 season working side by side. By this time, however, black workers were becoming a majority on the waterfront. To offset this trend, the Cotton Jammers had undertaken to absorb the Lone Star Association as a part of the amalgamation agreement. When the Lone Stars refused to give up their independence, the SBA found itself at a numerical disadvantage and summarily ended the agreement after just one season. This mutual distrust among rank-and-file members on both sides that surfaced in 1908 reappeared as this decision seemed to confirm that, in Galveston at least, economic self-interest was not sufficient to overcome the racial barrier. This rift was partly healed when the Lone Stars agreed to join the ILA. At least now all of Galveston's waterfront unions were within the biracial structure of the ILA, but the promise of amalgamation now remained out of reach for some sixty years.

Waterfront workers faced another challenge in the years immediately after the end of World War I as employers throughout America launched an attack on organized labor using the open shop as their chief weapon. Employers capitalized on the postwar anti-radical fervor to stigmatize unions and draw political and judicial support for their coercive measures. Galveston's coastwise workers felt the full force of this assault during 1920, when a largely peaceful strike by the white Southern Pacific workers and black Mallory workers was effectively ended by Gov. William Hobby's imposition of martial law. Mallory workers had fought a long struggle for their right to union recognition, but this defeat shattered both Mallory and Southern Pacific locals.

Galveston's deep-sea locals suffered far less at the hands of the open shop movement than the coastwise locals or their deep-sea counterparts in New Orleans. After the collapse of the amalgamation agreement in 1913, both white and black locals focused more on protecting their own share of the labor market than taking a united stand against employers. Ironically, the traditional conservatism and nonmilitant approach of these locals worked in their favor in the early 1920s. Unlike the New Orleans Steamship Association, Galveston's deep-sea employers saw little need to confront the power of its ILA locals. In truth, with the locals split by demarcation disputes rather than united in a biracial alliance, there was little left to confront. Galveston's Master Stevedores' Association sought only an end to restrictive practices, particularly the distinction between screwmen and longshoremen, along with a guarantee of long-term stability. There was a certain air of inevitability, then, to the agreements reached in 1924 and 1925, which served to confirm longstanding trends, most notably the passing of the screwmen's craft. With the amalgamation of the white screwmen and deep-sea longshoremen, the only remaining issue was the racial balance of the workforce. Faced with combined pressure from employers, local merchants, and white unions, the Lone Stars were forced to accept an uneven compromise of work sharing with the new white local. The Cotton Jammers, once at the forefront of biracial unionism, remained within the ILA but refused to enter into the work-sharing agreement. This final compromise in 1925 settlement set the pattern of biracial unionism on Galveston's waterfront for the next fifty years.

Employers undoubtedly held the upper hand after 1925, even though their victory was less complete than in New Orleans. White screwmen and deep-sea longshoremen lost their individual organizations, but they retained at least some of their former power, maintaining control over work rotation and hiring through the union hiring hall rather than the shape-up. By restricting membership, ILA locals in Texas were able to avoid the worst effects of casualization. Some of the screwmen's tradition and status also survived. Gilbert Mers, who began his longshoring career in Corpus Christi in the late 1920s, recalled that "The pervasive ambition was to work cotton." Hand-stowing cotton remained a physically demanding job, but it was also the highest paid. As Mers explained, the combination of high pay and masculinity kept cotton as the most prestigious and sought after of longshore work. Union rules continued to recognize cotton-stowing's place in the waterfront hierarchy by allowing a man to leave his assigned gang when offered cotton work. The bale limit was removed in 1929, which meant that the men could earn more by loading more, but the work required fewer gangs and became harder, especially for older hands. Despite the loss of this bastion of worker's control, other traditions continued. Although employers decided how many men would work a particular job, cotton-stowing continued to be done by the three-gang, fifteen-men system until at least 1987. Tradition survives into the present day, with screwmen and cotton jammers still listed among the skills of the current Galveston ILA Local 20.[3]

This pattern was ended not by the ILA or even employers but by the federal government, which achieved what segregation could not by bringing an end to biracial unions on the waterfront. In the early 1970s the government began a court action against the ILA, claiming that separate locals violated the 1964 Civil Rights Act. However, officials for black locals in the Gulf Coast District defended separation, arguing before the court that by having their own unions, black workers:

have been able to better themselves by being able to hold

high positions in their locals, and have been recognized in
the community as a separate, powerful voice for the Negro
communities, and has attained for them and the Negro
people of the community, a standing which they could not
have otherwise attained.

Like black longshoremen from an earlier era, these modern-day
counterparts still saw class identity as an important means of racial
advancement.[4]

· · ·

Unions in Galveston fulfilled several purposes for both white and black
workers: as benevolent society and social club as well as a means to protect wages and working conditions. For the men who joined the Cotton
Jammers and Galveston's other black waterfront unions, their association served as a means to advance their racial as well as class interests.
At first, unions represented a means of breaking the monopoly of the
white screwmen and longshoremen by taking advantage of the black
worker's position as cheap labor. However, for the Cotton Jammers, the
unions also became a means for seeking industrial, if not social, equality, and it was they who first tried to establish a working relation with
the port's leading white unions. Although white unionists rejected this
first approach, they faced a straightforward choice: recognize their economic self-interest and overcome prevailing racial attitudes to allow
them to accept the need to recruit the black worker, or allow employers
to gain the upper hand by playing one race against the other.

In comparing Galveston to New Orleans, we see how local conditions played a crucial role in this decision with the intense competition
in the latter port fostering a stronger biracial tradition. Black unions
faced a more ambivalent choice, and here, too, local conditions played a
decisive role. The volume of the cotton trade and structure of the industry in Galveston enabled the Cotton Jammers and the Lone Stars to
pursue alternate strategies. While the biracial agreement of the New
Orleans plan became the benchmark for the Cotton Jammers, the Lone

Stars remained less willing to trust the white union movement and continued to find work as cheap labor. The Cotton Jammers regarded its black rival as little more than scab labor, but as conditions changed, so, ironically, did the position of these two black unions. Even more ironically, this shift came at the high point of biracial cooperation as, for one brief season, men from the Cotton Jammers and the SBA worked abreast one another loading cotton. From that point on, biracial unionism in Galveston became more a means of dividing up the available work along racial lines than a joint strategy to protect wages and working conditions against the growing power of employers. This course was largely dictated by changes within the industry and the decline of cotton screwing as a craft. The division of work clearly favored white workers at the expense of the more numerous black longshoremen but, equally clearly, the stronger biracial compact in New Orleans led to the almost total defeat of both white and black unions. In Galveston, then, biracial unionism ultimately achieved little more than providing stability rather than posing any meaningful challenge to the racial codes of the South. Even this level of cooperation, however, represented a small but significant exception to the separation of Jim Crow. Moreover, for black workers in Galveston, unions gave them a standing they could not have otherwise obtained.

Notes

Introduction

[1] Edna Ferber, *A Kind of Magic* (New York: Doubleday, 1963), 102.

[2] For example: David G. McComb, *Galveston: A History* (Austin: University of Texas Press, 1986); Harold M. Hyman, *Oleander Odyssey: The Kempners of Galveston, Texas, 1854–1980* (College Station: Texas A&M University Press, 1990); Patricia Bellis Bixel and Elizabeth Hayes Turner, *Galveston and the 1900 Storm: Catastrophe and Catalyst* (Austin: University of Texas Press, 2000); Richard Payne and Geoffrey Leavenworth, *Historic Galveston* (Houston: Herring Press, 1985).

[3] Charles B. Barnes, *The Longshoremen* (New York: Survey Associates, 1915) gives one of the earliest and fullest accounts of the nature of longshore work in the port of New York at the turn of twentieth century. See also: Maud Russell, *Men along the Shore* (New York: Brussel & Brussel, 1966), 8–10; Ernest Poole, "The Ship Must Sail on Time," *Everybody's Magazine*, 19 (July, 1908), 176–186; Eric Arnesen, *Waterfront Workers of New Orleans: Race, Class, and Politics, 1863–1923* (New York: Oxford University Press, 1991), 38–42; Eric J. Hobsbawm, *Labouring Men: Studies in the History of Labour* (London: Weidenfeld and Nicolson, 1964), 204–230; John Lovell, "Sail, Steam and Emergent Dockers' Unionism in Britain, 1850–1914," *International Review of Social History*, 32, no. 3 (1987), 230–249; David Montgomery, *The Fall of the House of Labor: The Workplace, the State, and American Labor Activism* (Cambridge: Cambridge University Press, 1987), 96–109.

[4] Barnes, *The Longshoremen*, 54; Hobsbawm, *Labouring Men*, 207.

[5] Lovell, "Sail, Steam and Emergent Dockers' Unionism in Britain"; Barnes, *The Longshoremen*, 6.

[6] C. Vann Woodward, *Origins of the New South, 1877–1913* (Baton Rouge: Louisiana State University Press, 1951), 205–234 (1st quotation on 229); David R. Roediger, *The Wages of Whiteness: Race and the Making of the American Working Class* (London: Verso, 1991), 167–181; David R. Roediger, *Colored White: Transcending the Racial Past* (Berkeley: University of California Press, 2002), 151 (2nd quotation). See also: Sterling Dednhard Spero and Abram L. Harris, *The Black Worker: The Negro and the Labor Movement* (New York: Columbia University Press, 1931), 44; Arnesen, *Waterfront Workers of New Orleans*, 89–92.

[7] Eric Arnesen, "Biracial Waterfront Unionism in the Age of Segregation," in Calvin

Winslow (ed.), *Waterfront Workers: New Perspectives on Race and Class* (Urbana: University of Illinois Press, 1998), 20.

[8] Herbert Gutman, "The Negro and the United Mine Workers of America: The Career and Letters of Richard L. Davis and Something of Their Meaning, 1890–1910," in Julius Jacobson (ed.), *The Negro and the American Labor Movement* (New York: Anchor Books, 1968), 116–117; Eric Arnesen, "Following the Color Line of Labor: Black Workers and the Labor Movement before 1930," *Radical History Review*, 55 (Winter, 1993), 54–56; Herbert Hill, "Myth-Making as Labor History: Herbert Gutman and the United Mine Workers of America," *International Journal of Politics, Culture and Society*, 2 (Winter, 1988), 132–200; Barbara J. Fields, "Ideology and Race in American History," in James Morgan Kauser and James McPherson (eds.), *Region, Race and Reconstruction: Essays in Honor of C. Vann Woodward* (New York: Oxford University Press, 1982). For overviews of the debate on race and class in labor history see: Arnesen, "Following the Color Line of Labor," and Eric Arnesen, "Up from Exclusion: Black and White Workers, Race, and the State of Labor History," *Reviews in American History*, 26 (Mar., 1998), 146–174; and David R. Roediger, *Towards the Abolition of Whiteness: Essays on Race, Politics, and Working Class History* (London: Verso, 1994).

[9] Arnesen, "Following the Color Line of Labor," 54–56, and Eric Arnesen, "What's on the Black Worker's Mind? African-American Labor and the Union Tradition on the Gulf Coast," *Gulf Coast Historical Review*, 10 (Fall, 1994), 7–10; Robin D. G. Kelley, "'We Are Not What We Seem': Rethinking Black Working-Class Opposition in the Jim Crow South," *Journal of American History*, 80 (June, 1993), 76.

[10] Arnesen, *Waterfront Workers of New Orleans*, x–xi.

[11] Ruth Allen, *Chapters in the History of Organized Labor in Texas* (Austin: University of Texas Press, 1941), 187–210 (1st quotation on 187); Philip S. Foner and Ronald L. Lewis (eds.), *The Black Worker: A Documentary History from Colonial Times to the Present, Volume 4: The Black Worker during the Era of the American Federation of Labor and the Railroad Brotherhoods* (Philadelphia: Temple University Press, 1979), 2 (2nd quotation), 63–70; F. Ray Marshall, *Labor in the South* (Cambridge: Harvard University Press, 1967); Lawrence D. Rice, *The Negro in Texas, 1874–1900* (Baton Rouge: Louisiana State University Press, 1971); Allen Taylor, "A History of the Screwman's Benevolent Association from 1866 to 1924" (M.A. thesis, University of Texas at Austin, 1968); Ruth Evelyn Kelly, "'Twixt Failure and Success': The Port of Galveston in the Nineteenth Century" (M.A. thesis, University of Houston, 1975); Thomas Truel Barker, "Partners in Progress: The Galveston Wharf Company and the City of Galveston, 1900–1930" (Ph.D. diss., Texas A&M University, 1979); James V. Reese, "The Early History of Labor Organizations in Texas, 1838–1876," *Southwestern Historical Quarterly*, 72 (July, 1968), 1–20; James V. Reese, "The Evolution of an Early Texas Union: The Screwmen's Benevolent Association of Galveston, 1866–1891," *Southwestern Historical Quarterly*, 75 (Oct., 1971), 158–185; James C. Maroney, "Organized Labor in Texas, 1900–1929" (Ph.D. diss, University of Houston, 1975); Arnesen, "Biracial Waterfront Unionism in the Age of Segregation."

[12] Robert Stuart Shelton, "Waterfront Workers of Galveston, Texas, 1838–1920" (Ph.D. diss., Rice University, 2000); Ernest Obadele-Starks, *Black Unionism in the Industrial South* (College Station: Texas A&M University Press, 2000), 37–52. For the

most recent work see Robert S. Shelton, "'Which Ox is in the Mire': Race and Class in the Galveston Longshoremen's Strike of 1898," *Southwestern Historical Quarterly*, 110 (Oct., 2006), 219–239, and Joseph Abel, "Opening the Closed Shop: The Galveston Longshoremen's Strike of 1920–1921," *Southwestern Historical Quarterly*, 110 (Jan., 2007), 317–347.

[13] William Toll quoted in Milton Cantor (ed.), *Black Labor in America* (Westport, Conn.: Negro Universities Press, 1970), x–xi.

[14] For a full discussion of the transformation from workers' control to scientific management see Montgomery, *The Fall of the House of Labor.*

[15] Arnesen, "Biracial Waterfront Unionism in the Age of Segregation," 33–35.

Chapter One

[1] Taylor, "A History of the Screwmen's Benevolent Association," 19–23; McComb, *Galveston*, 5–6; Earl Wesley Fornell, *The Galveston Era: The Texas Crescent on the Eve of Secession* (Austin: University of Texas Press, 1961), 246–272; Thomas North, *Five Years in Texas* (Cincinnati: Elm Street Printing, 1871), 54 (quotation).

[2] *Houston Telegraph*, Aug. 19, 1837, in Charles W. Hayes, *Galveston: A History of the Island and the City* (2 vols.; Austin: Jenkins Garrett Press, 1974), 267 (1st quotation); McComb, *Galveston*, 68 (2nd quotation).

[3] Louis Tuffly Ellis, "The Texas Cotton Compression Industry" (Ph.D. diss., University of Texas at Austin, 1965), 52; McComb, *Galveston*, 68–69; Donald W. Meinig, *Imperial Texas: An Interpretive Essay in Cultural Geography* (Austin: University of Texas Press, 1969), 57 (quotation).

[4] James P. Baughman, *The Mallorys of Mystic: Six Generations in American Maritime Enterprise* (Middletown, Conn.: Weslayan University Press, 1996), 138–139; Marilyn McAdams Sibley, *The Port of Houston: A History* (Austin: University of Texas Press, 1968), 86; McComb, *Galveston*, 49–56.

[5] *Galveston Daily News*, Sept. 8, 1865 (1st quotation), May 3, 1866 (2nd, 3rd, 4th quotations); Kelly, "'Twixt Failure and Success,'" 44–53.

[6] Taylor, "A History of the Screwmen's Benevolent Association," 2, 20–21; John S. Spratt, *The Road to Spindletop: Economic Change in Texas, 1875–1901* (Dallas: Southern Methodist University Press, 1955), 19–36, 61–83; Edward Ayers, *The Promise of the New South: Life after Reconstruction* (New York: Oxford University Press, 1992), 13–15.

[7] Baughman, *The Mallorys of Mystic*, 131.

[8] James P. Baughman, *Charles Morgan and the Development of Southern Transportation* (Nashville: Vanderbilt University Press, 1968), 106, 128, 191–194 (quotations 192–193).

[9] Baughman, *The Mallorys of Mystic*, 138–143.

[10] Sibley, *The Port of Houston*, 65–66; Baughman, *Charles Morgan*, 194–195; Baughman, *The Mallorys of Mystic*, 150–155.

[11] Sibley, *The Port of Houston*, 92; Baughman, *Charles Morgan*, 196–197; Baughman, *The Mallorys of Mystic*, 150–155.

[12] Edward King, "Glimpses of Texas," *Scribner's Monthly*, 7 (Nov., 1873), 404 (1st quo-

tation); James P. Baughman (ed.), "Letters from the Texas Coast, 1875," *Southwestern Historical Quarterly*, 69 (Apr., 1966), 501 (2nd quotation).

[13] Fornell, *The Galveston Era*, 87–115; Elizabeth Hayes Turner, *Women, Culture and Community: Religion and Reform in Galveston, 1880–1920* (New York: Oxford University Press, 1997), 5–6, 25; Walter E. Grover, "Recollections of Life in Galveston During the 1880s and 1890s," Kincy Rygaard file, Special Collections Division (Rosenberg Library, Galveston); McComb, *Galveston*, 114–117.

[14] Reese, "The Early History of Labor Organizations in Texas," 1–13.

[15] SBA Constitution and By-laws, 1872, 5–27 (quotations on 14, 19, 23), Screwman's Benevolent Association Records, Galveston, Texas, 1866–1922 (Center for American History, University of Texas at Austin), hereafter cited as SBA By-laws; Taylor, "A History of the Screwmen's Benevolent Association," 51–53; Reese, "The Evolution of an Early Texas Union."

[16] Taylor, "A History of the Screwmen's Benevolent Association," 54–59; Reese, "The Evolution of an Early Texas Union"; SBA Minutes of Meetings, vols. 1–4, 1866–1922, I, 17 (quotation), Screwman's Benevolent Association Records, Galveston, Texas, 1866–1922 (Center for American History, University of Texas at Austin), hereafter cited as SBA Minutes.

[17] Reese, "The Evolution of an Early Texas Union"; SBA Minutes, I, 20, 54.

[18] Taylor, "A History of the Screwmen's Benevolent Association," 7–8, 30–39 (quotation on 7).

[19] Reese, "The Evolution of an Early Texas Union," 159–160; Taylor, "A History of the Screwmen's Benevolent Association," 32–39.

[20] Gilbert Mers, *Working the Waterfront: The Ups and Downs of a Rebel Longshoreman* (Austin: University of Texas Press, 1988), 15 (quotation); Hobsbawm, *Labouring Men*, 210.

[21] Taylor, "A History of the Screwmen's Benevolent Association," 39–44.

[22] Raymond Miller, "Dockworker Subculture," *Comparative Studies in Society and History*, 11 (June, 1969), 308 (quotation).

[23] Howard Kimeldorf, *Reds or Rackets? The Making of Radical and Conservative Unions on the Waterfront* (Berkeley: University of California Press, 1988), 13–14, 24 (quotation on 13).

[24] Barnes, *The Longshoremen*, 13–27 (1st quotation on 14); Poole, "The Ship Must Sail on Time," 176 (2nd quotation).

[25] William W. Pilcher, *The Portland Longshoremen: A Dispersed Urban Community* (New York: Holt, Rinehart, and Winston, 1972), 21. See also Mers, *Working the Waterfront*.

[26] Peter Way, *Common Labor: Workers and the Digging of North American Canals, 1780–1860* (Cambridge: Cambridge University Press, 1993), 6 (quotation), 174–175.

[27] William S. Red (ed.), "Allen's Reminiscences of Texas, 1838–1842," *Southwestern Historical Quarterly*, 18 (Jan., 1915), 290 (1st quotation); McComb, *Galveston*, 108–109; Jean M. Brown, "Free Rein: Galveston Island's Alcohol, Gambling, and Prostitution Era, 1839–1957" (M.A. thesis, Lamar University, 1998), 1; Turner, *Women Culture and Community*, 24; Ellen Beasley, *The Alleys and Back Buildings of Galveston: An Architectural*

and Social History (Houston: Rice University Press, 1996), 12; Grover, "Recollections of Life in Galveston" (2nd quotation); Ralph Albert Scull, "Black Galveston: A Personal View of Community History in Many Categories of Life," Special Collections Division (Rosenberg Library, Galveston); *Galveston Daily News,* Mar. 20, 1906.

[28] *Galveston Daily News,* Mar. 20, 1906; Longshoremen's Benevolent Union, Minutes, vols. 1–7, 1887–1913, V, 11, Screwmen's Benevolent Association Records, Galveston, Texas, 1866–1922 (Center for American History, University of Texas at Austin), cited hereafter as LBU Minutes; LBU Minutes, VI, 72, 77, 87; International Longshoremen's Association Local 310, Minutes, vols. 19–23, 1906–1918, XX, 62, 74, Screwmen's Benevolent Association Records, Galveston, Texas, 1866–1922 (Center for American History, University of Texas at Austin), cited hereafter as ILA Local 310 Minutes; SBA Minutes, III, 500 (quotation).

[29] Jon M. Kingsdale, "The 'Poor Man's Club': Social Functions of the Urban Working Class Saloon," *American Quarterly,* 25 (Oct., 1973); Way, *Common Labor,* 181–187.

[30] *Constitution and By-laws of the ILA Local 310* (Galveston: ILA, 1914).

[31] SBA Minutes, I, 97 (1st quotation), 207 (2nd quotation), 378 (3rd quotation); Taylor, "A History of the Screwmen's Benevolent Association," 60–78; Reese, "The Evolution of an Early Texas Union."

[32] SBA Minutes, I, 34.

[33] SBA Minutes, I, 54; McComb, *Galveston,* 85; Arnesen, *Waterfront Workers of New Orleans,* 14; Fornell, *The Galveston Era,* 115–125 (quotation on 116); Taylor, "A History of the Screwmen's Benevolent Association," 71; Susan Wiley Hardwick, *Mythic Galveston: Reinventing America's Third Coast* (Baltimore: Johns Hopkins University Press, 2002), 79.

[34] McComb, *Galveston,* 85; Bert C. Armstead, *Reminiscences of a Black Church in Galveston* (Galveston: n.p., 1989); Rice, *The Negro in Texas,* 145.

[35] Beasley, *The Alleys and Back Buildings of Galveston,* 7, 10; Stephen Paul Kretzman, "A House Built upon the Sand: Race, Class, Gender, and the Galveston Hurricane of 1900" (Ph.D. diss., University of Wisconsin, 1995), 183.

[36] *Galveston City Directory 1881–1882,* 60–62; *Galveston City Directory 1882–1883,* 101–102.

[37] Scull, "Black Galveston" (1st quotation); Jack Johnson, *Jack Johnson is a Dandy* (New York: Chelsea House, 1969), 32 (2nd quotation).

[38] King, "Glimpses of Texas," 403.

[39] Reese, "The Evolution of an Early Texas Union," 162 n14; Herman Bloch, "Labor and the Negro, 1866–1910," *Journal of Negro History,* 50 (July, 1965), 163 (quotation); Arnesen, *Waterfront Workers of New Orleans,* 4–7.

[40] Philip S. Foner, *Organized Labor and the Black Worker, 1619–1973* (New York: International Publisher's, 1976), 32 (quotation); Herman Bloch, "The National Labor Union and Black Workers," *Journal of Ethnic Studies,* 1 (Spring, 1973); William B. Hine, "Black Organized Labor in Reconstruction Charleston," *Labor History,* 25 (Fall, 1984), 507; Arnesen, *Waterfront Workers of New Orleans,* 17–18, 22–24, 28–30, 44, 51–53.

[41] Carl H. Moneyhon, *Republicanism in Reconstruction Texas* (Austin: University of Texas Press, 1980), 134, 159; Merline Pitre, *Through Many Dangers, Toils, and Snares: The*

Black Leadership of Texas, 1868–1900 (Austin: Eakin Press, 1985), 170–171; Reese, "The Early History of Labor Organizations in Texas," 11–13 (quotation on 13).

[42] Allen, *Chapters in the History of Organized Labor in Texas,* 137; *Galveston Daily News,* July 25, 28 (quotations), 1877.

[43] *Galveston Daily News,* July 31, Aug. 1, 1877; Marshall, *Labor in the South,* 66.

[44] Virginia Neal Hinze, "Norris Wright Cuney" (M.A. thesis, Rice University, 1965), 1–24 (quotation on 14), 57.

[45] *Galveston Daily News,* July 31, Aug. 1 (quotations), 2, 1877.

[46] SBA Minutes, I, 345.

Chapter Two

[1] Earle B. Young, *Tracks to the Sea: Galveston and Western Railroad Development, 1866–1900* (College Station: Texas A&M University Press, 1997), 3–4; Taylor, "A History of the Screwmen's Benevolent Association," 134; Ellis, "The Texas Cotton Compression Industry," 90; Harry Williams, "The Development of a Market Economy in Texas: The Establishment of a Railway Network" (Ph.D. diss., University of Texas at Austin, 1957), 380, 388; *Galveston Daily News,* Sept. 10, 1879 (quotation).

[2] Land and Thompson, *Galveston: The Commercial Metropolis and Principal Seaport of the Great Southwest* (Galveston: Land and Thompson, 1885), 56.

[3] Bernard Axelrod, "Galveston: Denver's Deep-Water Port," *Southwestern Historical Quarterly,* 70 (Oct., 1966), 217–228 (quotation on 227). See also Earle B. Young, *Galveston and the Great West* (College Station: Texas A&M University Press, 1997).

[4] Young, *Tracks to the Sea,* 5, 51–52.

[5] James P. Baughman, "The Evolution of Rail-Water Systems of Transportation in the Gulf Southwest, 1836–1890," *Journal of Southern History,* 34 (Aug., 1968), 373–379; Baughman, *The Mallorys of Mystic,* 156–158.

[6] Taylor, "A History of the Screwmen's Benevolent Association," 61, 100; SBA Minutes, I, 378, 396, 399; Arnesen, *Waterfront Workers of New Orleans,* 41; Mers, *Working the Waterfront,* 16.

[7] *Galveston Daily News,* Jan. 23, 1879.

[8] Lovell, "Sail, Steam and Emergent Dockers' Unionism," 239–240.

[9] Allen, *Chapters in the History of Organized Labor in Texas,* 20; *Galveston Daily News,* Sept. 2, 1881.

[10] *Galveston Daily News,* Nov. 30, 1882.

[11] Ibid., Jan. 4, 5 (quotations), 1883.

[12] Hinze, "Norris Wright Cuney," 1–22.

[13] *Galveston Daily News,* Mar. 16 (quotations), Apr. 4, 1883.

[14] Hinze, "Norris Wright Cuney," 23–26; Taylor, "A History of the Screwmen's Benevolent Association," 85–88; *Galveston Daily News,* Apr. 3–5, 1883 (1st quotation Apr. 5); SBA Minutes, I, 463–467 (2nd quotation on 465, 3rd quotation on 467).

[15] SBA Minutes, I, 471, 488 (1st quotation), 496 (2nd quotation).

[16] Taylor, "A History of the Screwmen's Benevolent Association," 92–93.

[17] SBA Minutes, I, 180, 305 (1st quotation), 311, 402, 463 (2nd quotation).

[18] Arnesen, *Waterfront Workers of New Orleans,* 61–65 (quotation on 63).

[19] SBA Minutes, I, 402–403 (quotation on 402), 469; *Galveston City Directory, 1881–1882;* 73; *Galveston City Directory, 1882–1883,* 102; *Galveston City Directory, 1884–1885,* 82; Eric Arnesen, "'It Ain't Like They Do In New Orleans': Race Relations, Labor Markets, and Waterfront Labor Movements in the American South, 1880–1923," in Marcel van der Linden and Jan Lucassen (eds.) *Racism and the Labor Market: Historical Studies* (Bern: Peter Lang, 1995), 62–72.

[20] Galveston Typographical Union, Minutes, vols. 1–2, 1875–1889, I, 180 (1st quotation), 204 (2nd quotation); II, 15, 23, Galveston Typographical Union Records (Center for American History, University of Texas at Austin), cited hereafter as GTU Minutes; SBA Minutes, I, 515; Allen, *Chapters in the History of Organized Labor in Texas,* 174.

[21] Jonathan Garlock, *Guide to the Local Assemblies of the Knights of Labor* (Westport, Conn.: Greenwood Press, 1982), 497; Arnesen, *Waterfront Workers of New Orleans,* 92; Allen, *The Great Southwest Strike,* 25.

[22] Philip S. Foner and Ronald L. Lewis (eds.), *The Black Worker: A Documentary History from Colonial Times to the Present, Volume 3: The Black Worker during the Era of the Knights of Labor* (Philadelphia: Temple University Press, 1978), 72 (quotation); Foner, *Organized Labor and the Black Worker,* 47–53; John H. Bracey, August Meier, and Elliot Rudwick (eds.), *Black Workers and Organized Labor* (Belmont, Calif.: Wadsworth, 1971), 6–21; Melton McLaurin, "The Racial Policies of the Knights of Labor," *Labor History,* 17 (Fall, 1976), 568–585; Kenneth Kann, "The Knights of Labor and the Southern Black Worker," *Labor History,* 18 (Winter, 1977), 47–70.

[23] McLaurin, "The Racial Policies of the Knights of Labor," 569, 573; Melton McLaurin, "Knights of Labor: Internal Dissensions of the Southern Order," in Gary M. Fink and Merle E. Reed (eds.), *Essays in Southern Labor History: Selected Papers, Southern Labor History Conference, 1976* (Westport, Conn.: Greenwood Press, 1977), 7; *San Antonio Light,* July 22, 1886 (quotation).

[24] Maud Cuney-Hare, *Norris Wright Cuney: A Tribune of the Black People* (1913; reprint; Austin: Steck-Vaughan, 1968), 44 (quotation); *Galveston Daily News,* Oct. 17–21, 1885.

[25] Baughman, *The Mallorys of Mystic,* 165–168 (1st quotation on 168, 2nd quotation on 167).

[26] Mallory Steamship Records, "A Comprehensive History of the Boycott, Galveston, 1866," Special Collections Division (Rosenberg Library, Galveston) (quotation); *Galveston Daily News,* Oct. 19, 1885.

[27] *Galveston Daily News,* Oct. 21–22, 28 (quotation), 1885.

[28] Cuney-Hare, *Norris Wright Cuney,* 44–45.

[29] *Galveston Daily News,* Nov. 3, 1885.

[30] Ibid., Nov. 4–6, 1885 (quotation on Nov. 5).

[31] Ibid., Nov. 6 (quotation), 7, 1885.

[32] GTU Minutes, II, 86–90 (quotation on 86).

[33] *Galveston Daily News,* Nov. 10 (quotation), 11, 1885.

[34] *Galveston Daily News,* Nov. 13, 1885 (quotations); Jan. 28, 1886; Mar. 6, 1886; GTU Minutes, II, 112.

[35] Foner, *Organized Labor and the Black Worker*, 53–63; Foner and Lewis (eds.), *The Black Worker: A Documentary History, Volume 3*, 114 (quotation); SBA Minutes, II, 9.

[36] Obadele-Starks, *Black Unionism in the Industrial South*, 37–40 (1st quotation on 40, 2nd quotation on 39).

[37] SBA Minutes, I, 571, 620–622 (1st quotation on 622, 2nd quotation on 621), 685; LBU Minutes, I, 23.

[38] SBA Minutes, I, 687–696 (1st and 2nd quotations on 687, 3rd quotation on 696), 731–733.

[39] Taylor, "A History of the Screwmen's Benevolent Association," 97; Foner and Lewis (eds.), *The Black Worker: A Documentary History, Volume 4*, n24; Douglas Hales, "The Cuneys: A Southern Family in White and Black" (Ph.D. diss., Texas Tech University, 2000), 86; *Galveston Daily News*, Jan. 30, 1898.

[40] Ernest Obadele-Starks, "Black Labor, the Black Middle Class, and Organized Protest along the Upper Texas Gulf Coast, 1883–1945," *Southwestern Historical Quarterly*, 103 (July, 1999), 53 (1st quotation); Rice, *The Negro in Texas*, 190; Charles Mac Gibson, "Organized Labor in Texas from 1890 to 1900" (M.A. thesis, Texas Tech University, 1973), 32; Hales, "The Cuneys," 26 (2nd quotation), 46–47, 51; Arnesen, *Waterfront Workers of New Orleans*, 52 (3rd quotation).

[41] LBU Minutes, I, 42, 43 (1st quotation), 48 (2nd quotation); *Galveston City Directory, 1886–1887*, 52; *Galveston City Directory, 1888–1889*, 59.

[42] LBU Minutes, I, 152 (1st quotation); SBA Minutes, I, 731–733 (2nd quotation on 733).

Chapter Three

[1] Barker, "Partners in Progress," iii–iv; Ellis, "The Texas Cotton Compression Industry," 158; *Galveston Daily News*, Nov. 24, 1894, Sept. 1, 1895.

[2] Barker, "Partners in Progress," 4; William A. Scharnwebber, *Facts about Galveston, Texas, the Deep Water Harbor of the Gulf of Mexico* (Galveston: n.p., 1899), 23 (1st quotation), 33 (2nd quotation).

[3] Scharnwebber, *Facts about Galveston*, 23, 33–35, 47; Clarence Ousley, *Galveston in 1900* (Atlanta: William C. Chase, 1900), 151 (quotation).

[4] McComb, *Galveston*, 47–49, 65–66.

[5] Andrew Morrison, *The Port of Galveston and the State of Texas* (St. Louis: G. W. Englehardt, 1890), 9 (1st quotation); SBA Minutes, II, 44 (2nd and 3rd quotations).

[6] SBA Minutes, I, 622.

[7] Nell Irvin Painter, *Standing at Armageddon: The United States, 1877–1919* (New York: W. W. Norton, 1987), 110–140; SBA Minutes, II, 99–103 (quotation on 100), 109, 138, 170.

[8] Ellis, "The Texas Cotton Compression Industry," 187, 196–197.

[9] Richard V. Francaviglia, *From Sail to Steam: Four Centuries of Texas Maritime History, 1500–1900* (Austin: University of Texas Press, 1998), 260; Lovell, "Sail, Steam and Emergent Dockers' Unionism in Britain," 238–241. For an account of the confrontation between craft workers and technology, see David Montgomery, *Workers' Control in*

America: Studies in the History of Work, Technology, and Labor Struggles (Cambridge: Cambridge University Press, 1979).

[10] SBA Minutes of Meetings of Executive Committee, vols. 1–3, 1893–1919, I, 3–5 (quotation on 3), Screwman's Benevolent Association Records, Galveston, Texas, 1866–1922 (Center for American History, University of Texas at Austin), hereafter cited as SBA Committee Minutes; SBA Minutes, II, 221, 229.

[11] SBA Minutes, II, 228 (quotation), 313, 329; SBA Committee Minutes, I, 8–9.

[12] SBA Committee Minutes, I, 17, 25–29; SBA Minutes, II, 325; Bracey, et al. (eds.), *Black Workers and Organized Labor*, 30 (quotation).

[13] Arnesen, *Waterfront Workers of New Orleans*, 120–145.

[14] Ibid.

[15] Ibid. (quotation on 120).

[16] SBA Committee Minutes, I, 25.

[17] SBA Committee Minutes, I, 25–28; SBA Minutes, II, 351, 372–373.

[18] SBA Committee Minutes, I, 25 (1st quotation), 28 (2nd quotation).

[19] SBA Committee Minutes, I, 26–28, 38–39 (quotations); SBA Minutes, II, 379, 382.

[20] SBA Minutes, II, 440, 446 (1st quotation), 561 (2nd and 3rd quotations).

[21] Woodward, *Origins of the New South*, 211–215 (quotation on 211); C. Vann Woodward, *The Strange Career of Jim Crow* (3rd. ed.; New York: Oxford University Press, 1974), 31–35, 70–71, 82–83, 97; Rice, *The Negro in Texas*, 140–150.

[22] Bradley Robert Rice, *Progressive Cities: The Commission Government Movement in America, 1901–1920* (Austin: University of Texas Press, 1977), 4–5.

[23] Hales, "The Cuneys," 172–181.

[24] LBU Minutes, I, 428–429 (quotation), 443, 447, 459; SBA Minutes, II, 415.

[25] *Galveston Daily News*, Dec. 10, 1897.

[26] *Galveston Daily News*, Jan. 14–16, 1894 (quotation on Jan. 16).

[27] Ibid., Jan. 15–17, 1894 (quotation on Jan. 16).

[28] Ibid., Jan. 16; Feb. 4, 1894.

[29] Ibid., Feb. 5, 1894.

[30] Ibid., Feb. 7, 13, 1894.

[31] *Galveston Daily News*, Sept. 12, 1894; *Galveston City Directory 1882–1883*, 102; *Galveston City Directory 1888–1889*, 213, 309.

[32] Arnesen, *Waterfront Workers of New Orleans*, 43; *Galveston Daily News*, Mar. 12, 1895 (quotations).

[33] *Galveston Daily News*, Mar. 12, 1895.

[34] Baughman, *The Mallorys of Mystic*, 180–188 (quotation on 183).

[35] *Galveston Daily News*, Aug. 31, 1898.

[36] *Galveston Daily News*, Aug. 31, 1898 (quotations); *Houston Daily Post*, Aug. 31, 1898.

[37] *Galveston Daily News*, Aug. 31, 1898.

[38] Gary Cartwright, *Galveston: A History of the Island* (New York: Atheneum, 1991), 154; *Galveston Daily News*, July 9–15, 20, 1894.

[39] *Galveston Daily News*, Aug. 31, 1898.

[40] *Galveston Daily News*, Aug. 31, Sept. 3, 1898 (quotation); SBA Committee Minutes, I, 38; *Houston Daily Post*, Aug. 31, 1898.

[41] *Galveston Daily News,* Sept. 1, 1898.

[42] Ibid.

[43] Ibid., Sept. 2, 1898.

[44] Bracey, et al. (eds.), *Black Workers and Organized Labor,* 25; Foner, *Organized Labor and the Black Worker,* 65 (quotation).

[45] Foner, *Organized Labor and the Black Worker,* 82–102; Bracey, et al. (eds.), *Black Workers and Organized Labor,* 26–40; Arnesen, "Following the Color Line of Labor," 62 (1st quotation); Arnesen, *Waterfront Workers of New Orleans,* 52 (2nd quotation), 85, 153; Paul Worthman, "Black Workers and Labor Unions in Birmingham, Alabama, 1897–1904," in Cantor (ed.), *Black Labor in America,* 60–61.

[46] *Galveston Daily News,* Sept. 3, 1898; Obadele-Starks, *Black Unionism in the Industrial South,* 41–43.

[47] SBA Minutes, II, 552, 556; *Galveston Daily News,* Sept. 6, 1898 (quotation).

[48] *Galveston Daily News,* Sept. 6–10, 1898 (1st quotation on Sept. 8); John Sealy, ALS to George Sealy, Sept. 13, 1898, Hutchings, Sealy and Company Papers, 1897–1927 (Special Collections Division, Rosenberg Library, Galveston, Texas) (2nd quotation).

[49] *Galveston Daily News,* Sept. 11 (quotations), 14, 15, 1898.

[50] *Galveston City Times* quoted in *Galveston Daily News,* Sept. 11, 1898.

[51] Ibid.

[52] *Galveston Daily News,* Sept. 18, 1898.

[53] Ibid., Sept. 23–25, 1898.

[54] Ibid., Sept. 25–28 1898 (quotation on Sept. 25).

[55] Rice, *Progressive Cities,* 4–5; Kretzman, "A House Built upon the Sand," 86. Campaign flyers for Jones in the mayoral race highlighted Fly's anti-labor record and role in suppressing the 1898 strike. *Galveston Daily News,* Sept. 16, 1898 (quotation).

[56] *Galveston Daily News,* Dec. 8, 1898 (quotation); Jan. 18, Apr. 28, May 8, 1900; *Galveston City Times,* Dec. 31, 1904.

[57] Alwyn Barr, *Black Texans: A History of Negroes in Texas, 1528–1971* (Austin: Jenkins Publishing, 1973), 145–146; Mozell C. Hill, "The All-Negro Society in Oklahoma" (Ph.D. diss., University of Chicago, 1946), 27–29 (quotation on 28); Edwin S. Redkey, *Black Exodus: Black Nationalist and Back-to-Africa Movements, 1890–1910* (New Haven: Yale University Press, 1969), 292.

[58] Labor Movement in Texas Collection, box 2E306, folder 7 (Center for American History, University of Texas at Austin); *Galveston Daily News,* Jan. 30, 1898, Nov. 1, 1889; Arnesen, *Waterfront Workers of New Orleans,* 59.

[59] Ayers, *Southern Crossing,* 430–432.

[60] SBA Minutes, II, 510, 514, 523–530 (quotation on 527–528), 542, 549; *Galveston City Directory 1893–1894,* 67; *Galveston City Directory 1896–1897,* 60; *Galveston City Directory 1898,* 285.

[61] *Galveston Daily News,* Sept. 21, 1899 (1st quotation); SBA Minutes, II, 610, 620; SBA Committee Minutes, I, 7–18 (2nd quotation on 13).

CHAPTER FOUR

[1] McComb, *Galveston*, 121–127; Beasley, *The Alleys and Back Buildings of Galveston*, 70–71; Barker, "Partners in Progress," 1–34; James Michael Claflin, "Two Communities, Two Responses: An Alternative Interpretation of Calamities Applied to Indianola and Galveston" (M.A. thesis, University of Texas at Austin, 1985).

[2] McComb, *Galveston*, 135–145; Hyman, *Oleander Odyssey*, 146–172; Beasley, *The Alleys and Back Buildings of Galveston*, 72–73; Barker, "Partners in Progress," 1–34; Rice, *Progressive Cities*, 3–19.

[3] Bixel and Turner, *Galveston and the 1900 Storm*, 76; Mers, *Working the Waterfront*, 84.

[4] Barker, "Partners in Progress," iii–iv (quotation on iv), 39–40; McComb, *Galveston*, 150–151.

[5] McComb, *Galveston*, 47–49; Kelly, "'Twixt Failure and Success,'" 80–82; Hyman, *Oleander Odyssey*, 173–195.

[6] Bixel and Turner, *Galveston and the 1900 Storm*, x–xi, 48, 59, 77–82; Kretzman, "A House Built upon the Sand," 140–182; McComb, *Galveston*, 129–130.

[7] Woodward, *The Strange Career of Jim Crow*, 82–85; Rice, *The Negro in Texas*, 67, 113–139; Bixel and Turner, *Galveston and the 1900 Storm*, 149–150.

[8] Beasley, *The Alleys and Back Buildings of Galveston*, 70–71, 83; Kretzman, "A House Built upon the Sand," 183; *Galveston Daily News*, Nov. 9, 1906 (quotation); Woodward, *The Strange Career of Jim Crow*, 49–51, 92–93.

[9] *Galveston City Times*, Jan. 28, 1905.

[10] Ibid., Dec. 26, 1903, Dec. 24, 1904 (quotation), June 17, 1905.

[11] SBA Committee Minutes, II, 16–24, 23–24; SBA Minutes, III, 21, 59–60, 99–100.

[12] SBA Minutes, II, 41, 49, 3:19, 23, 82, 99–100; Russell, *Men along the Shore*, 61–71; James C. Maroney, "The International Longshoremen's Association in the Gulf States during the Progressive Era," *Southern Studies*, 16 (Summer, 1977), 225–233.

[13] Russell, *Men along the Shore*, 71–72 (1st quotation); International Longshoremen, Marine, and Transportation Worker's Association, *Proceedings of the Tenth Annual Convention, 1901* (Toledo: ILA, 1901), 47–48 (2nd quotation), hereafter cited as ILA, *Proceedings*; SBA Constitution and By-Laws, 1872, 113 (3rd quotation); SBA Minutes, II, 49; *Galveston Daily News*, Jan. 2, 1901, Nov. 1, 1907.

[14] Galveston Labor Council Records, vols. 1–4, 1900–1967, I, 12, 21, 31, 32, 52, 73, 82, 111, 115 (Special Collections Division, University of Texas at Arlington Libraries); SBA Minutes, III, 71 (quotation), 94.

[15] Labor Movement in Texas Collection, box 2E304, folder 5; *Galveston City Directory, 1895–1896*, 67; SBA Minutes, II, 54; Gibson, "Organized Labor in Texas from 1890 to 1900," 179–180 (quotations).

[16] Galveston Labor Council Records, I, 126, 218; Screwmen's Benevolent Association, ILA Local 307, Records, vols. 1–4, 1870–1983, II, 31 (Special Collections Division, University of Texas at Arlington Libraries), hereafter cited as ILA Local 307 Records; Galveston Labor Council Records, II, 113 (1st quotation); *Galveston Labor Journal*, Mar. 5, 1907 (2nd quotation); SBA Minutes, III, 613, 625; LBU Minutes, VI, 158; LBU Min-

utes, V, 127; *Galveston Daily News,* Apr. 15, 1910 (3rd and 4th quotations); *Galveston Labor Dispatch,* Apr. 12, 1913.

[17] Grady Lee Mullenix, "A History of the Texas State Federation of Labor" (Ph.D. diss., University of Texas at Austin, 1955), 14–37, 138–144.

[18] Maroney, "Organized Labor in Texas, 1900–1929," 21–25; Bracey, et al. (eds.), *Black Workers and Organized Labor,* 30; Foner, *Organized Labor and the Black Worker,* 77; Worthman, "Black Workers and Labor Unions in Birmingham, Alabama," 60–61; Philip S. Foner, "The I.W.W. and the Black Worker," in Philip S. Foner, *Essays in Afro-American History* (Philadelphia: Temple University Press, 1978), 215. According to Foner, locals of the IWW's Marine Transport Workers existed in both Galveston and New Orleans.

[19] Mullenix, "A History of the Texas State Federation of Labor," 108 (1st quotation), 185–186 (2nd quotation on 185).

[20] Ibid., 185–189 (quotation on 187–188).

[21] SBA Minutes, III, 21 (1st quotation), 184; *Galveston Daily News,* Apr. 15, 1902 (2nd quotation).

[22] *Galveston Daily News,* Sept. 4, 1900, Sept. 2, 1902, Sept. 6, 1910 (quotation).

[23] Galveston Labor Council Records, I, 192, 196; ILA Local 307 Records, III, 90; LBU Minutes, II, 4–6; LBU Minutes, V, 9 (1st quotation); *Galveston Daily News,* Sept. 7, 1909 (2nd quotation); *Galveston Labor Herald,* Sept. 7, 1912.

[24] *Galveston Daily News,* July 10, 1902 (1st quotation), June 21, 1904 (2nd quotation), Sept. 4, 1900, Sept. 4, 1906, Sept. 7, 1909.

[25] Taylor, "History of the Screwmen's Benevolent Association," 101; SBA Minutes, III, 52, 62, 270–271, 406, 463, 646; SBA Committee Minutes, II, 45 (quotation), 54, 49.

[26] SBA Committee Minutes, II, 53; *Galveston Daily News,* July 31, 1902 (quotations).

[27] SBA Committee Minutes, II, 57; *Galveston Daily News,* Sept. 1, 1902.

[28] *Galveston Daily News,* Sept. 1, 1902.

[29] Ibid., Sept. 11–12, 1907 (quotation on Sept. 11).

[30] Ibid., Sept. 14, 17, 19 (quotation), 20, 1907.

[31] *Galveston Labor Journal,* Sept. 20, 1907.

[32] *Galveston Daily News,* Sept. 3, 1903; ILA Local 307 Records, II, 11, 19, 35–40, 73.

[33] Arnesen, *Waterfront Workers of New Orleans,* 153–169 (quotation on 163.

[34] Ibid., 196–203, 324–325 n105.

[35] SBA Minutes, III, 230, 235, 244–245; SBA Committee Minutes, II, 63, 65.

[36] SBA Minutes, III, 412, 441, 554, 558–560 (1st quotation on 560); LBU Minutes, III, 183; SBA Committee Minutes, II, 296 (2nd quotation).

[37] Arnesen, *Waterfront Workers of New Orleans,* 200; New Orleans Port Investigating Commission, "Minutes of Investigation Had in the City of Galveston, Texas, as to the Conditions Prevailing in That Port, January 9th, 10th and 11th, 1906," 40 (quotation), Manuscripts Department (Tulane University Libraries, New Orleans).

[38] New Orleans Port Investigating Commission, "Minutes of Investigation," 41–66 (quotation on 44).

[39] Ibid., 98–114 (quotation on 114).

[40] Ibid., 124–144; George Waverley Briggs, *The Housing Problem in Texas: A Study of*

Physical Conditions under Which the Other Half Lives (Texas: Galveston-Dallas News, 1912), 5 (quotations), 56; *Galveston Daily News,* Nov. 9, 1906.

[41] New Orleans Port Investigating Commission, "Minutes of Investigation," 124–144.

[42] Arnesen, *Waterfront Workers of New Orleans,* 201–202 (2nd quotation on 201); New Orleans Port Investigating Commission, "Minutes of Investigation," 48–56 (1st quotation on 56), 112–114, 135 (3rd quotation).

[43] Arnesen, *Waterfront Workers of New Orleans,* viii; Arnesen, "Biracial Waterfront Unionism in the Age of Segregation," 35.

[44] SBA Minutes, III, 564; SBA Committee Minutes, II, 117–123.

[45] SBA Committee Minutes, II, 117–123 (1st quotation on 119, 2nd quotation on 120).

[46] Ibid. (quotation on 120).

[47] Ibid. (1st and 2nd quotations on 122, 3rd and 4th quotations on 123).

[48] Ibid., 126.

[49] SBA Minutes, III, 570, 572; SBA Committee Minutes, II, 130 (quotation).

[50] SBA Committee Minutes, II, 134.

[51] SBA Committee Minutes, II, 140; SBA Minutes, III, 570, 573.

[52] SBA Minutes, III, 573, 599–600 (quotations), 607; SBA Committee Minutes, II, 140, 148–151.

[53] SBA Committee Minutes, II, 154–156 (quotation on 155), 161–162.

[54] SBA Committee Minutes, II, 564, 566, 637; Dock and Marine Council Records, 1909–1913, 3, 15, 21, 45, 89, 90–96 (Special Collections Division, University of Texas at Arlington), cited hereafter as Dock and Marine Council Records, 1909–1913; Galveston Labor Council Records, II, 297 (quotation).

[55] Dock and Marine Council Records, 1909–1913, 114, 122, 129, 178, 186, 196, 215.

[56] International Longshoremen's Association, Gulf Coast District Branch, *Minutes of the Convention of the Southern Locals, 1911* (New Orleans: ILA, 1911), 2 (quotation); *Galveston Daily News,* Sept. 13, 1912.

[57] Labor Movement in Texas Collection, box 2E304, folder 5; *Galveston Daily News,* Sept. 3, 1912.

[58] Labor Movement in Texas Collection, box 2E304, folder 5; *Galveston Daily News,* Sept. 3, 6, 7, 1912 (quotation on Sept. 6).

[59] *Galveston Daily News,* Sept. 7, 1912.

[60] ILA, *Proceedings, 1914,* 98–100; LBU Minutes, VI, 254.

Chapter Five

[1] *Galveston Daily News,* Sept. 2, 1913.

[2] Barker, "Partners in Progress," 90–91; International Longshoremen's Association, Gulf Coast District Branch, *Proceedings of the Annual Convention, 1915,* 11, 18, hereafter cited as ILA, Gulf Coast District, *Proceedings;* ILA, Gulf Coast District, *Proceedings, 1917,* 5; ILA, Gulf Coast District, *Proceedings, 1919,* 8; Ellis, "The Texas Cotton Compression Industry," 301–302.

[3] Barker, "Partners in Progress," iii–iv, 131; *Galveston Daily News,* Feb. 6, 10, 1924; Apr. 4, 1924.

[4] Dock and Marine Council Records, 1913–1920, vols. 1–2, I, 17, Screwmen's Benevolent Association Records, Galveston, Texas, 1866–1922 (Center for American History, University of Texas at Austin), hereafter cited as Dock and Marine Council Records, 1913–1920.

[5] ILA, *Proceedings, 1914,* 98–100; ILA, *Proceedings, 1915,* 127–128; SBA Committee Minutes, III, 26 (quotations).

[6] *Galveston Daily News,* Aug. 20 (quotation), 25, 1913; International Longshoremen's Association Local 310, Minutes, vols. 19–23, 1906–1918, XX, 68, Screwmen's Benevolent Association Records, Galveston, Texas, 1866–1922 (Center for American History, University of Texas at Austin), hereafter cited as ILA Local 310 Minutes; ILA, *Proceedings, 1914,* 11.

[7] *Galveston Daily News,* Aug. 25, 26, Sept. 2, 4, 8, 15, 1913; ILA Local 310 Minutes, XX, 68, 84.

[8] *Galveston Daily News,* Sept. 15, 16, 18, 21; ILA Local 310 Minutes, XX, 84, 98; ILA, Gulf Coast District, *Proceedings, 1914,* 19–20.

[9] ILA, *Proceedings, 1915,* 127–132; ILA, Gulf Coast District, *Proceedings, 1915,* 13 (quotation); Maroney, "Organized Labor in Texas, 1900–1929," 174–77; Baughman, *The Mallorys of Mystic,* 201–226.

[10] ILA, *Proceedings, 1915,* 127–132 (quotation on 129).

[11] Dock and Marine Council Records, 1913–1920, I, 55 (quotation); ILA Gulf Coast District, *Proceedings, 1914,* 10; ILA Gulf Coast District, *Proceedings, 1916,* 9–10; ILA Gulf Coast District, *Proceedings, 1917,* 6; ILA, *Proceedings, 1915,* 48, 63.

[12] Wendell Phillips Terrell, "A Short History of the Negro Longshoreman," box 2E304, folder 4, Labor Movement in Texas Collection; Charles J. Hill, *A Brief History of ILA Local 872: From the Files of Freemas Everett* (Houston: ILA, 1960); box 2E306, folder 7, Labor Movement in Texas Collection.

[13] Terrell, "A Short History of the Negro Longshoreman"; Hill, *A Brief History of ILA Local 872;* ILA Gulf Coast District, *Proceedings, 1916,* 9 (quotation), 11, 30–31; box 2E306, folder 7, Labor Movement in Texas Collection; Gulf Coast District, *Proceedings, 1919,* 14.

[14] Galveston Labor Council Records, III, 385; ILA, *Proceedings, 1915,* 12 (1st quotation); Dock and Marine Council Records, 1913–1922, I, 43, 148; ILA Gulf Coast District, *Proceedings, 1917,* 26; ILA Local 310 Minutes, XXII, 93, 97 (2nd quotation), 122.

[15] Maroney, "Organized Labor in Texas, 1900–1929," 211–212; Arnesen, *Waterfront Workers of New Orleans,* 221–222.

[16] Arnesen, *Waterfront Workers of New Orleans,* 222–224; ILA, *Proceedings, 1919,* 160–162, 251; ILA Gulf Coast District, *Proceedings, 1918,* 8–9; Labor Movement in Texas Collection, box 2E304, folder 7.

[17] Arnesen, *Waterfront Workers of New Orleans,* 228–234; Maroney, "Organized Labor in Texas, 1900–1929," 211–212.

[18] Regin Schmidt, *Red Scare: FBI and the Origins of Anticommunism in the United*

States, 1919–1943 (Copenhagen: Museum Tusculanum Press, 2000), 24–27. See also Robert K. Murray, *Red Scare: A Study in National Hysteria, 1919–1920* (Minneapolis: University of Minneapolis Press, 1955).

[19] Irving Bernstein, *The Lean Years: A History of the American Worker, 1920–1933* (Boston: Houghton Mifflin, 1960), 91, 144–157; Schmidt, *Red Scare,* 24, 32–35.

[20] *Galveston Union Review,* May 21, 1920 (1st quotation); ILA Gulf Coast District, *Proceedings, 1921,* 21–22 (2nd and 3rd quotations).

[21] ILA, *Proceedings, 1919,* 532; ILA, *Proceedings, 1920,* 15–16 (quotation); *Galveston Union Review,* Feb. 6, 1920; *Galveston Daily News,* Feb. 5, 1920; James C. Maroney, "The Galveston Longshoremen's Strike of 1920," *East Texas Historical Journal,* 16, no. 1 (1978), 34–38.

[22] *Galveston Daily News,* Feb. 5, 21 (quotation); Mar. 16, 19, 20; Apr. 9, 1920.

[23] *Galveston Union Review,* Apr. 23, 1920; *Galveston Daily News,* Apr. 21, 23 (quotations); May 6, 7, 1920.

[24] *Galveston Daily News,* May 6, 12–15, 1920; *Galveston Union Review,* May 21, 1920 (quotation).

[25] Lewis L. Gould, *Progressives and Prohibitionists: Texas Democrats in the Wilson Era* (Austin: University of Texas Press, 1973), xii–xiii, 270.

[26] Jay Littman Todes, "Organized Employer Opposition to Unionism in Texas, 1900–1930" (M.A. thesis, University of Texas at Austin, 1949), 24–49, 77–80; Michael Anderson, "Americanism, Unionism and the Galveston Longshoremen's Strike of 1920," paper presented at the annual Graduate Student Conference, Department of American Studies, University of Texas at Austin, Sept. 27, 2002, copy in author's possession; *Galveston Daily News,* June 8, 1920 (quotation).

[27] *Galveston Daily News,* June 3, 1920 (1st and 2nd quotations); James A. Clark, *The Tactful Texan: A Biography of Governor Will Hobby* (New York: Random House, 1958), 133 (3rd quotation).

[28] *Galveston Daily News,* June 4, 1920.

[29] Ibid., 1920.

[30] *Galveston Daily News,* June 3, 6, 1920 (quotation on June 6); William D. Angel Jr., "Controlling the Workers: The Galveston Dock Workers' Strike of 1920 and Its Impact on Labor Relations in Texas," *East Texas Historical Journal,* 23, no. 2 (1985), 15, 16.

[31] *Galveston Daily News,* June 9, 10, 1920.

[32] Ibid., June 7, 11, 1920 (quotation on June 7).

[33] Neil Foley, *The White Scourge: Mexicans, Blacks, and Poor Whites in Texas Cotton Culture* (Berkeley: University of California Press, 1997), 45–46, 51–59; Maroney, "Organized Labor in Texas, 1900–1929," 25.

[34] Grover, "Recollections of Life in Galveston"; Turner, *Women, Culture and Community,* 21; Galveston Labor Council Records, II, 243, 245 (1st quotation); ILA, *Proceedings, 1911,* 98; ILA, *Proceedings, 1919,* 388, 444 (2nd quotation).

[35] Anderson, "Americanism, Unionism and the Galveston Longshoremen's Strike of 1920"; ILA, *Proceedings, 1919,* 388, 444; *Galveston Daily News,* Apr. 6, June 17, Aug. 21, 1920 (quotation).

[36] McComb, *Galveston*, 152–155; Mary W. Remmers, *Going down the Line: Galveston's Red Light District Remembered* (Galveston: n.p., 1997), 11; *Galveston Daily News*, June 15, 17 (quotation), 21, 29; Aug. 31, 1920.

[37] *Galveston Daily News*, July 22 (quotation), 27, Aug. 3, 4, 24, 1920.

[38] Ibid., Aug. 16, 21 (quotation), 24, 19, 30, 1920.

[39] *Galveston Daily News*, Sept. 23, 1920, Todes, "Organized Employer Opposition to Unionism in Texas, 1900–1930," 79; Angel, "Controlling the Workers," 23–25 (quotation on 23).

[40] *Galveston Daily News*, Dec. 14, 1920; Maroney, "Organized Labor in Texas, 1900–1925," 219.

[41] Angel, "Controlling the Workers," 25–26; *Galveston Daily News*, June 11, 1920 (quotation).

[42] Herbert Roof Northrup, *Organized Labor and the Negro* (2nd ed.; New York: Harper, 1944), 138; ILA Local 310 Minutes, XXII, 106; International Longshoremen's Association Local 310 Executive Council Minutes, vol. 4, 3-6 (Special Collections Division, University of Texas at Arlington Libraries), cited hereafter as Local 310 Executive Council Minutes; Local 307 Minutes, 1922–1931, 27, 54, 70–79 (Special Collections Division, University of Texas at Arlington Libraries), cited hereafter as Local 307 Minutes, 1922–1931.

[43] Arnesen, *Waterfront Workers of New Orleans*, 204–210, 236–249.

[44] *Galveston Daily News*, Sept. 16, 24; 1923; Arnesen, *Waterfront Workers of New Orleans*, 244–249.

[45] *Galveston Daily News*, Sept. 22, 24, 27; Oct. 1, 2, 1923.

[46] *Galveston Daily News*, Oct. 11, 14, 16, 17, 1923; ILA Gulf Coast District, *Proceedings, 1924*, 19–21; ILA, *Proceedings, 1923*, 296.

[47] ILA Gulf Coast District, *Proceedings, 1924*, 19–21; *Galveston Daily News*, Oct. 19–21; Nov. 15, 1923 (quotation).

[48] ILA Local 307 Minutes, 1922–1931, 125, 133–136, 172.

[49] *Galveston Daily News*, Aug. 6, 1924.

[50] ILA Local 307 Minutes, 1922–1931, 200.

[51] *Galveston Daily News*, Apr. 4, 1914; ILA Local 307 Minutes, 1922–1931, 24, 38, 63, 64, 78.

[52] ILA Local 307 Minutes, 1922–1931, 208; *Galveston Daily News*, Sept. 30, Oct. 9, 1924 (quotation).

[53] *Galveston Daily News*, Oct. 10 (1st quotation), 11, 21; Nov. 1, 1924; ILA Local 307 Minutes, 1922–1931, 212, 214–216, 225; Obadele-Starks, *Black Unionism in the Industrial South*, 46–47 (2nd quotation).

[54] *Galveston Daily News*, Oct. 11 (quotations), Nov. 1, Dec. 14, 1924.

[55] *Galveston Daily News*, Sept. 29, Oct. 6, 1925; ILA Gulf Coast District, *Proceedings, 1926*, 28–30.

Conclusion

[1] Arnesen, *Waterfront Workers of New Orleans*, 253–255.

[2] Ibid., 64.

[3] Lester Rubin, *The Negro in the Longshore Industry* (Philadelphia: University of Pennsylvania Press, 1974), 125; Mers, *Working the Waterfront*, 9–27; ILA Local 307 Records, Working Rules, 1956.

[4] Rubin, *The Negro in the Longshore Industry*, 134.

Bibliography

PRIMARY SOURCES

Manuscript Collections
Center for American History, University of Texas at Austin.
Screwmen's Benevolent Association Records, Galveston, Texas, 1866–1922:
    Dock and Marine Council Records, Vols. 1–2, 1913–1920.
    Longshoremen's Benevolent Union, Minutes, Vols. 1–7, 1887–1913.
    International Longshoremen's Association Local 310, Minutes, Vols. 19–23, 1906–1918.
    SBA Constitution and By-laws, 1872.
    SBA Minutes of Meetings, Vols. 1–4, 1866–1922.
    SBA Minutes of Meetings of Executive Committee, Vols. 1–3, 1893–1919.
Galveston Typographical Union Records:
    Minutes, Vols. 1–2, 1875–1889.
Labor Movement in Texas Collection:
    Box 2E304–2E306.
Special Collections Division, University of Texas at Arlington Libraries
Dock and Marine Council, Galveston, Texas. Records, 1909–1913.
Galveston Labor Council. Records, Vols. 1–4, 1900–1967.
Screwmen's Benevolent Association, ILA, Local 307, Galveston, Texas. Records, Vols. 1–4, 1870–1983. Also known as International Longshoremen's Association, Locals 310, 317, and 307 Records.
Local 310 Executive Council, Minutes, Vol. 4.
Local 307, Minutes, 1922–1931.

Special Collections Division, Rosenberg Library, Galveston

Hutchings, Sealy and Company Papers, 1897–1928.

Mallory Steamship Records. "A Comprehensive History of the Boycott, Galveston, 1886."

Grover, Walter E. "Recollections of Life in Galveston during the 1880s and 1890s." Kincy Rygaard file.

Scull, Ralph Albert. "Black Galveston: A Personal View of Community History in Many Categories of Life."

Manuscripts Department, Tulane University Libraries, New Orleans

New Orleans Port Investigating Commission. "Minutes of Investigation Had in the City of Galveston, Texas, as to the Conditions Prevailing in That Port, January 9th, 10th and 11th, 1906."

Published Works

Constitution and By-laws of the International Longshoremen's Association Local 310. Galveston: ILA, 1914.

Galveston City Times. 1904–1905.

Galveston Daily News. 1865–1925.

Galveston City Directory, Galveston: Morrison and Fourmy, 1882–1904.

Galveston Labor Dispatch, 1913.

Galveston Labor Herald, 1912.

Galveston Labor Journal, 1907.

Galveston Union Review, 1920.

Houston Daily Post, 1898.

International Longshoremen, Marine, and Transportworker's Association. *Proceedings of the Tenth Annual Convention, 1901.* Toledo: ILA, 1901.

International Longshoremen's Association. *Proceedings of the Annual Convention, 1911–1923.*

International Longshoremen's Association, Gulf Coast District Branch. *Minutes of the Convention of the Southern Locals, 1911.* New Orleans: ILA, 1911.

———. *Proceedings of the Annual Convention, 1914–1926.*

San Antonio Light, 1886.

SECONDARY SOURCES

Abel, Joseph. "Opening the Closed Shop: The Galveston Longshoremen's Strike of 1920–1921." *Southwestern Historical Quarterly*, 110 (Jan., 2007), 317–347.

Allen, Ruth. *Chapters in the History of Organized Labor in Texas*. Austin: University of Texas Press, 1941.

Anderson, Michael. "Americanism, Unionism and the Galveston Longshoremen's Strike of 1920." Paper presented at the annual Graduate Student Conference, Department of American Studies, University of Texas at Austin, Sept. 27, 2002.

Angel, William D. Jr. "Controlling the Workers: The Galveston Dock Workers' Strike of 1920 and its Impact on Labor Relations in Texas." *East Texas Historical Journal*, 23, no. 2 (1985), 14–27.

Armstead, Bert C. *Reminiscences of a Black Church in Galveston*. Galveston: n.p., 1989.

Arnesen, Eric. *Waterfront Workers of New Orleans: Race, Class, and Politics, 1863–1923*. New York: Oxford University Press, 1991.

———. "Following the Color Line of Labor: Black Workers and the Labor Movement before 1930." *Radical History Review*, 55 (Winter, 1993), 53–87.

———. "What's on the Black Worker's Mind? African-American Labor and the Union Tradition on the Gulf Coast." *Gulf Coast Historical Review*, 10 (Fall, 1994), 7–30.

———. "Up From Exclusion: Black and White Workers, Race, and the State of Labor History." *Reviews in American History*, 26 (Mar., 1998), 146–174.

Axelrod, Bernard. "Galveston: Denver's Deep-Water Port." *Southwestern Historical Quarterly*, 70 (Oct., 1966), 217–228.

Ayers, Edward L. *The Promise of the New South: Life after Reconstruction*. New York: Oxford University Press, 1992.

Barker, Thomas Truel. "Partners in Progress: The Galveston Wharf Company and the City of Galveston, 1900–1930. Ph.D. diss., Texas A&M University, 1979.

Barnes, Charles B. *The Longshoremen*. New York: Survey Associates, 1915.

Barr, Alwyn. *Black Texans: A History of Negroes in Texas, 1528–1971.* Austin: Jenkins Publishing, 1973.

Baughman, James P., ed. "Letters from the Texas Coast, 1875." *Southwestern Historical Quarterly,* 69 (Apr., 1966), 499–515.

_____. *Charles Morgan and the Development of Southern Transportation.* Nashville: Vanderbilt University Press, 1968.

_____. "The Evolution of Rail-Water Systems of Transportation in the Gulf Southwest, 1836–1890." *The Journal of Southern History,* 34 (Aug., 1968), 357–381.

_____. The *Mallorys of Mystic: Six Generations in American Maritime Enterprise.* Middletown, Conn.: Wesleyan University Press, 1972.

Beasley, Ellen. *The Alleys and Back Buildings of Galveston: An Architectural and Social History.* Houston: Rice University Press, 1996.

Bernstein, Irving. *The Lean Years: A History of the American Worker, 1920–1933.* Boston: Houghton Mifflin, 1960.

Bixel, Patricia Bellis, and Elizabeth Hayes Turner. *Galveston and the 1900 Storm: Catastrophe and Catalyst.* Austin: University of Texas Press, 2000.

Bloch, Herman. "Labor and the Negro, 1866–1910." *Journal of Negro History,* 50 (July, 1965), 163–184.

_____. "The National Labor Union and Black Workers." *Journal of Ethnic Studies,* 1 (Spring, 1973), 13–21.

Bracey, John H., August Meier, and Elliot Rudwick, eds. *Black Workers and Organized Labor.* Belmont, Calif.: Wadsworth, 1971.

Briggs, George Waverley. *The Housing Problem in Texas: A Study of Physical Conditions under Which the Other Half Lives.* Texas: Galveston-Dallas News, 1912.

Brown, Jean M. "Free Rein: Galveston Island's Alcohol, Gambling, and Prostitution Era, 1839–1957." M.A. thesis, Lamar University, 1998.

Cantor, Milton, ed. *Black Labor in America.* Westport, Conn.: Negro Universities Press, 1969.

Cartwright, Gary. *Galveston: A History of the Island.* New York: Atheneum, 1991.

Claflin, James Michael. "Two Communities, Two Responses: An Alternative Interpretation of Calamities Applied to Indianola and Galveston. M.A. thesis, University of Texas at Austin, 1985.

Clark, James A. *The Tactful Texan: A Biography of Governor Will Hobby.* New York: Random House, 1958.

Cuney-Hare, Maud. *Norris Wright Cuney: A Tribune of the Black People.* 1913. Reprint; Austin: Steck-Vaughan, 1968.

Ellis, Louis Tuffly. "The Texas Cotton Compression Industry." Ph.D. diss., University of Texas at Austin, 1965.

Fink, Gary M., and Merle E. Reed, eds. *Essays in Southern Labor History: Selected Papers, Southern Labor History Conference, 1976.* Westport, Conn.: Greenwood Press, 1977.

Foley, Neil. *The White Scourge: Mexicans, Blacks, and Poor Whites in Texas Cotton Culture.* Berkeley: University of California Press, 1997.

Foner, Philip S. *Essays in Afro-American History.* Philadelphia: Temple University Press, 1978.

_____. *Organized Labor and the Black Worker, 1619–1973.* New York: International Publisher's, 1976

Foner, Philip S., and Ronald L. Lewis, eds. *The Black Worker: A Documentary History from Colonial Times to the Present, Volume 3: The Black Worker during the Era of the Knights of Labor.* Philadelphia: Temple University Press, 1978.

_____. *The Black Worker: A Documentary History from Colonial Times to the Present, Volume 4: The Black Worker during the Era of the American Federation of Labor and the Railroad Brotherhoods.* Philadelphia: Temple University Press, 1979.

Fornell, Earl Wesley. *The Galveston Era: The Texas Crescent on the Eve of Secession.* Austin: University of Texas Press, 1961.

Francaviglia, Richard V. *From Sail to Steam: Four Centuries of Texas Maritime History, 1500–1900.* Austin: University of Texas Press, 1998.

Garlock, Jonathan. *Guide to the Local Assemblies of the Knights of Labor.* Westport, Conn.: Greenwood Press, 1982.

Gibson, Charles Mac. "Organized Labor in Texas from 1890 to 1900." M.A. thesis, Texas Tech University, 1973.

Gould, Lewis L. *Progressives and Prohibitionists: Texas Democrats in the Wilson Era.* Austin: University of Texas Press, 1973.

Hales, Douglas. "The Cuneys: A Southern Family in White and Black."

Ph.D. diss., Texas Tech University, 2000.

Hardwick, Susan Wiley. *Mythic Galveston: Reinventing America's Third Coast.* Baltimore: Johns Hopkins University Press, 2002.

Hayes, Charles W. *Galveston: A History of the Island and the City.* 2 vols. Austin: Jenkins Garrett Press, 1974.

Hill, Charles J. *A Brief History of ILA Local 872: From the Files of Freemas Everett.* Houston: ILA, 1960.

Hill, Herbert. "Myth-Making as Labor History: Herbert Gutman and the United Mine Workers of America." *International Journal of Politics, Culture and Society,* 2 (Winter, 1988), 132–200.

Hill, Mozell C. "The All-Negro Society in Oklahoma." Ph.D. diss., University of Chicago, 1946.

Hine, William B. "Black Organized Labor in Reconstruction Charleston." *Labor History,* 25 (Fall, 1984), 504–517.

Hinze, Virginia Neal. "Norris Wright Cuney." M.A. thesis, Rice University, 1965.

Hobsbawm, Eric J. *Labouring Men: Studies in the History of Labour.* London: Weidenfeld and Nicolson, 1964.

Hyman, Harold M. *Oleander Odyssey: The Kempners of Galveston, Texas, 1854–1980.* College Station: Texas A&M University Press, 1990.

Jacobson, Julius, ed. *The Negro and the American Labor Movement.* New York: Anchor Books, 1968.

Johnson, Jack. *Jack Johnson is a Dandy.* New York: Chelsea House, 1969.

Kann, Kenneth. "The Knights of Labor and the Southern Black Worker." *Labor History,* 18 (Winter, 1977), 47–70.

Kauser, James Morgan, and James McPherson, eds. *Region, Race and Reconstruction: Essays in Honor of C. Vann Woodward.* New York: Oxford University Press, 1982.

Kelley, Robin D. G. "'We Are Not What We Seem': Rethinking Black Working-Class Opposition in the Jim Crow South." *Journal of American History,* 80 (June, 1993), 75–112.

Kelly, Ruth Evelyn. "'Twixt Failure and Success': The Port of Galveston in the Nineteenth Century." M.A. thesis, University of Houston, 1975.

Kimeldorf, Howard. *Reds or Rackets? The Making of Radical and Conserva-*

tive Unions on the Waterfront. Berkeley: University of California Press, 1988.

King, Edward. "Glimpses of Texas." *Scribner's Monthly*, 7 (Nov., 1873), 401–431.

Kingsdale, Jon M. "The 'Poor Man's Club': Social Functions of the Urban Working Class Saloon." *American Quarterly*, 25 (Oct., 1973), 472–489.

Kretzman, Stephen Paul. "A House Built upon the Sand: Race, Class, Gender, and the Galveston Hurricane of 1900." Ph.D. diss., University of Wisconsin, 1995.

Land and Thompson. *Galveston: The Commercial Metropolis and Principal Seaport of the Great Southwest*. Galveston: Land and Thompson, 1885.

Lovell, John. "Sail, Steam and Emergent Dockers' Unionism in Britain, 1850–1914." *International Review of Social History*, 32, no. 3 (1987), 230–249.

Maroney, James C. "Organized Labor in Texas, 1900–1929." Ph.D. diss., University of Houston, 1975.

_____. "The International Longshoremen's Association in the Gulf States during the Progressive Era." *Southern Studies*, 16 (Summer, 1977), 225–232.

_____. "The Galveston's Longshoremen's Strike of 1920." *East Texas Historical Journal*, 16, no. 1 (1978), 34–38.

Marshall, F. Ray. *Labor in the South*. Cambridge: Harvard University Press, 1967.

McComb, David G. *Galveston: A History*. Austin: University of Texas Press, 1986.

McLaurin, Melton. "The Racial Policies of the Knights of Labor." *Labor History*, 17 (Fall, 1976), 568–585.

Meinig, Donald W. *Imperial Texas: An Interpretive Essay in Cultural Geography*. Austin: University of Texas Press, 1969.

Mers, Gilbert. *Working the Waterfront: The Ups and Downs of a Rebel Longshoreman*. Austin: University of Texas Press, 1988.

Miller, Raymond. "Dockworker Subculture." *Comparative Studies in Society and History*, 11 (June, 1969), 302–314.

Moneyhon, Carl H. *Republicanism in Reconstruction Texas*. Austin: University of Texas Press, 1980.

Montgomery, David. *Workers' Control in America: Studies in the History of Work, Technology, and Labor Struggles*. Cambridge: Cambridge University Press, 1979.

_____. *The Fall of the House of Labor: The Workplace, the State, and American Labor Activism*. Cambridge: Cambridge University Press, 1987.

Morrison, Andrew. *The Port of Galveston and the State of Texas*. St. Louis: G. W. Englehardt, 1890.

Mullenix, Grady Lee. "A History of the Texas State Federation of Labor." Ph.D. diss., University of Texas at Austin, 1955.

Murray, Robert K. *Red Scare: A Study in National Hysteria, 1919–1920*. Minneapolis: University of Minneapolis Press, 1955.

North, Thomas. *Five Years in Texas*. Cincinnati: Elm Street Printing, 1871.

Northrup, Herbert Roof. *Organized Labor and the Negro*. 2nd ed. New York: Harper, 1944.

Obadele-Starks, Ernest. "Black Labor, the Black Middle Class, and Organized Protest along the Upper Texas Gulf Coast, 1883–1945." *Southwestern Historical Quarterly*, 103 (July, 1999), 53–65.

_____. *Black Unionism in the Industrial South*. College Station: Texas A&M University Press, 2000.

Ousley, Clarence. *Galveston in 1900*. Atlanta: William C. Chase, 1900.

Painter, Nell Irvin. *Standing at Armageddon: The United States, 1877–1919*. New York: W. W. Norton, 1987.

Payne, Richard, and Geoffrey Leavenworth. *Historic Galveston*. Houston: Herring Press, 1985.

Pilcher, William W. *The Portland Longshoremen: A Dispersed Urban Community*. New York: Holt, Rinehart, and Winston, 1972.

Pitre, Merline. *Through Many Dangers, Toils, and Snares: The Black Leadership of Texas, 1868–1900*. Austin: Eakin Press, 1985.

Poole, Ernest. "The Ship Must Sail on Time." *Everybody's Magazine*, 19 (July, 1908), 176–186.

Red, William S., ed. "Allen's Reminiscences of Texas, 1838–1842." *Southwestern Historical Quarterly*, 18 (Jan., 1915), 287–304.

Redkey, Edwin S. *Black Exodus: Black Nationalist and Back-to-Africa Movements, 1890–1910*. New Haven: Yale University Press, 1969.

Reese, James V. "The Early History of Labor Organizations in Texas,

1838–1876." *Southwestern Historical Quarterly*, 72 (July, 1968), 1–20.

_____. "The Evolution of an Early Texas Union: The Screwmen's Benevolent Association of Galveston, 1866–1891." *Southwestern Historical Quarterly*, 75 (Oct., 1971), 158–185.

Remmers, Mary W. *Going down the Line: Galveston's Red Light District Remembered.* Galveston: n.p., 1997.

Rice, Bradley Robert. *Progressive Cities: The Commission Government Movement in America, 1901–1920.* Austin: University of Texas Press, 1977.

Rice, Lawrence D. *The Negro in Texas, 1874–1900.* Baton Rouge: Louisiana State University Press, 1971.

Roediger, David R. *Towards the Abolition of Whiteness: Essays on Race, Politics, and Working Class History.* London: Verso, 1994.

_____. *The Wages of Whiteness: Race and the Making of the American Working Class.* London: Verso, 1991.

_____. *Colored White: Transcending the Racial Past.* Berkeley: University of California Press, 2002.

Rubin, Lester. *The Negro in the Longshore Industry.* Philadelphia: University of Pennsylvania Press, 1974.

Russell, Maud. *Men along the Shore.* New York: Brussel & Brussel, 1966.

Scharnwebber, William A. *Facts about Galveston, Texas, the Deep Water Harbor of the Gulf of Mexico.* Galveston: n.p., 1899.

Schmidt, Regin. *Red Scare: FBI and the Origins of Anticommunism in the United States, 1919–1943.* Copenhagen: Museum Tusculanum Press, 2000.

Shelton, Robert Stuart. "Waterfront Workers of Galveston, Texas, 1838–1920." Ph.D. diss., Rice University, 2000.

_____. "'Which Ox is in the Mire': Race and Class in the Galveston Longshoremen's Strike of 1898." *Southwestern Historical Quarterly*, 110 (Oct., 2006), 219–239.

Sibley, Marilyn McAdams. *The Port of Houston: A History.* Austin: University of Texas Press, 1968.

Spero, Sterling Dednhard, and Abram L. Harris. *The Black Worker: The Negro and the Labor Movement.* New York: Columbia University Press, 1931.

Spratt, John S. *The Road to Spindletop: Economic Change in Texas, 1875–1901.*

Dallas: Southern Methodist University Press, 1955.

Taylor, Allen. "A History of the Screwmen's Benevolent Association from 1866 to 1924." M.A. thesis, University of Texas at Austin, 1968.

Todes, Jay Littman. "Organized Employer Opposition to Unionism in Texas, 1900–1930." M.A. thesis, University of Texas at Austin, 1949.

Turner, Elizabeth Hayes. *Women, Culture, and Community: Religion and Reform in Galveston, 1880–1920.* New York: Oxford University Press, 1997.

Van der Linden, Marcel, and Jan Lucassen, eds. *Racism and the Labor Market: Historical Studies.* Bern: Peter Lang, 1995.

Way, Peter. *Common Labor: Workers and the Digging of North American Canals, 1780–1860.* Cambridge: Cambridge University Press, 1993.

Williams, Harry. "The Development of a Market Economy in Texas: The Establishment of a Railway Network." Ph.D. diss., University of Texas at Austin, 1957.

Winslow, Calvin, ed. *Waterfront Workers: New Perspectives on Race and Class.* Urbana: University of Illinois Press, 1998.

Woodward, C. Vann. *Origins of the New South, 1877–1913.* Baton Rouge: Louisiana State University Press, 1951.

_____. *The Strange Career of Jim Crow.* 3rd ed. New York: Oxford University Press, 1974.

Young, Earle B. *Galveston and the Great West.* College Station: Texas A&M University Press, 1997.

_____. *Tracks to the Sea: Galveston and Western Railroad Development, 1866–1900.* College Station: Texas A&M University Press, 1999.

Index

COLOPHON

The text of this book is set in Adobe Caslon. Adobe Chizel Solid
is used for display type. William Caslon released his first typefaces in
1722. Caslon's types became popular throughout Europe and America.
The first printings of the American Declaration of Independence and
the Constitution were set in Caslon. The book was printed by
Edwards Brothers, Inc., of Ann Arbor, Michigan,
on 50# EB Natural paper.